BROOKE AT THE BAR

Honorary Proclamation

BILL RITTER, JR.
GOVERNOR

Brooke Wunnicke Day
May 9, 2008

WHEREAS, Brooke Wunnicke will celebrate her 90th birthday on May 9, 2008, having achieved many plaudits, launched new innovations, and broken barriers throughout her illustrious life; and

WHEREAS, after graduating from Stanford University in 1939, and the University of Colorado School of Law in 1946, Brooke moved north and was admitted to the Wyoming State Bar later that year – the first woman to ever practice trial law in the State of Wyoming; and

WHEREAS, throughout her distinguished career, Brooke has received numerous awards and honors, including the 1999 national award from the Defense Research Institute, the 1999 Colorado Bar Association Award of Merit, the 2004 Denver Bar Association's Award of Merit, the 1997 William Lee Knous Award, and membership to the American Bar Association – some of the most honorable awards each respective institution bestows upon nominees; and

WHEREAS, Brooke has led a life dedicated to the law and judicial system, having served as a lawyer, taught as a professor, guided as a mentor, and imbued her sense of the law to others as an author; and

WHEREAS, Brooke was a loving wife and mother, and continues to maintain her close familial ties with her daughter Dianne; and

WHEREAS, on Brooke's 90th birthday, May 9, 2008, her closest friends and family will honor her lifelong work and intrepid character at her birthday party, and join together to reminisce the many memories each person has had with this kind and devoted lady;

Therefore, I, Bill Ritter, Jr., Governor of the State of Colorado, do hereby proclaim May 9, 2008, in honor of

BROOKE WUNNICKE DAY

in the State of Colorado.

GIVEN under my hand and the Executive Seal of the State of Colorado, this ninth day of May, 2008

Bill Ritter, Jr.
Governor

Figure 0.1. Colorado Governor's Proclamation of Brooke Wunnicke Day on May 9, 2008.

A Governor's Proclamation

The person who imparted upon me the importance of being ethical above all else is Brooke Wunnicke. Those of us whom Brooke mentored owe her a debt of gratitude that can never be paid in full. She was our Grand Dame. God bless Brooke for the considerable contribution she made to building a better world for us all.

Governor Bill Ritter Jr., of the State of Colorado (2007–2011),
September 29, 2014

Figure 0.2. Governor Bill Ritter Jr. reads his Proclamation of Brooke Wunnicke Day, May 9, 2008, with Brooke at his side, to guests at her ninetieth birthday party.

MEET "BROOKE AT THE BAR"
As Others Write about Brooke

[COMPILER'S NOTE: Here, the Reader may "Meet Brooke" from a few excerpts of letters in her archives.]

Brooke Wunnicke was a dynamo . . . a force of nature, if you will. And a rare gift to all of us and our profession. And by anyone's definition she was "one of a kind." And sometimes out here in the Wild, Wild West in places like Wyoming and Colorado, "one of a kind" can beat even a royal flush.
   Robert J. Kapelke, Colorado Court of Appeals Judge 1994–2005, from his Brooke Wunnicke Memorial Remarks in October 2015

Brooke . . . is the very finest. [I]ntegrity and ability are taken for granted if you know Brooke. She goes beyond this to humility, common sense and profound intelligence.
   Harry D. Heist, A & C Feed Company, Cheyenne, Wyoming, 1969

Brooke Wunnicke, our Chief Appellate Deputy District Attorney, is the best all-round and appellate lawyer I have ever known. . . . As the single most knowledgeable person in this office, her counsel is sought from lawyers around the state.
   Dale Tooley, District Attorney, Second Judicial District. Denver, Colorado, 1978

Brooke is one of those rare individuals who captivates audiences with her passionate, witty, and professional presentation of ethics.
   Robert C. Dorr, Cofounder of International Practicum Institute, Denver, Colorado, 2003

[The following are from "children" Brooke mentored in the Denver District Attorney's Office.]

Many years later, I am still proud to say, I am one of her "children" . . . Brooke was our cheerleader, encouraged us, and was concerned for us. Her wit and her hearty laugh cheered even the gloomiest of days.
   Christopher Cross, Judge, Arapahoe County Court; September 2003

We called her the "velvet hammer." . . . We worked for her as legal interns . . . her "children." The great thing about working with Brooke was that she had seen it all. . . . She took us into the trials courtrooms and appellate courts and mentored us . . . to give respect to the courts and to be a good advocate. She is a jewel in my life.
   Mark A. Fogg, Past President, Denver and Colorado Bar Associations

Brooke is one of those rare persons who positively touches the lives of all those with whom she has contact. . . . I think Colorado lawyers would vote to clone Brooke. I and many other lawyers who have benefited from her tutelage seek to emulate Brooke, a feat that, frankly, is impossible.
   Velveta Howell, Regional Manager, Office for Civil Rights, US Department of Health and Human Services, 2003

When I phrase a legal finding, analyze an ethical issue, or approach a difficult client or lawyer, I often think: "How would Brooke do it?" But mostly, it is your smile, the gleam in your eye, your infectious love of law, and your kindness to others that I recall.
   William (Bill) G. Meyer, Retired Denver District Court Judge, Managing Arbiter, Judicial Arbiter Group, Denver, Colorado, 2013

Brooke Wunnicke has been my mentor and "My Mother-In-The-Law" since my 2nd year of law school. [H]er half century record of legal excellence easily qualifies her as one of the great legal minds of our time.
   J. Wallace (Wally) Wortham Jr., Denver City Attorney, 2000

Brooke
at the Bar

Inside Our Legal System

BROOKE WUNNICKE

(1918–2014)
Member of the Bar
State of Colorado (1969–2014)
and
State of Wyoming (1946–2014)

UNIVERSITY PRESS OF COLORADO
Denver

© 2023 by Diane B. Wunnicke

Materials for *Brooke at the Bar* compiled by Diane B. Wunnicke

Published by University Press of Colorado
1580 North Logan Street, Suite 660
PMB 39883
Denver, Colorado 80203-1942

 The University Press of Colorado is a proud member of
Association of University Presses.

The University Press of Colorado is a cooperative publishing enter-
prise supported, in part, by Adams State University, Colorado State
University, Fort Lewis College, Metropolitan State University of Denver,
University of Alaska Fairbanks, University of Colorado, University of
Denver, University of Northern Colorado, University of Wyoming, Utah
State University, and Western Colorado University.

∞ This paper meets the requirements of the ANSI/NISO Z39.48-1992
   (Permanence of Paper).

ISBN: 978-1-64642-419-1 (hardcover)
ISBN: 978-1-64642-420-7 (ebook)
https://doi.org/10.5876/9781646424207

Cataloging-in-Publication data for this title is available online at the
Library of Congress.

Cover photograph by Jim Wunnicke

Contents

Figures

Many of the original photographs included in this book are now part of the Brooke Wunnicke Papers, archived at the Denver Public Library Western History/Genealogy Department.

Brooke Wunnicke

AUTOBIOGRAPHY AND COMMENTARY
ON THE AMERICAN LEGAL SYSTEM

Thomas J. Noel

T his is a candid account of the downs as well as the ups of a tiny 5' 1", less-than-100-pound attorney who looms large in Wyoming and Colorado legal history. It includes her experiences, discussions of judicial procedures, the roles of courtroom actors and thoughts on the US legal system including the US Constitution and Bill of Rights. Warm, witty, and wise, Brooke may make you repent all those lawyer jokes.

After undergraduate study at Stanford, Brooke graduated first in her class from the University of Colorado School of Law in October 1945. She was admitted in May 1946 to practice law in her home state of Wyoming. Starting out as an attorney she had to "solo" because no man then wanted to practice with a woman lawyer. Brooke also encountered and opposed discrimination against ethnic groups. So, in the early 1960s, she was pleased to be included as the guest speaker at the first chapter meeting with banquet of the National Association for the Advancement of Colored People in Cheyenne. A few years later, she also was the guest speaker at the first meeting of a Mexican American business group in Wyoming (now the Wyoming Hispanic Chamber of Commerce).

Brooke vividly recalls her courtroom adventures including lawyers "whose droning voices could have brought slumber to the most afflicted insomniac." Then there was the divorce case where her client's witness, asked about previous husbands, said "I buried all of mine." Yet another client could not stop weeping when discussing her case. Brooke realized that such behavior on the stand would gain jury sympathy. And in another case, her brilliant defense of an impoverished, unfortunate client even led jurors to cry. Her clear, compassionate writing may lead you to cry too, as well as laugh. A "brief" in legal terms, she admits, is often "an amusing misnomer" for a document "impressive more for length than content."

After twenty-three years as a successful business, trial, and appellate attorney in the Cowboy State, Brooke and her husband moved to Denver where she practiced for over thirty years, both in private law firms and at the Denver District Attorney's Office. She also lectured for twenty-five years, authored books, and served as a law school professor at the University of Denver Law School. Brooke seems proudest of the more than sixty law students and young lawyers whom she mentored while serving as the Chief Appellate Deputy District Attorney in Denver. These mentees became known as "Brooke's children," because her hope was to "spare them some of the wounds and scars that she sustained as a young lawyer." She gave the time to do one-on-one mentoring because she knew that most law firms seldom provided mentoring because that time could not be charged as billable hours to clients. "Brooke's children" became a governor, six district court judges, five elected district attorneys, five recipients of Distinguished Alumni Awards, past presidents of the Denver and Colorado Bar Associations, successful trial and appellate attorneys, and administrators in public offices.

In addition to her daytime practice, Brooke also began, as an Adjunct Professor of Law, a course named Problems in Legal Practice, two hours in the evening for two nights a week at the University of Denver (DU) College of Law. To make teaching the Problems course more challenging, there was no textbook. This book fills that gap. Furthermore, DU's old downtown law school building had unreliable heating and air conditioning, leaving her alternately freezing or perspiring. She loved teaching but was alarmed by how poorly some of her students wrote. So she prescribed that old classic, William Strunk and E. B. White's *The Elements of Style*. Brooke soon shifted to courses she knew well and loved—Oil and Gas Law and Future Interests. She taught at DU Law for twenty years with rave student evaluations and two prestigious DU Law awards.

Brooke taught that reading faces was important, especially a judge's face. She also read faces of her students. Finding one in distress, she asked why. He explained that his employer would not let him off early enough to get to her class on time. Brooke offered to share her notes with him and gave him her home number and assurance that he could call her for help. "A painting of his face," she ends that story, "could have been entitled 'Gratitude.'"

On the last day of her law school classes, she treated her students to sandwiches and nuts (no peanuts) on paper plates and wine in paper cups. One last day of class, appreciating Brooke's quotes from Shakespeare, a group of her students brought in a large sheet cake with the icing inscribed with these words:

Oils Well that Ends Well
Thanks,
It has been a Gas
Class of '96

After serving as Chief Appellate Deputy District Attorney for Denver from 1973 to 1986, Brooke returned to private practice with the large, regional Hall & Evans litigation firm in downtown Denver. She was "Of Counsel" for that firm's trial and appellate practices. She also continued to write, teach, and give lectures across the nation. Hall & Evans prized Brooke's work, giving her a roomy, sunny office, a conference room named for her, and scholarships in her name at the University of Colorado School of Law.

Brooke was a scholar as well as a lawyer, teacher, and nationally recognized lecturer on ethics. Her book, *Ethics Compliance for Business Lawyers* (John Wiley & Sons, 1987) was praised as "the most practical and definitive resource" on that topic. With her daughter, Diane Wunnicke, Brooke also wrote *Standby and Commercial Letters of Credit* (Wolters Kluwer, 1989–2013); and with her friend, A. Sydney Holderness Jr., she wrote the *Legal Opinion Letters Formbook* (Wolters Kluwer, 1994–2011). Her works should be required law school reading.

While generally praising the legal system, especially the jury system, Brooke does have a few complaints. One is the politicized system of appointing State Supreme Court justices. Another is the recent use of "Discovery" whereby depositions can be taken ahead of a trial. The proliferation of innumerable depositions, she maintains, has clogged up and made ever more expensive the legal process. She argues that the number of pre-trial depositions should be strictly limited. She also contends that the number of pre-trial motions should be strictly limited, or they too can go on *ad infinitum*.

Brooke became a nationally prominent lecturer on practice and ethics, arguing for accuracy, brevity, clarity, and integrity. Greater adherence, she suggests, would help improve the reputation of the law, lawyers, and judges.

Brooke's book includes both a refresher on the law, our Constitution, and our Bill of Rights and advice on the very different roles people play at trials. From her hundreds of cases, she provides examples including what to do—and not to do. Much of this is entertaining as well as instructive. For example, in discussing the different types of witnesses, she covers babbling, hostile, and arrogant witnesses and how they will impact judges and juries.

Brooke says her main reason for writing this book was to alert all Americans about their rights and to educate us on the legal system and process. The rights of all Americans, as she shows, are under continual attack and must be defended.

Readers and students interested in civics and history as well as people facing jury duty, and—most important to Brooke, citizens concerned about their legal rights—should find this book entertaining as well as informative.

Thomas J. Noel, Emeritus Professor of History, University of Colorado Denver, is also known as Dr. Colorado for his many books, columns, tours, and talks on the Highest State.

Brooke's Welcome to the Reader, a Letter to Brooke's Friends and Colleagues, and a Song about Brooke

BROOKE'S WELCOME TO YOU, THE READER

I HAVE always tried to live by three mottos:

> » As a person, my parents' guidance: "Do what thou hast to do and to thine own self be true."
> » As a lawyer, my guidance is Marcus Aurelius during AD 171–175: "Never esteem aught of advantage which will oblige you to break your faith or to desert your honor."
> » As an American, John Locke's 1689 warning: "Where-ever [*sic*] law ends, tyranny begins."

I love the law, warts and all. I know there are many things wrong with our legal system today, things that I deplore. Yet I know it's the best legal system ever known to mankind.

I truly believe that for the last six thousand years, the law has been and will continue to be civilization's hope for the world. In the United States of America, we have three branches of government, but it is the judiciary that speaks for the law. Congress, presidents, can't protect freedom. But lawyers and judges can.

This book is in three parts:

» Part One: A short author's biography so you will know your tour guide (me) to "Inside Our Legal System."
» Part Two: Memories of my life as Wyoming's first woman trial and appellate lawyer, followed by my life in Denver, Colorado, as a lawyer, advisor, mentor, adjunct law professor, national and regional lecturer, and published author.
» Part Three: The Law: What the law means for you; inside the workings of our courts, trials, and appeals; what's important in the law for us; our Constitution with its Bill of Rights.

Ralph Waldo Emerson's precept was that " 'Tis the good reader that makes the good book." Your help with this book is appreciated.

Cordially,
Brooke Wunnicke, your author, 2014

Figure 0.3. Brooke in 1998.

BROOKE'S HEART was fearless and full of love for the law and for her many loyal and caring friends and colleagues.

Always busy with important activities, including writing her published law books and many lectures, Brooke found time to write your voyage "inside our legal system." She wrote from 2000 until just before she, at home, peacefully died in her sleep in September 2014. When others and I were concerned that, in her nineties, she might not finish her book, she would cheerfully comment, "It's done, but never the end," as she continued writing her memoirs and her essays about the law. In the general folder for her book, I found her undated, handwritten note, perhaps as she mused about the years writing her book: "Speed in the beginning may mean delay in ending."

This book answers the question so often asked over the years by those same friends and colleagues, "How's your book coming?"

My acknowledgments for Brooke's book are a pleasure to write. The University Press of Colorado (UPC), led by its long-time director Darrin Pratt, has an excellent, gracious staff that edited and designed all phases of *Brooke at the Bar*. I had compiled Brooke's 2014 text with materials from her archives for its figures. Tom Noel gave its first edit and a referral to UPC. Rachael Levay streamlined the manuscript's layout; Allegra Martschenko guided the many details to acceptance by UPC's editorial board; Robert Ramaswamy edited the manuscript for Brooke's "Reader" to enjoy knowing her and its information. Laura Furney is UPC's assistant director and was a very fine managing editor for this book. Dan Pratt may win another award for his design of this book. He selected the cover's photograph of Brooke, lovingly taken by her husband, Jim. Beth Svinarich, directs, with wisdom and creative flair, UPC's marketing and sales department. Last but not least is LaDonne Bush for years of encouraging Brooke for her book's writings and for collaborating with me for its arrangements; her "I suggest" was invariably followed.

Diane B. Wunnicke
2023 in Denver, Colorado

PS: To nonlawyers reading this, before you sign anything, remember Brooke's lifelong wise legal counsel to me: "The big print gives it to you, and the small print takes it away."

A SONG ABOUT BROOKE

OVER HER long career, Brooke received many awards and many tributes. A musical tribute captured her spirit as a lawyer, mentor, and professor. The lyrics were written by Bob Kapelke and sung by him and Brenda Taylor—both good friends of Brooke—to the tune of *Mame* at an event posthumously honoring her in October 2015.

> Who wowed those all-male juries with grace? Brooke.
> Who found the way to win every case? Brooke.
> Who had opponents reeling the moment she said "May it please the
>   Court?"
> No one was more appealing when arguing with just the right retort.
>
> Who taught young lawyers how to write well? Brooke.
> Who was adored by her clientele? Brooke.
> Who made a future interest class livelier than any class you took?
> Through efforts inconceivable, who made our dreams believable and life
>   success achievable? Brooke.
>
> Who came through ev'ry battle unbowed? Brooke.
> Who made women lawyers feel proud? Brooke.
> Her style was smooth as satin—she always had a twinkle in her eye,
> From Cheyenne to Manhattan, her legal reputation was sky high.
>
> Which Bar star did all judges admire? Brooke.
> Who set those ethics lessons afire? Brooke.
> Who made us better lawyers and proud we passed that Bar exam we
>   took?
> Her friendship was sensational, her lessons educational,
> her life was inspirational
> Brooke, Brooke,
> (Our) Brookie!

BROOKE AT THE BAR

Part One

Meet the Author for Your Voyage

"Inside Our Legal System"

> "Do what thou hast to do and to thine own self be true."
> *Parents of Brooke von Falkenstein (née) Wunnicke, in*
> *guidance soon after her marriage, early 1940. Paraphrased*
> *from William Shakespeare,* Hamlet, *Act 1, Sc. 3*

WELCOME. MY brief autobiography will introduce me to you, before joining me on our voyage inside our legal system, as I have long dreamed of sharing with my fellow Americans.

Figure 1.1. Brooke in 1919, age one.

Figure 1.2. Brooke at age two in the garden at her family home in Dallas, Texas.

I Am a Westerner

I was born in Texas and, at the age of three, moved with my family to Southern California, where I was raised and educated.

I married a fellow college student from Wyoming, where I lived and practiced law for twenty-three years. Then we moved to Colorado, where I practiced law for forty-plus years until retirement in 2011. As an adult, I was never farther east in the United States than Chicago until I was thirty-five years old, when I was in New York on business.

This book, therefore, explains for you how the majority of American lawyers practice law and citizens experience the law and courts in small and medium-size towns and cities. I have no experience with very large firms in major cities, where some firms have hundreds of lawyers and many branch offices here and abroad. I have no experience with nationally famous cases or as a judge on the highest court in the country.

Instead, I shall share with you an insider's look at the law in America from the second half of the twentieth century to the first decade of the twenty-first century. Our Founding Fathers emphasized that we have a government of laws, not of men. So, come visit with me to learn—or remind yourself—what we have done with that sage advice on how to live as a free people.

Figure 1.3. Brooke at age three is already photogenic for this 1921 professional photograph by Melbourne Spurr Portraiture, then in Hollywood, California.

Figure 1.4. Brooke's parents in back of their West Hollywood stucco house, in the late 1920s or early 1930s.

Early Life

GROWING UP IN THE GREAT DEPRESSION

T he term "autobiography" seems too pompous for this brief sketch of
my life, included as an aid to reading and hopefully liking my book.
In 1918, I was born in Dallas, Texas.

My family moved to Los Angeles when I was three years old and that is
where I lived until I was twenty years old, in a pleasant Spanish-style house
with a large back garden, located in West Hollywood.

I was the youngest of three children, a brother seventeen years older and
a sister six years older. I was fortunate in having a loving family, parents and
my older siblings. I was unfortunate to be unathletic, and Readers with the
same problem may be comforted to know that they can still have happy, successful lives.

MY FAMILY

ACCORDING TO what my parents told me, their backgrounds differed sharply.
My father was born in 1878 in Frankfurt-am-Main, Germany, and came to the
United States when he was twelve years old. My mother was born in 1880 in
Atlanta, Georgia, orphaned when five years old and raised by maternal grand-
parents in their home, which was on Sherman's March to the Sea during the
Civil War. My parents were married in 1901.

My father was the youngest of five children and was christened Raphael
von Falkenstein, being named after the great Italian artist. He told me that

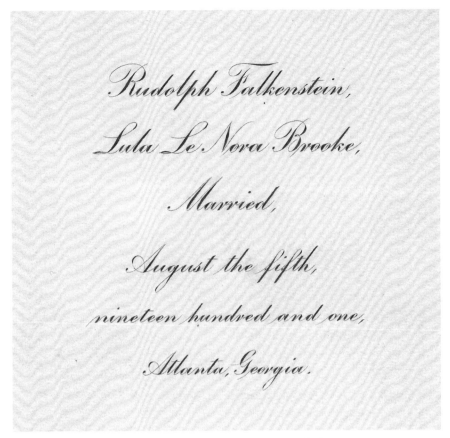

Figure 1.5. Announcement card that Rudolph Falkenstein and Lula Le Nora Brooke married on August 5, 1901, in Atlanta, Georgia.

his father's uncle was General Vogel von Falkenstein, who served with Otto von Bismarck. I was quite impressed when I learned about this and checked on my father's family in genealogy books at the library. When I told my father how impressed I was with the family history, I shall never forget my father's reply. He told me that the von Falkensteins were the second oldest German family, only the Hohenstauffens were older. Then he said that German people had given us three of the world's greatest musicians, Bach, Beethoven, and Brahms. They had also given us giants of literature, Schiller and von Goethe. But, he said that all the von Falkensteins had done through the centuries was fight, "warriors, nothing but warriors."

My father's father, who died long before I was born, loved art and did not believe in war. At the time of my father's boyhood, Germany was conscripting boys at age thirteen for military service. My paternal grandfather sent his sons to America before they were thirteen, my father being sent at age twelve. At Ellis Island in about 1890, the immigration authorities "Americanized" his name to Rudolph von Falkenstein. Alas, decades later when the Nazis came to power, they tracked down my father in California and pressured him to support the Nazi regime because of his family's "great military history"! My father was appalled. He was always so proud of being an American citizen, very patriotic, and insistent that his children must always exercise their right to vote. Then the Nazis began threatening him and his family, insisting that he was German, and his family's centuries of notable military service required his return to Germany. He understandably became frightened. My family had never had any involvement in politics or with the law. I was away from home at this time, in my senior

Figure 1.6. Lula Le Nora and Rudolph von Falkenstein in about 1904 with Brooke's brother Rudolph Jr., who used the first name Robert or Bob.

year of college at Stanford. When they called to tell me of this frightening situation, I said that they needed to notify the FBI and volunteered to do so for them. The FBI was wonderful, sent two agents to my family's home, and gave them adequate protection. I found out later that they became fond of my mother, who was charming and made delicious food, and they kept her free from fear. I shall always be grateful for the safety that the FBI provided to my dear, unworldly parents.

An interesting note: while Nazis were threatening my parents, I read in the *San Francisco Chronicle* about a big party honoring a Nazi high-ranking officer visiting in the Golden Gate City. People in our country had not yet realized that the mounting Nazi military victories and the imminent invasion of England posed a threat to our national security.

I have many memories of my father, several becoming fond only with time. He was very artistic, and business was always an alien world for him, with consequent unsuccessful results. He was impractical, always kind and gentlemanly, except when offended artistically. He also had an unfortunate inability to recall the surnames of my dates and later, even that of my husband.

As to my father's intolerance for "bad art," I remember when dear neighbors invited all five of our family to dinner to see the new picture that the wife had bought for their newly redecorated living room. We always enjoyed going to their home for dinner because we liked them very much, and she was an excellent cook. The husband was the well-paid head of the local division of a major corporation. They liked us, had no children, and enjoyed having our family with them. This night, however, we worried because the couple had no interest in art, and her home decorating taste was at best unfortunate. So, we urged our father not to say anything derogatory about the new picture she had bought, no matter how dreadful. He assured us that, of course, he would not be rude or hurt her feelings. When I saw the new picture, I feared that we were in trouble. It was painted in garish colors on black velvet! My father walked up close to this framed travesty, pulled out the small magnifying glass that he kept in his coat pocket, and peered at the picture. I held my breath, but it was not necessary because my father promptly said in an accusing tone: "Eva, who sold you this thing?" Not responding to his question, she made matters worse by saying, "I thought the picture would be nice because its colors go with the new carpet." Nonetheless, after this chilly interchange, our hostess served us a delicious dinner. My father's extreme lack of tact gave me a lifelong lesson to be polite and tactful.

My mother's background was entirely different from that of my father. Lula Le Nora Brooke was born in Georgia to a very old American family, with an ancestor who had signed the Declaration of Independence. My mother, the next to youngest of five children, was orphaned when she was only five years old and does not remember either parent. The Brooke children were not brought up together. As a result, I never knew aunts or uncles or cousins—the family was splintered. I remember my mother telling me that she never knew her two oldest siblings. She had heard that her oldest brother, Jasper Brooke, became a lawman in some western territory. Her older sister, Roxane, had married an Englishman and moved to England. The next sibling, Arthur Lee Brooke, lived in Atlanta, and occasionally he and my mother corresponded. The youngest child, O. A. Brooke, became a physician and practiced in the

Midwest. He would never disclose the names for his initials, and I started to tell them here—but I don't blame him, and my conscience would hurt if I told. My little orphaned mother went to live with her maternal grandparents, who still lived in their old plantation home that had been ransacked during Sherman's famous (and in the South, infamous) March to the Sea. She was raised by grandparents who had lived through the invasion during the Civil War. Thus, she was brought up in an earlier generation than if she had been raised by her parents. Her maternal grandfather was Zachariah Pinckney, a strict Scotch Presbyterian and a fervent hater of Yankees. The Pinckneys were loving grandparents but inculcated my dear mother with a distrust of Northerners and a lifelong detestation for General Sherman and his ravaging March to the Sea. When I was a child driving with my parents, we had to detour around a Los Angeles suburb that had the unfortunate name of Sherman Oaks. This was so unlike my mother in all other respects because she had a capacious heart and mind. She read widely, primarily history and biography with an occasional classical philosopher. I tell you truthfully: my mother was the loveliest person who I have ever known. I never heard her raise her voice in anger; she was always loyal and loving, intelligent, and eager to learn more. She was the epitome of a Southern lady of the nineteenth century in her taste, manners, and charm.

Many years later, when she was a sad new widow, I took her for her first visit to Washington, DC. She proudly watched my 1958 admission to practice before the Supreme Court of the United States; because of my Wyoming appellate practice, I had applied. My mother much enjoyed Mount Vernon and was thrilled to visit the home of Robert E. Lee, whose multivolume biography by Douglas Freeman she had recently read. I was still living in Wyoming at the time of our Washington trip, and I had prearranged a visit with our then senator, Frank Barrett. He invited us to lunch with him in the Senate Dining Room. He introduced us to a Southern senator, stating that my mother was from the South. My mother acknowledged the introduction in her usual gracious manner, and I still remember what ensued. The Southern senator excused himself and returned with two more Southern senators, later joined by still two others. Senator Barrett and I just looked at each other—we were nonexistent! Finally, he murmured, "I guess it's true, what they say about the charm of Southern ladies." Yes, it is true. My mother, free from any affectation, graciously made you feel good and want to be with her.

My mother tried very diligently to bring me up as a lady, in my manners, taste, and attitudes. I never acquired a fraction of her charm, but her teachings have always remained with me, even as to such details as a lady did not go forth without a hat and gloves. I did not realize how deeply she had inculcated the requirements for a lady until after my marriage and move to Wyoming. Then a lawyer, I was driving from Cheyenne to Casper to argue several motions, when I had my first and only serious auto accident. I learned the hard way that a hill that is clear on one side can be icy on the other. As I came to the top of the hill, the heavy dark red Hudson Hornet convertible went into a four-wheel skid, sailed into the air, and rolled over twice. As traffic stopped, and drivers rushed down the hill to pick up the body, I emerged from the total wreck. I was shaking, with my hat askew, and when asked, "Are you all right?" I responded, true to my mother's teachings, "No, I left my gloves in the car."

I very much want the Reader to be able to visualize my mother. A friend of my big brother's, who had become a successful playwright in New York, told me that when my mother was in her twenties, "She was the most beautiful lady whom I have ever seen." All my life she seemed beautiful to me and apparently to all around her. Every plant in our garden seemed to respond to her. We had a large bush covered with pink Cecil Bruner roses, a lovely big lilac tree, yellow roses, large hydrangeas, big ginger flowers, fuchsias, and many more humble and exotic flowers. Everything bloomed in profusion, as if to please my mother. Our fruit trees reacted the same: a giant apricot tree with the best apricots I have ever eaten, purple and white fig trees, orange and lemon trees, and a favorite peach tree. Again, like the flowers, the fruit grew and ripened in profusion. I always think of my mother when I read *The Sensitive Plant*, a memorable poem by Percy Bysshe Shelley that describes a beautiful garden and the lovely lady who tended and loved it. So many cherished memories of my wonderful, elegant, loving, and lovely mother, who so influenced me and my life. I wish that you could have known her. I now say good-bye here to my mother, whose death in 1967 left a permanent hole in my heart.

My childhood home was unusual in one notable respect, which I did not realize until after I had left my family home. All of us loved to read, and we had books everywhere: our living room, two bookcases in our dining room, the top two shelves of our linen closet, the top shelves of our kitchen cabinets, and of course in each of our bedrooms, both in bookcases and on bedside tables. Books, books everywhere. A culture shock for me was finding out that a houseful of books was not always to be found. Indeed, I was astounded when as an adult I visited in homes that apparently had no books. Classical music was also part of my family life. Even during the depths of the Depression, when we could afford meat only once a week, we had season tickets to the Los Angeles Philharmonic and to the Hollywood Bowl Summer Season, the latter then charged only twenty-five cents per individual ticket! Classical music was a necessity for us. Art, every form of it, was loved by all of us. We used to visit the Huntington Library and Art Museum, which had a far better collection than our city's then art museum.

The most vivid memory of my childhood and early teens is of the Great Depression. In 1929, along with millions of other Americans, my family suddenly went from financial comfort to utter poverty. Soon thereafter: the family printing and engraving business became insolvent; the trauma cost my father his hearing, and his business partner absconded with the few remaining assets; and then burglars stripped our home of all family heirlooms, including silver, fine china, and paintings; and the burglars even poisoned our dear spaniel Tyloe.

THREE YEARS IN GRAMMAR AND MIDDLE SCHOOLS

BY 1929, my brother had completed his education. My sister had been educated by private tutors, a highly competent Englishwoman and a French tutor. I had been home schooled; my first clear memory is of my loving and lovely mother teaching me my letters and how to read, together with basic arithmetic. By age four, I was able to read and have enjoyed reading throughout my life. I also audited my sister's sessions with her tutors. When I was five, my brother taught me the Greek alphabet, and I enjoyed learning all the (what I thought of as "cute") little alphabet characters. I learned from *Harvey's Rules of Grammar*. When I was ten, my father's business partner absconded with all the firm's assets, my father lost his hearing, and my big brother left college to help support the family. The next year, the Great Depression erupted. So, at age ten, I became the first girl in either of my parent's families to attend a public school. I was placed in the fifth grade. I hated it because it was boring, being already a fluent reader with a basic knowledge of French, Latin, and Greek.

My father declared that I forgot more in my first year of public school than all I had previously learned.

I was enrolled in Rosewood Grammar School, grades one through six, and it was a horrid experience for me. I hated school from the first day. The school was a long five block walk from my home, an unpleasant trip in chill, rainy weather. Because of my age, I was enrolled in the fifth grade. My first day at school, in a room with twenty-nine boys and girls, we were ordered to go into the schoolyard for morning recess and exercise. I had been a frail child, had not played outdoors, and the schoolyard was covered with gravel, whereas the garden at home had soft green grass. I looked at all that gravel with hot sun beating down on it and yelped, "No!" This led to my first, but not last, trip to the principal's office. The principal was unsympathetic to my plea, so outside I went, slipped and fell, and I still have a scar on my knee from my first day in public school. This was the first of my problems with having no athletic ability and the requirements of public schools—a separate discussion follows in this narrative of my life in " 'Fizz-Ed': A Tragic Tale of No Athletic Ability." This was my first encounter with, to me still, the basic fallacy of "If we do it for you, we would have to do it for everyone else."

Grammar school was downhill from my knee injury. I was bored as the lessons covered what I had previously learned. The only subject that I could not learn was the Palmer method of penmanship. The Palmer method, as taught to us, required filling pages with loops and squiggles of remarkable similarity, made possible we were told by a small muscle on the underside of the forearm. To this day, I believe that my arm does not have that little muscle. I could not learn that fancy penmanship. From my start and to this day, I always wrote a round, very legible backhand, with letters that slope to the left instead of to the right. This caused friction between the teacher and me, but I was incapable of doing that fancy slanting, illegible writing. Then Parents' Night was scheduled, when the children's "artwork" would be pinned up all around the classroom, with captions to identify what was depicted. The teacher asked me to write the captions because my handwriting was so easy to read! I refused. Back to the principal's office I went. He was not happy to see me and made me feel unpatriotic if I continued to refuse. My reward was that no further criticism of my handwriting ensued.

The fifth grade had other memorable experiences for me. An interesting one was when a local bank sent an officer to speak to our class about the importance of "Thrift," how important for us always to be "Thrifty," and gave each of us a piggy bank to inspire us to "Save." His message proved to be very important throughout future years of adversity.

Still a travail for me in the fifth grade was the sewing class, compulsory for all girls. We were each required to make a bean bag (I still don't know what that is), a pair of bloomers (yes!), and a dress. I don't know how huge my bloomers would have been because we were told to measure from the waist to just below the knee, double that figure, and buy that much yardage. My mother's opinion was that the result would be an immense pair of bloomers. But I never progressed that far. When all the other girls were sewing on their dresses, I was still struggling with the bean bag. Finally, the teacher, who always wore a smock printed with large, bright designs of dubious taste, took me by the ear to the principal. She said to him, "I can't stand her one more day. She's hopeless in sewing." I hope that I have aroused the sympathy of every Reader who, like me, was born with no manual dexterity whatsoever. The principal was ready for me this time and said, "All right. She's out of sewing and in the boys' woodshop class." I found that the boys were all carving interesting little items for their fathers, but after two weeks, the instructor gave me a large piece of used plywood with which to do something. Anyway, he was nice to me. So ended the fifth grade. The school had me skip the sixth grade, and I have always been suspicious of the motive for this decision.

Grammar school had taught me that authority demands conformity without exception, and later world history confirmed this truth.

Next, I entered a public junior high school, grades seven through nine, with only one year of grade school behind me.

I walked two blocks to get a streetcar that took me two blocks from the school, Bancroft Junior High. Junior high school was another memorably unpleasant experience. The classes were designed to teach the most mentally dull students, leaving the others learning nothing and restless. Again, physical education was mandatory, and as always, I was hopeless. I was small, rather thin, and hated "fizz-ed," as we called this school requirement. The teacher was always sarcastic about my ineptitude, and I dreaded the class.

The one bright spot in junior high school was my very excellent English teacher. I wish that Mr. Field could know how he started me in writing well, so that I later adopted "Accuracy, Brevity, Clarity" as my ABCs for legal writing. At just turned twelve years old when I entered junior high school, I was proud of my vocabulary, acquired during home teaching. So, I affected the use of big words when I wrote a school composition, even using with pride "sesquipedalian." I was graded an "A" probably for effort, but Mr. Field wrote on my paper, "Don't wear all your jewels to an afternoon tea." I never forgot that advice, and even wrote a chapter in one of my law books about the basics of legal writing, stressing simplicity.

Figure 1.7. Brooke at age twelve, in second row middle, with her classmates in seventh-grade Room 204 at Bancroft Junior High School.

A much less bright memory was the special yard recess to see a farm animal that the Board of Education had bought to take to all the schools so students could see one. The back of a small truck opened, a ramp was let down, and a man said as he led it down the ramp, "Children, this is a pig." Alas, this was during the Great Depression, and the school board could not afford to buy a cow. I saw my first live cow when I went as a bride to Wyoming and saw a herd of cows that were all black! I had expected live cows to be brown and white like in picture books that I had seen. I misunderstood my husband and, when I later told him how surprised I was by "Agnes" the cow, he was shocked. He said, "And you a Phi Beta Kappa! It is Angus, not Agnes!" I later represented a fine Angus cattle rancher in Wyoming.

A final but unpleasant memory of my last year in junior high school: our ninth grade was allowed to elect class officers. In a contested election for class president, I received many more votes than my opponent, Betty (whose last name I shall omit mentioning). The election was over shortly before afternoon recess and, as I was leaving to go outside, a teacher stopped me. She said, "You cannot be president. Betty will be president." I responded, "The class did not

Figure 1.8. Brooke in spring 1931, in front row, middle, with her ninth-grade classmates at Bancroft Junior High School.

want Betty. My classmates elected me." The teacher replied, "Betty's father is a member of the Los Angeles Board of Education, and so she will be president instead of you." Furious, I went outside to the schoolyard. There for the first and last time in my life, I hit someone. I walked up to Betty, who was much taller than I, willowy and hopelessly pithy, stood on my tiptoes and hit her on the chin as hard as I could. This time, my parents had to join me in the principal's office. My parents, of course, were shocked. I was very relieved when the ninth grade was over and that I need never see that junior high school again.

Junior high school had taught me that life was not fair, it was stupid to lose one's temper, and the English language could be written well.

AGE TWELVE: I DECIDE TO BE A LAWYER

RESERVING THIS paragraph all to itself is my decision when I was twelve years old to be a lawyer and devote my life to the law. Why? No one in my family, present or ancestors, had been lawyers; my family had never used a lawyer, sued or been sued; and did not care for lawyers. I had checked out from

Figure 1.9. Brooke, about age twelve, at an entrance to the downtown Los Angeles County Library Building, then recently built with unique architecture.

the public library, which I visited regularly, biographies of several lawyers, including *For the Defence: The Life of Sir Edward Marshall Hall*, the noted nineteenth-century English barrister, and the life of our great American jurist, John Marshall. Next, I started checking out from the library such books about law as I could comprehend. And so, inspired by these books, at age twelve I made the decision that I have never regretted: I would be a lawyer and "The Law" would always be a cherished, integral part of my life.

HIGH SCHOOL: TEACHERS, DEBATE, ORATORY, GRADUATION

AT AGE thirteen, I entered Hollywood High School, with only three years of public schooling, the fifth, seventh, and ninth grades; I did not attend grammar school until the fifth grade and skipped the sixth and eighth grades. I soon was delighted with my new school, Hollywood High School, located on

Sunset Boulevard just two blocks south of Hollywood Boulevard. The school occupied a whole city block, with different buildings. We had over 2,000 students, with few exceptions, excellent teachers, and it was a haven for all of us. The Great Depression engulfed us all for years to come with grueling, frightening poverty. At least, we were all poor together.

For the first time, I was in a school where I was taught much about many new areas of knowledge. My English teacher, Mr. Black, was a former Canadian college professor who "retired" to Southern California. He was a superb teacher of grammar, rhetoric, and literature.

My Latin teacher deserves special mention. Our class of thirty students adored her, and we all learned really to like Latin. Although she was not pretty, we thought her cute with her cheerful, sparkling personality. As the Great Depression continued to make our lives harsh, our Latin teacher always made us feel happier. As teenagers will, boys and girls alike, we wondered why she was not married—we thought her a special prize. When our two weeks' Christmas vacation was imminent, our Latin teacher told us that she had been saving money for many years to afford a cruise and that now she was going to spend her Yule holiday on a cruise. When we returned to school after the Christmas holiday, we learned that our Latin teacher had married the captain of the cruise ship. As impoverished as we all were, we were determined to buy her a wedding gift. For many of us, this would require missing some of our cheap lunches, but the sacrifice was worth it. One of our glamorous classmates said that she could buy a nice gift at a big discount at one of the stores on Hollywood Boulevard, which was only two blocks north of our high school. She said that the store had really pretty garments, and we all wanted to give a personal gift. We gave her our money, and the great day came when we put the elegantly wrapped box with a big shiny bow on our Latin teacher's desk, together with a large card that every member of the class had signed with a short message of admiration. Our teacher was so surprised when she saw the box, and we called out, "Open it! Open it!" *So she did, and I can still see the gift that she took out of the box.* It was the sexiest black nightgown that you can imagine, extremely sheer with very open black lace.

Our dear teacher exclaimed in words that I have often found useful, "Thank you. I have never seen anything like it." She smiled through sudden tears and said, "Tomorrow is my last day with you because my husband must return to his ship. You will have a substitute teacher for the rest of the term. My dears, I thank you from my heart." The next day was a sad one, but our beloved teacher brightened us when she said, "My husband thought your gift was splendid and said that he would really like to meet this Latin class. Thank you again, my dears, from my heart. I shall never forget you." And I am sure that she never did.

As always, my school life was tainted with mandatory physical education. In tenth grade, the girls were put in dancing class that was the first class of the day at 8:15 a.m. I still remember standing at the bar, being required to bend over to touch the floor and then bend back as far as one could—this before breakfast had been digested. Ugh! Also, in tenth grade I had my only two dismal high school teachers. My geometry teacher could have made Euclid hate geometry. My history teacher simply made us learn dozens of dates, leaving me with a disinterest in history until I married a history devotee and realized how fascinating history was.

In the eleventh grade, my then record in public speaking caused the school to plan to send me to various men's service clubs as a speaker to raise funds to buy an organ for the school's fine 2,500-seat auditorium, completed in 1928. Also, in eleventh grade, the required Physical Education class for girls was basketball. I protested against playing because I would get hurt, due to most of the girls being bigger than I was. As usual, my protest was to no avail. On the second day of the hated basketball class, I was accidentally hit so hard in the mouth that it loosened one of my front teeth. So this time, I took myself to the principal's office to tell him that I could not speak to raise funds for the school organ because of my loose front tooth—due to the required basketball class. He was understandably upset and said that the school would pay to send me to a fine dentist to see what could be done. The upshot was no speeches for six months, "leave that tooth alone"; later, I spoke repeatedly and raised money for the organ.

Eleventh grade was notable in two more respects. First, I shall tell you briefly about my chemistry class, where I quickly proved that science was not my intended area. One of our laboratory activities involved hydrogen. My maiden surname was "von Falkenstein," and my one-half Germanic inheritance caused me to want everything to be what I considered orderly. So, with the chemistry experiment, I did not follow the instructions given but neatly plugged every outlet in the widget I was using. It exploded with a loud noise. One of the girls in the class screamed and another one seemingly fainted. Emergency equipment came, sirens screeching. In retrospect, I probably made a small prototype for the hydrogen bomb. Enough of chemistry!

Eleventh grade also brought me my assured ticket to a college education. I doubt if any public high school class in my area ever had more straight "A" students than mine did. We knew that we could not go to college unless able to get scholarships, so all college-ambitious students worked very hard to get excellent grades. To assure a scholarship, therefore, the student had to have top grades, *plus*. For boys, the *plus* could hopefully be found in athletics or the sciences. For girls, the *plus* was difficult to find. So, in the eleventh grade, I decided to take Debate and Oratory, where I was the only girl in the class.

I was on the debate team that won the state high school debate contest, and I was the winner of the state oratorical contest. Then, in my last semester of high school, I participated in a city-wide high school extemporaneous speaking contest, sponsored by a local William Randolph Hearst newspaper, the evening *Herald-Express*. The contest was held on a wretchedly rainy night in the large auditorium of the University of Southern California. After drawing my topic from a fishbowl, I was taken through the rain to another building where I was locked in a small cubicle for one hour in which to prepare my speech. I was determined to win.

The auditorium seemed huge, with the second balcony very far away, and we had a then state-of-the-art microphone with a temperament of its own. I gave my all to that audience—with arms outstretched and a voice that reached to the very top row of the top balcony. After all the contestants had spoken, the wait began for the judges' decision. The wait was long, grew longer, the audience became restless, the newspaper sponsors could be seen arguing with the judges. Then we could see that both the judges and the sponsors were angry with each other, and more argument ensued.

Finally, the awards were made. First place went to a young man whose family was prominent and who attended a socially prestigious high school. Second and third places were awarded—and I had won nothing. Then the sponsors stepped to the front of the stage, called me up, and presented me with the huge horseshoe-shaped bouquet that had been the stage decoration for the occasion—I felt like a winning horse when they sort of draped it over me. One of the sponsors announced that the newspaper thought I was the best and would ensure me a proper award, and the audience's loud applause gratified my young heart and pleased the sponsors. And the newspaper did later give me a fine award of a trophy and cash.

Our debate and oratory coach was a recent arrival from Iowa to Hollywood High School. He was a fine teacher, and a kind, decent man. We wanted to

Figure 1.10. Hollywood High School 1935 graduating class in their matching sweaters on the front steps of the school. This is an excerpt from a larger photo, so we can identify Brooke in front row, center, kneeling.

do something special for him, despite the depths of the Great Depression, like take him out to dinner. In 1933, Prohibition was still in effect, and one of our group said that speakeasies had good, cheap food, making their money on the illegal sale of liquor. The decision was thus made to take our admired debate coach out to dinner at a speakeasy two blocks from the school, and one of our group made prearrangements with the place of our choice. Our teacher looked very surprised when a slot was pulled open in the locked entrance door to where we were dining. The appetizer that evening was a delicious steamed baby artichoke, which led to my shameful deed for which I can never forgive myself. Our teacher had never seen an artichoke before and asked what it was. He looked at it for several moments and then, because he obviously trusted me, leaned over and whispered: "How do I eat it?" I shamefully replied, "With a knife and fork." I truly hope that somewhere and somehow, he has forgiven me.

Twelfth grade continued an excellent high school education and with more debate and oratory for me. Our senior class wanted to enjoy some of the pleasures customary for a senior class, but we were all very poor. Our usual lunch was an undersized "pint" of ice milk for which we paid a dime. We decided that we could manage class sweaters and, because we had many more boys than girls in our class, the boys made the choice. The sweaters met the requirement of cheap, but I have never seen the like,

Figure 1.11. Brooke's February 1935 high school graduation book's portrait; as were other classmates, her eyes and mouth were altered by the photo-artist.

before or since. They were an odd shade of gray with long strands like hair hanging down so that we looked like grizzled apes in them.

We also wanted a high school annual book like previous senior classes always had, but we could not afford photographs. One of our classmates said that her uncle was a fine artist who did portraits and that he would do a portrait of each of us for only $1.00 apiece. We happily accepted and cheerfully put together the text for our annual. So off to the printer went the text from us and our portraits from the artist. I still have that high school annual and will show it only to very close friends. All of our senior class look alike: large, almond-shaped, slightly slanted eyes and identical mouths.

We were appalled when we first saw them and finally decided to laugh, saying to each other that we had the only really unique high school annual. Still true!

The last day of class we could not, of course, afford a party such as is the custom today in many schools. We so wanted to do something together after last class that would cost nothing. I had an idea: we all had, or could borrow, skates. Bicycles were an expensive rarity at that time. So I said, let's all bring skates tomorrow and after last class, we can all skate together, blocking traffic, down Hollywood Boulevard. The "yes" vote was unanimous, and the next day we had a fine time as we skated for some distance down the famed boulevard, until finally police herded us back to the high school, where the principal awaited us. I still remember that kind man's name, Mr. Foley. He told the police that they could leave and that he would "take care of us." He looked at us, suddenly downcast, in our shabby clothes and shoes, and said, "Well, that was not the right thing to do. But you had fun, and now it's time to look forward to your graduation tomorrow evening. Class dismissed." Bless him!

Our high school graduation ceremony in February 1935 was different. We were our high school's first class to graduate in caps and gowns. The high school had rented this attire because so many of the boys had no jackets, and the girls no nice dresses. Instead of the former big baskets of flowers on stage, we had garden marigolds laid flat in front of the footlights. I was the commencement speaker, and my dear mother had made me a pretty new dress for the occasion. After the ceremony, the school had a party for us of punch and cookies made by parents and teachers. In contrast, today on high school prom night, parents tell me the boys buy corsages for their dates and that their graduates rent limousines and are limousine-driven to a fine dinner, followed by dancing until the wee hours of the morning. No comment.

College and Working in the Great Depression

I have never known whether my college scholarship was the result of the newspaper sponsors' efforts or merely a fortuitous event. Anyway, soon after the memorable extemporaneous speaking contest, the University of Southern California (USC) offered me a full scholarship. No debate scholarship would be available until the fall, and I had graduated in February. But USC let me enter spring semester on an available men's track scholarship. Fortunately for both the university and for me, I was not expected to participate in track! (More about me and athletics in " 'Fizz-Ed': A Tragic Tale of No Athletic Ability.")

SNAP COURSE: "LIFE AND TIMES OF JESUS"; MEETING "A KRAFT CHEESE"

I REMEMBER my first day on campus. I was sixteen years old and bewildered by the elaborate process of registration. A big and burly young man came up to me and said: "Looking for a snap course, little girl? Take Life and Teachings of Jesus for two units." Grateful for his caring, I was nonetheless shocked by his message. I later learned that "Two-Ton" Tony (whose last name I omit) was a star on USC's football team which, predating the pass attack, played power football, and Tony looked powerful. That first day I did not know anyone at USC and so went by myself to one of the nearby campus cafes. A young woman, also alone, invited me to sit with her, and introduced herself: "My mother was a Kraft cheese." I began to feel like Alice in Wonderland after Tony's advice and my lunch companion's introduction. Would everyone on campus be this different from the students whom I had known before? But both were friendly, and the young woman, who was also an entering freshman, and I became good friends.

MY NASTY DEBATE COACH

ALTHOUGH USC spared me track during my first semester, I was required to participate in debate. The women's debate coach I also remember well—but not fondly. He took an instant dislike to me because he had not chosen me for a scholarship, and my small stature was not impressive. His favorite debater was a talented young woman who was everything I was not: tall, blonde, blue-eyed, with an almost musical speaking voice. So, the coach tried desperately to transform me into a carbon copy of this fair goddess, not in appearance which would have been impossible, but in style of presentation. My first debate contest in college rolled around late that spring semester: a regional contest with six rounds of debate. The partner whom the coach paired with me was not very good, and I was worse as I tried to look tall and utter my arguments in pearly tones. We lost every round.

HAT AND WHITE GLOVES, SIXTEEN, LANDING MY FIRST OFFICE JOB

THE GREAT Depression was getting no better, so I needed a summer job to help buy textbooks and to help out with home expenses. I have read that now high schools train young people how to dress and to apply for a job. In 1935, this was not the case. Indeed, I was the first woman in my family—and in its history—to seek a job in an office. So, at age sixteen, I put on my Easter Sunday outfit, topped with my Easter bonnet, a round straw hat with a bunch of pretty white flowers right in the middle front, and snowy white cotton gloves. My beloved mother was from the South and most particular about my dress and manners. I decided that I would prefer an attractive office so I went to Spring Street in downtown Los Angeles, which was our equivalent to Wall Street. I selected the finest looking stock brokerage building, entered, approved of the deep carpet and rich furnishings, and told the receptionist that I would like to see the president. I handed her my calling card, "Brooke von Falkenstein." Eyeing the flowers bobbing on my hat and my white gloves, the receptionist justifiably had no clue that I was a job applicant. So I was ushered into the president's office and was struck mute at the sight of the "Distinguished Executive" seated behind a "Distinguished Desk." For a moment he also was struck mute at the sight of me, poor fellow. Then he kindly asked me to sit down and asked what he could do for me. I told him that I wanted and needed a job, did not know how to do anything in an office, but would work hard to learn. Then I stopped breathing. Bless his heart, how kind he was! He called the Los Angeles Stock Exchange next door and said that he would appreciate their interviewing me. So next door I trotted—flower-trimmed hat, white gloves, and all—interviewed and was hired.

A PARIAH WINS THE DEBATES

USC RENEWED my scholarship of my freshman year for the fall semester. My first day that semester, I ran into the debate coach who said, "What are you doing here? I made sure that you did not get a debate scholarship." USC had awarded me, however, an academic scholarship with a request that I continue to participate in debate. No wonder that I know what it is to be treated like a pariah. The debate coach ignored me except to assign me a hopelessly inept partner. The good part was that he did not coach me. So, we won every round of the next tournament, further debate championships, and I also won oratory and extempore. The coach was a sort of perverse motivation for me to excel.

THE STOCK EXCHANGE DURING
THE GREAT DEPRESSION

I WAS fortunate to be hired by the Los Angeles Stock Exchange, not only for my first summer in college but on a part-time basis during the school year. I worked at the Stock Exchange every summer and Christmas and other holiday breaks until, having transferred from USC, I was graduated from Stanford in 1939. I also remember the shock at the Exchange when I celebrated my eighteenth birthday, which they thought was my age when hired. I had not been truthful because of California's strict child labor laws, and I had needed the job so much.

How patient they all were at the Exchange! I learned much about the securities business. I remember when daily trading was so slack on the New York Stock Exchange that a bad day would see only 35,000 shares traded! What a comparison to today's hundreds-of-millions or even billion shares that may be traded in a day. The traders would say, "Well this is a good day—we made lunch money." On a good trading day, they would sometimes buy me lunch, which was a special treat. My usual was a ten-cent malt with ice milk instead of ice cream, together with a five-cent sandwich, either cheese or tuna fish. Remember, this was the time when unemployment was rampant. I still remember the people who sold red apples on the corner for a nickel as their means of support—capable people from every walk of life, with no jobs. To this day, although I love to eat apples, my least favorite is a red apple because it evokes sad remembrances. The Exchange was a patient employer. Sometimes a boyfriend or a group of college friends would drive by the back of the Exchange building and call out: "Can Brooke come out awhile—to go get a Coke or something?"

I have always regretted my mean act toward the traders who were so solicitous of me. I was one of those chosen at USC to usher at our Saturday afternoon football games. The girl ushers were clad in special sweaters with the Trojan emblem, which is USC's logo, and we were proud of our special status. When the traders came to the game, they were so pleased to know one of the Trojan ushers and would call out a greeting to me. But I would pretend not to hear them. I did not want my peers to know that I knew these "Old Men"— mostly in their thirties and even forties. They would now forgive me, I'm sure, if they knew how warmly I remember their many kindnesses to me.

In addition to my job at the Stock Exchange, I had three other jobs that I could do "on my own time," which was really nonexistent because I carried a full load of courses at USC. But I wanted to provide some financial help at home because my family, as did so many throughout the country, had lost everything in 1929. My ambition was to be elected to the Phi Beta Kappa academic honorary society but, after several years of my grueling schedule, my ambition changed to wanting sufficient sleep. And, of course, I wanted and enjoyed a happy social life. Although USC was then a very Greek-letter campus, a sorority was out of the question for me because of economic and work-related reasons. But the fraternity boys could and did ask me to dances and other festive occasions.

DON'T SPEND SAVINGS ON DANCING SHOES

ACROSS THE street from the Los Angeles Stock Exchange's building was a small, sound, and very conservative bank where I had started a minuscule savings account. Every cent that I could scrimp, I put into that account. One day I went to make my first withdrawal. The elderly teller seemed displeased and asked me what I was going to do with the money. When I answered that I was going to buy a pair of evening sandals for dancing, he shook his head somberly and disapprovingly doled out my cash. Probably for my own good, but nonetheless that teller left me with a permanent sense of guilt whenever I draw cash from an account.

MEMORABLE FACULTY

NOT TO be preachy, but snobbery about universities to me seems a hallmark of personal insecurity. A student at any officially accredited university can obtain a splendid education. You get out of a university what you put into it. I had three wonderful years at USC. Although I remember several miserable incidents, the overall experience was intellectually challenging. For those of you still in college or still smarting from slights inflicted there, remember you are not alone. You will never forget but they cease to bother, and on a good day, you can even feel sorry for a person cut on so small a scale.

I remember one professor who had a small class, in which I had enrolled, comprised of obviously well-off students. My presence bothered the professor like a persistent itch, until one day he addressed me in class to say, "People like you don't really belong in college because you don't have the money." I didn't, but I had a full tuition scholarship, and he inspired me to get the highest grade in the class. This was my first exposure to what I consider the infamous Bell Curve of grading which I again met and resisted many years later when I was an Adjunct Professor of Law. Anyway, this unpleasant professor did not give me an "A" despite my earning the highest grade. One of only two times that I ever squawked about a grade, I squawked. The professor's response: "The Bell Curve allows me only three A's for this class, you would make four, so I awarded the A's alphabetically. Your name, beginning with 'V' is last, so you are out." I retorted, "The von in my name is a small 'v', the first letter is capital 'F', so I am in. And the university's registration records will confirm my alphabetical status." He was furious—but I got my deserved "A."

REMEMBERING FINE TEACHERS

FOR THOSE of you who are caring and capable teachers, be assured that your students will always remember you fondly. I remember with much gratitude my science professor. We were required to have one year of science, and I

Figure 1.12. Brooke in 1938, wearing her Phi Beta Kappa key, as awarded in her junior year at the University of Southern California.

avoided a "lab" course because of my unfortunate high school experience in chemistry with the hydrogen experiment.

Anyway, at USC, I opted to take geology, which seemed a safer choice than chemistry. The professor, Arthur Tieje, despite a rather dusty dry manner, excited my lifelong interest in geology. More importantly, he taught effectively "how to analyze," that proved indispensably useful to me as a lawyer. I wish he could know how often I have thanked him for imparting analytical skills. He was a retired petroleum geologist who had searched for oil all over the world in exotic places that I yearned to visit. He was very knowledgeable and often testified as an expert witness in oil litigation. He taught us about analyzing with scientific precision. I then took the other courses that he taught, vertebrate paleontology and invertebrate paleontology. And I am quite serious: Professor Tieje's teaching has served me well throughout my over half-century as a lawyer.

I remember bemoaning in paleontology that I could not remember all the long Latin names for the fossils. His response was that the names were not important, but what was important were the distinctive, distinguishing characteristics. What did I see that enabled me to distinguish one fossil from another? And so it is with law. When searching for a court opinion that supports my client's case, how do I determine if the opinion really applies? Or, opposing counsel cites an opinion claimed to be against my client's position, how do I determine if it applies? By using the precise fossil analysis that Professor Tieje taught us, I look for key facts that are similar or distinguishable from my case. What may first seem an apples and oranges situation may be analyzed to fit—if fruit is what is needed. Or, scrutiny may disclose facts distinguishing the supposedly adverse case from mine.

I was elected to Phi Beta Kappa in my junior year. In this book, for

Figure 1.13. Brooke in 1938, wearing her cap and gown for the occasion of her graduation from Stanford University.

the first time, I admit that I do not recall the installation ceremony because I was so tired from all my jobs plus school that I went to sleep. I would really like to know what, if any, official ritual occurs when installed as a member of Phi Beta Kappa. But I still wear my key with pride, although the engraving of name and year on the reverse side is now obliterated by time.

At the end of my junior year in 1938, I transferred to Stanford University at the behest of a wealthy family friend (anonymous to me) who thought it more appropriate for me—and would foot the bill.

I was happy at Stanford and did not mind contributing funds to my family at home. I earned money by developing and selling several accounting systems in San Francisco, including one to a bank for its trust department. Affiliated with the Stanford chapter of Phi Beta Kappa after my first batch of grades, I became used to a type of university and campus different from USC. Both provide excellent opportunities for learning, if that is the student's objective.

Law School

A WOMAN LAW STUDENT IN THE 1940S

My most important event at Stanford was that I met James M. Wunnicke.

I HAVE always said that I married him for his money, and this was reported in a flattering 1986 article in the Denver Bar Association's publication, *The Docket*. The article gave all the financial facts: he had twenty dollars when we eloped, and I had five dollars. Soon after meeting, he proposed to me. I did not answer yes or no, but said, "Only if I can be a lawyer." And he agreed, a commitment that he nobly honored until his untimely death in 1977. With love, I always called him "Jimmie."

Jim was a native of Cheyenne, Wyoming, and thence we went to establish our home and raise a family. I was to go to law school when our children were in school. But events were otherwise. In 1941, when our daughter was born, I did not do well, being hospitalized some while before and after. We were blessed with having a particularly fine daughter, Diane.

Jim and I both worked because we needed two incomes in the hope of elevating our financial status to that of the proverbial church mouse. We were finally able to purchase, with a big mortgage, a nice little brick house and have some money around the edges for recreation. Then, on December 7, 1941, the Pearl Harbor attack struck our country. Jim had his first lieutenancy in the infantry courtesy of his high school ROTC, but he became unacceptable because he had contracted undulant fever. The navy also rejected him, but finally the Coast Guard accepted him and away he went to war. Diane and I took the train to Los Angeles to live with my parents. I was to enroll in law school so that I could support us in the sad event that he did not return from war.

I WELL remember my first day in 1943 at USC's College of Law. I arrived long before class, at 7:30 a.m., after an hour's travel via two streetcar transfers. I walked into the law library, with the sun streaming through the windows on all those mysterious but wonderful law books that I would learn how to use. I said silent prayers for my loved ones and the last one for me, that I could and would become a worthy lawyer and appellate judge.

As I recall, two other women were in my law class. We were not greeted warmly, but only one professor overtly showed his dislike. At the first class with him, he announced, "You may have heard that I do not like women. That is true. But I particularly do not like women in my law class." He soothed his irritation by never calling on any of the women to recite. I think that this allowed him to pretend happily that we were not there. On my final examination, he noted that my paper had the highest grade that he had given in twenty-five years. Thereafter, when this professor met me in the hall, he would quickly turn his head away as far as he could without snapping it off his neck—a notably visible snub. When some of the students asked if I did not resent his treatment, I answered "No." I would have resented him if he had denied me the grade that I had earned—that would have been discrimination. But this professor was not obligated to like me, and he did not because I had the fatal flaw of being a woman law student.

I have related this episode to some young Black and Hispanic law students or lawyers from many backgrounds—whom over the years I mentored—who are often justifiably hurt by not being liked. Law firms may be more careful not to discriminate, so as to avoid financial liability or adverse publicity. And I tell these talented young people, so long as you are treated fairly, accept the fairness but realize that you cannot compel those people to like you. And I feel no sympathy for those who cannot bring themselves really to like the minorities whom they feel obligated to hire. I know that by not becoming friendly with my uniquely talented and delightful "children," these narrow spirits have deprived themselves.

After I had completed half of my law school courses, I transferred to the University of Colorado School of Law in Boulder, Colorado. The end of World War II was believed to be near, and Boulder is only about a hundred miles from Cheyenne. The belief of imminent peace was erroneous, but I finished my law education in Colorado—about one month after the war ended, and

Figure 1.14. A portrait photograph of Brooke, probably 1945, wearing the strand of graduated-size pearls given to her by Jim Wunnicke. She very often wore them.

Figure 1.15. Jim Wunnicke with their daughter Diane, about 1945.

my Jimmie came home. I was number one in my law class at USC and also at Colorado, so was very happy to be awarded Order of the Coif, which is the law school equivalent of Phi Beta Kappa. And "my Jimmie" was able to come to my law school graduation on October 20, 1945.

MY ADMISSION TO THE BAR—THE JUDGE'S DOG KNOWS MORE LAW THAN I?

AS WAS true for hordes of young couples, my husband and I started anew after World War II. We could no longer afford a house in the Cheyenne neighborhood where we had bought before because prices had escalated during the war. And servicemen did not make much money while at war. But we had confidence that somehow we would make a good life for us and our daughter. First, I had to take and pass the dreaded Bar exam, which I did.

On May 7, 1946, I was admitted to the practice of law in the State of Wyoming. Such a cold, bald sentence to describe a magnificent event in my life. Today's admission ceremonies are far different. Hundreds of lawyers take the Bar examination in each state twice a year and, of course, the result is that our country is notoriously over-lawyered. The state admission ceremonies are held in auditoriums or theaters, usually with the state's appellate judges sitting on stage and one of the judges giving a welcoming speech.

In 1946, admission to the Wyoming Bar was a highly personal affair. The clerk of the Wyoming Supreme Court called me to come to his office to be sworn in as a lawyer. My husband was at work and could not come. I took Diane, then five years old, with me, but she does not recall the occasion. The clerk's office had a high counter so Diane could not really see what was going on, except when I raised my hand and took the oath. The clerk then told me that the chief justice wanted to see me in his chambers. The clerk, Fred S. Fobes, was a thoughtful gentleman and offered to keep Diane with him, where he entertained her with the wonderful clockworks that he made by hand.

I went into the august precinct of the justices' chambers, wondering if something had gone wrong. Then Chief Justice Fred H. Blume greeted me graciously and invited me to be seated. He always brought his dog with him to work, although never actually into court. The dog, which varied as to breed over the years, would always lie alongside his desk. In 1946, Justice Blume's dog was a very large, dark brown, curly-haired dog of a breed I did not know.

Justice Blume welcomed me to the Wyoming Bar and visited with me. He was internationally known as a Greek and Latin scholar and for having single-handedly created what is still today the only known translation of and notes to Justinian's Code made from the standard Latin edition, and with extensive notes on Roman law. He was a great scholar of the law. He asked me if I were familiar with Justinian's Code, and I replied "Yes." While still an undergraduate, I had saved to buy a used copy of Justinian's Code, because I had learned that this code of Roman law undergirded law in Western Europe and some of the English common law. The justice said, "I am very pleased. The young lawyers today never seem to be familiar with Justinian's Code." Then he asked, "Are you familiar with the Theodosian Code?" Although I could identify it, I certainly was not familiar with it and replied "No, your honor, I am not." And the Justice's dog growled at me.

At dinner that night, I faithfully reported to my husband the events of my admission to practice law in Wyoming, including my discomfiture because the Justice's dog seemed to know more law than I did.

OATH OF ADMISSION TO THE BAR

FINALLY, A message about an Oath of Admission to the Bar. In our United States of America, the states vary the wording of the oath for a lawyer being admitted to the bar of that state and to practice law and appear in their courts. Over the many years of my lectures to lawyers, and teaching law school students, I have reminded them that regardless of where or when: For twenty-four-hours a day, every day of the year, until the lawyer dies, retires, or is disbarred, you are "at the Bar." Thus, for you the Reader, my title of this book is *Brooke at the Bar*.

"Fizz-Ed"

A TRAGIC TALE OF NO ATHLETIC ABILITY

Dedicated to those with NO athletic ability.

I AM certain that my Readers include some, to whom this dedication is addressed, who have little athletic ability. They will find comfort in knowing that they have company, who managed later to have happy, successful lives.

I was the youngest in my family, arriving rather late in my parents' lives. I was petite, being a delicate way of saying that I was short and thin.

On my very first day in the fifth grade of the public school (I was ten), over my strenuous objections, I was ordered outside by the principal for a morning recess and exercise.

The exercise started with a game of tag and, on the first order to run, I fell on the gravel, and a piece embedded in my kneecap. The pain was dreadful, and I am a "bleeder." The school had to call an ambulance, and as I was laid on a stretcher, I looked up into the face of the anxious principal. Shamefully, I croaked: "I told you so."

Worse was yet to come in junior high school Physical Education (pronounced "fizz ed"), which was a mandatory class. I was among the smallest of the girls in my class. In addition, I lacked even the most basic coordination. Fizz-Ed was a daily tragedy for me at school. I was always first academically and by-far-the-last athletically. Then came the climax of my athletic career at junior high school. Our "gym" teacher, a tall, robust woman who wore a middy blouse and large, black bloomers, soon singled me out as inferior talent. She had us engage in a "decathlon," with events differing from those in the Olympics but equally formidable for me. I remember only two of the ten. One was the broad jump, in which one was supposed to jump over a small sandbox and as far beyond as possible. I, of course, always landed in the near side of the sandbox.

The other event was my Waterloo. We were instructed to throw a hard baseball as far as we could. When my turn came, the teacher taunted me in front of all the other girls, predicting with laughing disparagement how pitiful my throw would be. Fury at the public taunt gave me amazing strength. I threw the ball with all my might, and it sailed out of the school yard, over the fence, and broke a window in the laundry building next door. Not content with that, I shouted, "My parents are not going to pay for the window; the damn school is going to pay." This was the first time that I had ever used a swear word aloud—and it felt good under the circumstances. The result: not only another visit to the principal's office, but also a meeting with both my mother and father with the principal. She was a tall, haughty woman, who told my parents that I was "the best student that the school had ever had, but the worst citizen!" My parents were shocked, protesting what a well-behaved child I always was at home. I knew that was true because I loved them both and wanted to make them happy. Those emotions did not extend to the adult denizens of my junior high school. Anyway, I served only two of my three years' sentence there, skipping the eighth grade and finishing the ninth without any athletics.

Even the fine Hollywood High School had a terrible flaw in my opinion: mandatory physical education, although with a new variety of choices. I chose ballet as my first class of the day, to get the hated hour over and done with for the day. My sister was a very talented ballet dancer, whose expensive lessons continued during those dark financial days of the Great Depression. I certainly had none of her talent, seemingly having a spine that did not bend and two left feet. Anyway, class always started by holding on to a bar, gracefully (ha!) bending down, and then bending back with your arm gracefully over your head. Impossible! Plus, trying to bend to-and-fro so soon after my breakfast made me sick. The next year as I entered the eleventh grade, I learned that physical education for girls required us to play baseball (hardly a post-school sport to enjoy) for the first semester and basketball for the second semester.

By my second semester in the eleventh grade, several important events had happened to me. I had won the state high school oratorical contest for juniors and had been on the winning state high school junior year debate team. The high school had a fine, new, large auditorium, seating 2,500 persons, completed just before the 1929 stock market crash. The school very much wanted an organ for the auditorium but could not afford to buy one. Then for the first time in my school days, I was called to the principal's office to be asked to bestow a favor. The school wanted me to speak at the different men's service club luncheons, such as those of Rotary, Kiwanis, and Lions, to raise money for the organ. I responded that I would be pleased to give the requested talks but had a problem in doing so. I told the principal that I was required in this new semester to play basketball, and I was sure that I would get hurt and be unable to help raise the organ money. Poor fellow! He had no way of knowing what a hopelessly clumsy person I was. So thence to the basketball court I went. Sure enough, in my second game, a very large guard hit me accidentally across the mouth and loosened one of my two front teeth. I returned to the principal's office to explain "no talks" and to say that the school, not my parents, should pay a dentist to look at my loose front tooth. The principal was very sorry about my injury and arranged for my dental visit. The dentist told me to keep my hands off the loose tooth, it would gradually tighten, and I would be able to give a public speech in about six months. (Yes, I did later give speeches and helped raise money for the organ.) So ended my high school athletic career. Again, I graduated with all A's—except for a bare pass in Physical Education.

I entered the University of Southern California on a full scholarship and elsewhere tell you about my travails and joys there. To my horror, I found out that college, for the first two years, also had mandatory physical education. I had no coordination, no muscle strength, and negative coordination skills. We had no choices in the first semester of our freshmen year, so I dutifully tried to do all the prescribed exercises and, of course, failed abysmally. The teacher was kind, however, and gave me an undeserved "Pass." For the second semester, I chose Morris Dancing, which the university's catalogue described as a popular English folk dance of the sixteenth century. I thought, aha, that should be about my speed. Ho! Was I wrong! I wonder how many Brits, good and true, lost their lives engaging in Morris Dancing. I found out that you dance around quickly while carrying very tall sticks, so I soon knew that I would fall victim—which I did, flattened by a flailing stick.

By my sophomore year, I had already, to my parents' distress, decided on economics with accounting and statistics for my sub-majors. My parents believed that I should major in more usual liberal arts, but I wanted assurance of a job and earning enough to go to law school. Anyway, way back then, I was the only girl in my classes, which were held in a small building all the way across campus from the women's gym building. The only women's physical education class available to me during the one hour that I had open in my required academic curriculum was Soccer and Baseball for Physical Education Majors.

Readers, you will be incredulous when I describe how frightening the soccer was to me. You may be right. Perhaps with time my soccer experience has become more frightening than it really was, and the teacher and my soccer opponent were not really as large as I remember them. I can share only my uncorrected memory. The teacher was a tall, muscular woman, who was always clad in gym suits, her shirt and bloomers starched stiff, and in jarring pastel colors of pink, blue, or lavender. I can still visualize my opponent rushing down the field toward me while vigorously kicking the ball. In memory she seems the size of a defensive end in the National Football League, her long legs like big logs kicking that ball. The teacher would shout: "Brooke, get the ball from Dorothy!" And I would fervently shout back: "Dorothy can have it!"

When the next semester came, the women's physical education department, having suffered me for three of the four required semesters, registered me for my last semester of women's gym in "rest." I'm serious: *rest*. We had ten minutes between classes, so when the bell rang for the end of my immediately preceding class, I ran as fast as I could across campus to the women's gym building. When I got there, I ran to my locker, off with my street clothes and on with my gym shirt and big bloomers; then I would run up a flight of stairs to a pallet on which I was to *rest*. I would lie there panting. After panting, I calmed to heavy breathing and just as I was about to breathe normally, it seemed the bell would ring for end of rest. Up I would jump, quickly to reverse the process I had just undergone, and run back to my class building. When my grades came, I had all A's—except in rest, in which I received a C minus. In one of the only two times that I ever questioned a grade (I tell you about the other time in Part One's "College and Working in the Great Depression," about Memorable Faculty), I asked how I could get such a low grade in rest. The response was cryptic and memorable: "You don't rest well."

The end of college does not end this Tragic Tale of No Athletic Ability. The years went by happily and busily as a practicing lawyer. When in 1969 my husband retired from business, he wanted us to move from his hometown of Cheyenne, Wyoming, to Denver, Colorado. I continued to practice law, with his encouraging approval, and had become a respected lawyer of ripe age. Our beloved daughter joined us in Denver. My husband and daughter decided that it would be healthy for me to exercise. I no longer did trials and led a contentedly sedentary existence as an appellate and transaction lawyer. We were members of the Denver Athletic Club, a very old downtown club. The club, however, began to modernize and hired a woman to provide athletic training for women. Unfortunately, the club sent out an announcement of a new after-work gym class for "mature business and professional women." My husband and daughter urged me to go, verbally painting me a picture of my blooming youthful health once I had taken the class.

My husband and daughter were so earnest about how wondrous this class would be for me, and I loved them so much, that I agreed to join the class. They said that I needed to buy a "workout suit." I could think of no item of clothing on which I would be more reluctant to spend money than a workout suit. So I went to a low-priced but respectable downtown store to buy my "costume" for the class. The store did not have my size but had one, only one, just one size larger. I soon found out why the garment had not yet sold: it was a very dismal grey, probably the grey of a very old elephant. I thought that the garment would probably shrink if washed in very hot water, but it did not shrink—it grew. Well, I wasn't training for a fashion show, and off I went to my first class. When I arrived, I was unhappy to see that all the other "mature" women were young, tall, lithe creatures, dressed in form-fitting stylish workout clothes, and in tip-top physical condition. Nonetheless, I plodded on, week after week. My little family was proud of me. As the weeks dragged on, my workout suit grew larger and baggier with each washing. The other class members grew more lithe and elegant looking. The teacher, however, was a bright spot because she was a very nice and patient woman probably in her late forties. She tactfully hid her pity for my ineptitude, and I did try to do well.

Then she announced we would do swimming classes. I was thrilled because I had always wanted to be able to swim. Indeed, when I entered Stanford, I was told that being able to swim was mandatory for a Stanford graduate. I fielded that one by saying, "Well, I was raised in Southern California, so what do you think?" The truth is that I could not learn to swim because I sink too fast, like a big anchor. In fairness, I warned the nice teacher of my current class. She said that she had been teaching swimming for twenty-five years and had never failed in teaching a student to swim. I was filled with new hope. Never afraid of water and always yearning to swim in a beautiful blue swimming pool, I had stood dry and wistful on the sidelines. The teacher offered to stay after our class for a half-hour to train me to swim. My family was happy for me, and so the project began. At the end of two weeks, she sadly said: "Brooke, dear, all I seem able to do is keep scraping you up from the bottom of the pool. You are my first failure."

Finally, the teacher announced that the next class would be our last one. We had been "cleared" to run on the track that ran around the mezzanine in the men's gym. She said that the schedule was to run four times around the track and emphasized that there might even be "*a few Men*" running around the track. I heard a murmur of pleasure from attractive young women who were my classmates. To my relief, the last class came, and we went across the hall to the men's gym. I saw a few men throwing basketballs and hoped none of them were lawyers who knew me. As we trooped up to the mezzanine, I heard a man's voice say, "Look, there's Brooke, Brooke Wunnicke. Hi, Brooke!" Then another voice, "You're right! Hi, Brooke!" I looked, two lawyers whom I knew, and I wanly waved my hand. Then we began the race around the track. I ran what I thought a fast pace so as to keep up with the rear of the class, loping clumsily in my very baggy "sweats" costume. Again, to my mortification, one of the men runners said, "Brooke! I didn't recognize you at first. Hello!" And then yet another lawyer on the track looked at me, arrayed in my baggy gray sweats, and said, "Why it's you Brooke! I didn't recognize you at first!" About this time, we passed our teacher who called out to me, "Brooke, I don't think that you should try to run more than once around the track." And something within me snapped—I guess that it was my pride waking up. So I found sudden new energy to speed up, determined to run all four laps and *win!*, which I did, passing the men and my young classmates to come in *first!* Thus ended my fleeting moment of athletic glory and also the very last time in my life that I exercised.

Spotlight

LOOOOONG ARM OF THE LAW

Lawyer's professional passion burns bright after 54 years. 3D

Denver Rocky Mountain News ◆ Thursday, September 28, 2000

Figure 2.1. *Rocky Mountain News*, Spotlight, September 28, 2000, full cover page close-up photo of Brooke with the article about her professional passion burning bright after fifty-four years.

Part Two

The Lawyer, 1946–2011

Never esteem aught of advantage which will oblige you
to break your faith or to desert your honor.
  Marcus Aurelius, Meditations, *Third Book, VII*

A Lifetime of Law

Pioneer attorney still practicing after 60 years

By Mary Angell

Women were "about as common as an aardvark in the courtroom" when Brooke Wunnicke started practicing law in Cheyenne.

The year was 1946, and Wunnicke was Wyoming's first female trial attorney.

"In those days, reporters were all men. Jurors were all men," she told the *Wyoming Lawyer* recently. "I tried jury cases to (male) judges, always. I tell you truthfully, I never felt it prejudiced my clients. When they saw I was there for real and prepared and doing my job, I could feel the support. It was literally palpable to me."

Now, at the age of 88, Wunnicke is the oldest active member of the Wyoming Bar and one of the oldest in the Colorado Bar. She serves as Of Counsel for the firm of Hall & Evans, L.L.C., located in the Chase Building in downtown Denver. Though she's practiced in Colorado since 1969, Wyoming mementos — including documentation from the Wyoming Supreme Court of her acceptance to the Wyoming Bar and a crystal plaque commemorating her 60 years as a member — are prominent fixtures there.

Over the years, Wunnicke has specialized in diverse areas of the law. She gained extensive trial and appellate experience and served as Chief Appellate Deputy in the Denver District Attorney's office for more than 12 years. She has authored and co-authored books on business law, taught law classes at the University of Denver College of Law and lectured on a variety of subjects, chiefly professional ethics.

When Wunnicke talks about her years in the legal profession, her love of the law is obvious.

"I've gotten so much joy from it," she said of her career. "I have a lot of memories. You never forget your victories and you never forget your defeats — which are always unjustified. You never forget anything funny or sad, so you have to say the trivia is not worth recording."

Wunnicke stands about 5 feet tall. Her white hair and gentle countenance may remind younger lawyers of their grandmothers, but her discussion of the law is as sharp as the plum and gray hounds tooth suit she wore for her *Wyoming Lawyer* interview.

Wunnicke proudly displays her Wyoming Supreme Court certification as well as a crystal plaque honoring her 60-year membership to the Wyoming State Bar.

Figure 2.2. Article about Brooke for her sixty years at the Bar (1946–2006) was aptly titled *A Lifetime of Law*, and this is the first-page excerpt from the *Wyoming Lawyer* magazine, of December 2006.

The Wyoming Lawyer (1946–1969)

Let no action be done at random, nor otherwise than in complete accordance with the principles involved.
Marcus Aurelius, Meditations, *Fourth Book, II*

Figure 2.3. Brooke 2006 Special Honoree in Laramie at the University of Wyoming Law School with its Dean and the President of the Wyoming State Bar. Brooke also gave a morning lecture for law school students and, for the Bar, an afternoon lecture about ethics.

First Woman C C Director Elected

By KIRK KNOX

Mrs. Brooke Wunnicke said today she was pleased and proud at her election last night to the board of directors of the Chamber of Commerce—the first woman to be so honored here.

Four other b o a r d members were also elected at the Chamber's annual meeting.

Obviously elated at her election, Mrs. Wunnicke, who is a Cheyenne attorney, said "I am proud and pleased at the opportunity to serve the Chamber and our community, and I appreciate the confidence shown."

Others elected to the board were Ed Krumm, Leonard H. Treber, Howard H. Hembrey and R. L. Esmay. Krumm's nomination came from the floor by Carl Halliday.

Members voted on ten board candidates presented by a nominating committee and on the lone floor nomination.

Gus Fleischli, appearing for Frontier Committee Chairman Lou Domenico, told the annual meeting 1964 was a "very successful" year for the city's big rodeo. Domenico was unable to attend.

Frontier Days' gross income was down by approximately one per cent, Fleischli said. He pointed out that other such shows reported revenues for last season down by as much as 5 to 10 per cent.

The 1964 week of rodeo saw the largest single day's attendance in the event's long history, Fleischli said, the new mark being set on Saturday. He said he did not have the exact figure for the day, but that it would be published in November along with the Frontier Committee's financial report. Printing of the report was not completed in time for presentation to the annual gathering of the Chamber.

A 10 per cent increase in the number of general admissions tickets for the 1964 rodeos was seen by Fleischli as indicating a more conservative approach to entertainment expenditures b y tourists.

He labeled "very doubtful" the prospects for continued national television coverage of Frontier Days. "The Rodeo Cowboys Association's entire TV program is in some trouble," he explained, "and in our opinion will have to undergo a complete overhaul before any of the networks will sign a contract with them."

He said the Frontier Committee would, nonetheless, continue efforts to obtain national televising of the rodeo.

He outlined improvements to the physical plant at Frontier Park which were made in 1964. They included construction of two tunnels under the track, con-

A FORMER OFFICIAL of the Cheyenne Chamber of Commerce, Willard Murfin, at left, receives a distinguished service award from Col. Leo I. Herman, chamber secretary-manager. Murfin for years was secretary-manager of the organization here. Herman made the presentation on behalf of Chamber of Commerce Executives of Wyoming. A similar award was made by Herman to Bob Hanesworth, also a former secretary-manager of the chamber.   (Photo by Brammar)

☆ ☆ ☆   ☆ ☆ ☆   ☆ ☆ ☆

NEW DIRECTORS of the Cheyenne Chamber of Commerce were elected last night at the group's annual meeting at the Hitching Post. Pictured, from left, are Howard Hembrey, Gen. R. L. Esmay, Brooke Wunnicke, Ed Krumm and Leonard M. Treber.

At right is Clyde Gaymon, out Krumm was elected to the boa the meeting floor. The others dates submitted by the nomina

☆ ☆ ☆   ☆ ☆ ☆   ☆ ☆ ☆

pointed out. He said, however, that expense of operating the facility was also higher at $11.-

"I have thoroughly enjoyed this year, and I can say to you members, 'try it sometime.'"

should be known as "payroll development" rather than industrial development, asserting that

Figure 2.4. 1964 local headline news when Brooke was elected the first woman to the Board of Directors of the Cheyenne Chamber of Commerce.

DIRECTORS

Immediate Past President: Clyde W. Gaymon	Ralph C. Ausman	Dr. Francis A. Barrett, Jr.	William A. Corson, Jr.	Lt. General R. L. Esmay	William G. Fleischli
Howard H. Hembrey	E. H. Krumm	Frank J. Martini	J. Douglas Reeves, Jr.	Leonard M. Treber	Mrs. Brooke Wunnicke

Figure 2.5. Cheyenne Chamber of Commerce 1964–65 annual report page of its Board of Directors includes a photograph of Brooke.

OFFICIALS OF THE Greater Cheyenne Chamber of Commerce and the city of Cheyenne are shown at the organization meeting of the "Committee of 100" held last night in the Frontier Pavilion. The committee will co-ordinate the work of the Citizens Industrial Council of Laramie County and the Industrial Development Association of Cheyenne. Heads of the committees were announced last night and the coordinating program launched. Left to right are Bob Kays, secretary-manager of the Chamber; Val Christensen, head of the Industrial Park sub-committee of the "Committee of 100;" Tom Powers, general chairman of the committee; Mrs. Brooke Wunnicke, Chamber board representative; E. H. Krumm, Chamber president; and Herb Kingham, mayor of Cheyenne. Story at top of page.

(Photo by Brammar)

Figure 2.6. Committee of 100 in Cheyenne, including Brooke as Chamber of Commerce's Board representative; November 1966 local news article.

"Committee of 100" Off and Running!

Officials of the Greater Cheyenne Chamber of Commerce and City of Cheyenne are shown at the organization meeting of the "Committee of 100" held at the Frontier Pavilion on Nov. 14. Shown, left to right are: Tom Powers, general chairman of the Committee of 100; Brooke Wunnicke, Chamber Board Representative; Chamber President E. H. Krumm and Cheyenne Mayor Herb Kingham.

The "New Industry" sub-committee is shown here with Ivan Heimsoth, chairman: Abe Rosenberg, Earl Barton, Richard Kroll and Jack Nathenson discussing how the sub-committee was to develop its program.

"Ambassadors" sub-committee is shown here projecting their program for the coming year. Shown are Bill Tyrrell, Jim Tilker, Chairman Fred McCabe, Don Correll and Curtis Williams.

At the organization meeting, Board Representative Brooke Wunnicke is shown explaining the committee's functions and goals. The new committee will combine the work of the Industrial Development Association of Cheyenne and the Citizen's Industrial Council of Laramie County and will act as a cooperating and coordinating body for the two groups.

"Industrial Park" sub-committee Chairman Val Christensen leads the discussion with C. B. Coolidge, Sam Levine, Dr. K. L. McShane and Nick Dudash.

Ralph Johnson, chairman of the "Existing Industry" sub-committee is shown here with Dean Dunlap, Phil Kahle and Bob Cheever, planning the sub-committee's aims and goals.

Other sub-committee chairmen not pictured are F. H. Gilroy, chairman of the "Research" sub-committee; Bill Anderson, "Promotion" sub-committee; Bill Veta, chairman of the City-County planning and zoning sub-committee; Art Abbey, chairman of the "Presentation" sub-committee; John Veta, chairman of "Rural Trade" sub-committee; Bard Ferrall, chairman of "Industrial Relations" sub-committee; and Doug Reeves, chairman of the "Regional Industrial Conference" sub-committee.

Figure 2.7. Chamber of Commerce report page about the Committee of 100, with Brooke as the Board's representative in two small photographs: with chairman, Chamber's president, and Cheyenne's mayor; and Brooke explaining the group's functions and goals.

CHEYENNE CHAMBER OF COMMERCE

307 - 638-3388 P. O. BOX 1147 CHEYENNE, WYOMING 82001

September 24, 1968

Mrs. Brooke Wunnicke
203 Teton Building
Cheyenne, Wyoming, 82001

Dear Brooke:

When the Board of Directors accepted your resignation yesterday, its members expressed their deep regret
that you will be moving to Denver.

You have always done a splendid job as Chairman of
the National Affairs Committee, and it will be difficult
to replace you. All of us know that you have done far
more than your duties required both as a Chairman, a
committee member and as a member of the Board of Directors. We appreciate your excellent work, as well as the
cooperation you have always given.

Though we shall be sorry to see you and Jim leave
us, you should have the pleasure of knowing you both
take with you our best wishes for success and happiness.
You can be sure we're going to miss our charming, sparkling booster!

With best personal regards,

Wally

WALLACE K. REED
President

Area on the Move

Figure 2.8. Cheyenne Chamber of Commerce commendation letter dated September 1968 when Brooke resigned after she and Jim decided to relocate to Denver.

[*EDITOR'S NOTE: Francis E. Warren Air Force Base, the main gate almost adjacent to Cheyenne, is one of three strategic missile bases in the United States. The base is the oldest continuously active military installation in the Air Force; in 1867, the US Army established the base. In 1947, the facility was transferred to the United States Army Air Forces. In 1959, the first Atlas D missile to deploy away from Vandenberg Air Force Base (AFB), California, went to the missile squadron stationed at Warren AFB. After the earlier Atlas ICBM missile squadrons, from 1963–1974, the ninetieth SAC program for Missile Wing Minuteman missile squadrons were active.*]

DEPARTMENT OF THE AIR FORCE
HEADQUARTERS 90TH STRATEGIC MISSILE WING (SAC)
FRANCIS E WARREN AIR FORCE BASE, WYOMING 82001

SPECIAL ORDER   10 March 1967
T-335

Each of the civilians listed below, addresses indicated, is invited by
the Secretary of the Air Force to travel by military aircraft on space
available basis from Francis E Warren AFB, Wyo 82001, to March AFB,
Calif 92508 and Vandenberg AFB, Calif 93437 and return, on or about
20 Mar 67. Travel is necessary in public service and is authorized per
AFR 190-13 and Hq 15AF Information Plan 67-1. Travel performed under
this order is at no expense to the government.

BROOKE WUNNICKE, 3300 Carey Ave, Cheyenne, Wyo 82001

Figure 2.9. Here's an unusual form of invitation. Dept. of the Air Force, Headquarters 90th Strategic Missile Wing (SAC) Francis E. Warren Air Force Base (Warren AFB), Wyoming, Special Order T-335 March 10, 1967, by invitation from Secretary of the Air Force, for named civilians on or about March 20 to visit Vandenberg Air Force Base (AFB), California. For this image, Brooke's name is excerpted from the list of thirty-two other community leaders from Cheyenne and the nearby area.

Figure 2.10. Brooke, in front row (second on the left), with the other Cheyenne area community leaders, visiting Vandenberg AFB in March 1967.

Figure 2.11. Brooke, at top of the airplane's boarding stairs, with the other visiting Cheyenne area community leaders, who all traveled to Vandenberg AFB in March 1967.

Figure 2.12. Brooke at Warren AFB Officers Awards party, as reported in the November 1967 Chamber of Commerce *Cheyenne Action*, page 4.

The "Old West Bar" and Some Firsts for Me

EARLY CAREER AS A WOMAN LAWYER IN WYOMING

THE "OLD WEST BAR"

THE "OLD West Bar" was before my time as a lawyer, but when I began to practice in 1946, some of the elder Wyoming lawyers either remembered or had heard first-hand about the early lawyers' Bar association. Of course, I was always eager to hear about lawyers and judges in the early days.

Some of the tales about law in the early territorial days were memorable. One of my favorites was the territorial judge who knew no law whatsoever but had appropriate political connections, so he was appointed a judge. He had a lawyer friend who was a poker crony and who practiced in the judge's district. The judge asked him, "What do I do if a lawyer says, 'I object' because I hear lawyers do that sometimes." His friend replied, "Don't worry. We don't have many lawyers around here, and I'm usually one of the lawyers who'll be in the case. If the other lawyer says, 'I object' look at me, and if I pull my handkerchief up a bit out of my breast pocket, you say 'Objection overruled.' If I push my handkerchief down, then you say 'Objection sustained.'" This system apparently worked well for some time, until the trial when opposing counsel said, "I object" and the judge's friend sneezed. The judge is reported to have said, "What the hell do I do now?"

Another rather private (private at least from judicial earshot) joke among our Bar was to comment, "That judge needs a new deck of cards," when one of our colleagues had suffered from a badly wrong evidentiary ruling. The origin of the comment was another story from Wyoming's territorial days. A territorial judge was notoriously ignorant of the law of evidence. He kept a deck of cards at the bench and during trial would entertain himself with playing solitaire, interrupting himself only to admit into evidence that which he should not and to exclude from evidence that which should have been admitted. The local Bar took up a collection to buy the judge a book on the law of evidence. The judge accepted the Bar's gift, kept it on the bench with him, but his evidentiary rulings became even worse after he dabbled in the reference. After six months, the local Bar bought the judge a new deck of cards.

When I was admitted to the Wyoming State Bar, the state had only one federal district judge—and this was still true when I moved to Colorado twenty years later. The judge, T. Blake Kennedy, was a truly fine judge and man, and you will read more about him in this book as well as his equally fine and beloved successor, Ewing T. Kerr. Judge Kennedy was from New York and arrived in Cheyenne in 1903 to practice law. Judge Kennedy told me that on his second day in Cheyenne, as he walked out of the then prominent InterOcean Hotel, a bullet whizzed by his head.* He also told me that he had been junior counsel in the famous trial of Tom Horn, the notorious "hired gun" of the cattle ranchers in their continuing war to get rid of the sheep ranchers. Tom Horn was convicted and hung on the site of the courthouse in Cheyenne where I practiced years later, from 1946 to 1969. The old timer who was Clerk of Court when I started practicing law told me: "Brooke, if you could drop a plumb line right from this second-floor office where you are standing right down to the ground, well, that would be just about where the gallows were on which Tom Horn was hung."

Judge Kennedy told me that although he attended the entire Tom Horn trial, about all he did as junior counsel was to carry the briefcases. The senior defense lawyers did an excellent job, but Tom Horn "dropped the noose around his own neck." Wide-eyed, I said, "Tell me about it." His response was that the key fact for the defense was that a reliable witness had seen Tom Horn on his horse at Point A at a certain hour, and the young victim, a twelve-year-old boy as I recall, was shot dead at Point B several hours later. The defense was that the distance between Point A and Point B was too great for a person to have been at both Point A and Point B at the crucial times.

---

* EDITOR'S NOTE: The InterOcean Hotel burned in 1916; nearby, opened in 1911, the Plains Hotel is still a leading historic downtown hotel.

When Horn testified in his own defense, his lawyer asked him if any person could possibly ride his horse from Point A to Point B in the time involved. Horn did drop the noose around his neck with his reply, "No ordinary person could—but I could." I have always regretted that none of the biographers of Tom Horn ever talked to Judge Kennedy and taped his account of this historic trial—although several had the opportunity.

WOMAN'S SUFFRAGE IN THE TERRITORY OF WYOMING AND ADMISSION TO THE UNITED STATES

I OWN a copy of the first session of the legislative assembly of the Territory of Wyoming, held in Cheyenne, Wyoming, in October 1869. Chapter 31, enacted at that session and approved December 10, 1869, granted every woman of the age of twenty-one the right to vote at every election. Chapter 31 also declared: "And her rights to the elective franchise and to hold office shall be the same under the election laws of the territory, as those of electors." Wyoming was not admitted to statehood until 1890, and that is an interesting story also. Wyoming was the first territorial state to allow women the right to vote, but the US Congress was unwilling to admit Wyoming into the Union unless the Territory of Wyoming withdrew that right. The original proceedings of the Wyoming Constitutional Convention record that women's right to vote was hotly debated. One of the territorial legislators eloquently declaimed, "If we are going to disenfranchise half of our state, let us not disenfranchise the better half." This eloquence saved the day for women suffrage, Wyoming held firm, and Wyoming was admitted as a state, including that its women could vote.

NO WOMEN JURORS

WYOMING WAS one of the last states to allow women jurors. Although, in 1869, Wyoming became the first state or territory to permit women to serve as jurors, this ended after three court terms when the judge who had initiated it resigned in 1871 and was replaced by a judge opposed to women's suffrage. For years, I practiced before juries of only men. And some judges expected that, because women wore hats to church, I should wear a hat in their courtrooms.

After Wyoming's legislature passed the so-called "Woman Jury Bill" in 1949 (Chapter 61, *Session Laws of Wyoming*), the Wyoming Supreme Court held it

Figure 2.13. Brooke in one of her winter hats, if required by the judge to appear in court in the 1950s and 1960s.

Figure 2.14. Brooke in one of her summer hats, if required by the judge to appear in court in the 1950s and 1960s.

constitutional the next year in *Wyoming v. Yazzie*, 281 P.2d 482 (Wyo. 1950). If added to the rolls of eligible jurors and if summoned for jury duty, women then could serve on the state courts' juries.

SOME FIRSTS FOR ME

I DID not start practicing law immediately after my admission to the Bar but waited until our daughter entered first grade in the fall. This gave me the pleasure of teaching her the alphabet and her numbers as well as time to read a lot to her—and play with her.

First Law Office

IN THE fall of 1946, I opened my own humble, small law office and literally hung out a shingle, "Brooke Wunnicke, Attorney at Law." No lawyer had invited me to join his firm, and I had not expected any offers. My expectation was that it would take me at least five years to get as far in my practice as a man would get in two or three years. I was wrong because it only took about four years, but I was not bitter. I was a lawyer practicing law and loving it—as I still do.

For all Readers who feel that their appearance is so hopelessly unimpressive that they cannot aspire to succeed in a profession, let me offer cheer. I topped out at five feet one and one-half inches. When asked about my stature, I always rounded out my reply to five feet two inches. But as I write, honesty compels me now to answer five feet one inch, having shrunk a bit with age. I have never weighed very much either. With brown hair and brown eyes, a naturally husky voice, and short—I had no inborn "presence" to bring into a courtroom. But hard work in preparing for court and just being oneself in court can overcome the disadvantages of size or rather lack thereof, to inflict a legalism.

First Local Bar Meeting

WYOMING HAS what used to be called an Integrated Bar. A lawyer could not practice in any court in Wyoming unless a member of the Wyoming State Bar. Hence, I was a member of that Bar and received notices sent to members. When I received my first notice of a monthly Bar meeting, I thought that as a lawyer I would be welcome. When I entered the dining room, where about two dozen lawyers were assembled, total silence occurred. I looked at them while they looked at me. Then, the Honorable T. Blake Kennedy, at that time Wyoming's only federal judge, rose, came to me, and extended me his arm, saying: "Brookie, will you do me the honor of sitting next to me?"

Judge Kennedy's greeting was a surprise because I did not know him except for his formal admission of me to practice in the federal bar. But after his surprising welcome, I was immediately accepted by my fellow lawyers. And when Judge Kennedy retired many years later, I told him how I remembered with much gratitude his thoughtfulness in welcoming me to my first Bar meeting. I became active in the local Bar association and eventually served as Secretary, Treasurer, Vice President, and President.

Serving on a Funeral "Honor Guard": An Indulgent Meditation

AS SOON as you have read the title for this memory, you probably decided not to read further. No hard feelings if you skip this. But before you make your decision, I want to tell you that reading this may help to explain the feelings of a lawyer who is deeply devoted to the law.

During my years of practice in Wyoming, 1946 to mid-1969, Wyoming had three state Supreme Court justices and no law clerks. When I began practice, the justices were Fred H. Blume (the scholar discussed in Part One's "My Admission to the Bar—The Judge's Dog Knows More Than I"), William A. Riner, and Ralph Kimball and the court was nationally recognized for its excellence. When I had my first argument in the Wyoming Supreme Court, still a very young lawyer, the court clerk took me to the room where the lawyer waited until the lawyer's case was called up for argument. It was a cold snowy day, and I remember sitting alone in that dimly lit room, with snow swirling down outside its windows, and being scared about my first appellate argument. I looked about me in the room where the walls were hung with old, faded photographs of the court's former justices. Most of the justices had long white beards, and those who did not had big bushy mutton-chop whiskers. If you think that saying your heart sank to your toes is absurd, I assure you that is not true. I thought that I could hear my heart beating under my toenails when the clerk entered to announce the court was ready to hear my case.

Elsewhere, I have described my first—and shoeless—argument out of eventually over 250 appellate arguments (see Part Two's "The Wyoming Lawyer," about The Appellate Lawyer). I think it fair to tell you that the justices were truly learned and always courteous to the lawyers who appeared before them. They were both knowledgeable and wise and hence free from judicial arrogance. This has all been a preface to my subject here.

When I was still a junior lawyer, Justice Riner died and lay in state in the courtroom of the Supreme Court where he had served with distinction for many years. The Bar Association called the lawyers who were to serve as an "honor guard" for the justice as he lay in his casket in the courtroom. Senior lawyers were designated for this honor, with the exception of one junior lawyer: me. I learned that this had been a wish of Justice Riner, who had requested that I be one of the lawyers. My shift was from 4:00 p.m. to 10:00 p.m. I appeared at the appointed time and was assigned to stand at the foot of the open casket with a senior lawyer standing at its head. He was a kindly lawyer, for which I was grateful.

Because I had never before seen a dead person, I was dreading looking at the deceased justice. But as I took my first look, my mind flooded with how dedicated he had been to the law, how hard he worked on each case, and I felt that he—with his fellow justices on the court—really strived to be fair in reaching a right result. And I remembered gratefully how encouraging he had been to me. As dusk came, dim lamps lit up the courtroom. I still think it was an elegantly simple and beautiful courtroom. To be impressive at the taxpayer's expense, it did not depend on marble and bronze and a gorgeous, large justices' bench with very high-backed leather chairs. Instead, the bench, counsel tables, and wood-paneled walls were of Oregon myrtle. As I watched the daylight fade in the courtroom, and then looked at the justice, I felt a renewed commitment to be a good lawyer always faithful to the highest ideals of our profession and the legal system that it serves. I thought of my privilege and my obligations in serving as a lawyer.

So, I here thank Justice Riner for including this young, then rarity, a woman-lawyer, in his honor guard. Standing guard in the darkening courtroom evoked meditations on the nobility of a good system of law for free people and the vow to serve the law to the best of my ability always.

First Lecture Fee as a Lawyer: Why Did the Coal Company Need a Woman Speaker?

FOR A lawyer, as is true for everyone starting his or her own small business, "getting known" is essential to economic survival. Common advice to young lawyers was to "get active in your church," which offended me by what I considered its cynicism. I attended church every Sunday and taught Sunday School for seventeen years, because a spiritual dimension to my life was essential. I was delighted, of course, by any slight community recognition that came my way, which leads me to share with you a truly memorable experience.

In these days of billion-dollar mergers and acquisitions and when "everyone who is anyone" talks in terms of millions and hundreds of millions, let me tell you the story of my $500 speaking fee. Sixty-plus years ago, when noncontested divorces cost under $100 in our town, $500 was an exciting fee. And my husband and I would then have qualified as poor relatives of church mice. I had been practicing only a few months when I received a telephone call from an executive of the Union Pacific Coal Company, headquartered in Rock Springs, Wyoming. He asked if I would be willing to be the keynote speaker at the company's semiannual safety banquet, all expenses paid and a $500 fee. I accepted and could hardly wait that evening to share the good news with my husband, "Jimmie." He had a helpful penchant for seeing the dark side of the moon. He asked, "Why do you suppose the coal company called you when you are such a new, young lawyer? Maybe that's the reason." But I had no interest in the reason for my incomprehensible selection.

The appointed day arrived. I left Cheyenne in the morning on a Union Pacific train for the ride to Rock Springs, arriving shortly before lunch. I was picked up at the train depot, taken to the hotel to check in, and then to lunch. At that time Rock Springs had a fully justified bad reputation for the food available in its limited cafes. But I have been blessed with a digestive system comparable to that of a goat and even have had recommended that, at death, I donate my digestive system to medical science. Even I could not cope with what the company executive insisted on ordering for me—ghastly is an understatement.

After lunch, I was taken back to my hotel to "rest" before the big occasion of the evening. I have never, before or since, been as violently nauseated as I was all afternoon—crawling from bed to bathroom and return. I kept thinking that no way would I be able to speak that night because I would probably be dead before the scheduled time.

Worse was yet to come. The telephone rang, I was being picked up for dinner, and we returned to the scene of the crime. The same executive again ordered for me, "Little girl, I want you to eat a big steak—you have a rough evening ahead of you." My protests went unheeded and, as I write this, I can still see that steak: a T-bone, overcooked to a dirty taupe, with greasy bubbles all over it and so massive that it draped over both ends of the platter. And, French fries, I use the phrase loosely, greasy enough to fill a crankcase. "Now I want you to eat every bit of that—you will need it." I did, and we departed for the auditorium.

The auditorium, which is still there and now on the National Register of Historic Places, was called the Slovenski Dom. At that time, Rock Springs and its five satellite coal company towns had a very diverse ethnic population. I had been told that thirty-three different languages were spoken there. The Slovenski Dom was large, gloomy and, when I arrived, was already filled with about 1,200 miners. The miners had been on strike for months, but a settlement of the strike was supposed to be imminent, so the safety meeting, with its prizes and awards, was scheduled as usual. John L. Lewis was then President of the United Mine Workers of America and, on the afternoon of the meeting, his brother had committed suicide. As a result, strike settlement negotiations had stopped, and the miners were restive.

When I was seated on the big stage, I saw that on the floor of the auditorium, ringed around the stage, were uniformed National Guard soldiers with their rifles cradled in their arms "at the ready." After the coal company's vice president got the meeting underway, he called on a minister to give an opening prayer.

The minister, who was seated next to me on the stage, was newly graduated from an Ivy League theological seminary. He had recently arrived out West for the first time and for his first ministerial assignment, Rock Springs. I remember that his invocation was short and unfortunate, concluding with "Lord, please help each of the men present to each day do a good day of work." It seemed to me that a soft, ominous growl emanated from the audience. When he sat down, a tall and still rather gangly young man, he leaned over to me, clasping his long, trembling hands and asked: "Did I do all right?" And I could not help but lie because he looked so anxious and caring. I answered, "Yes. You did just fine."

Next was my turn, and I thought that all went very well. The audience seemed very pleased at the end and, when the program was over, some of the men came up toward the stage and waved at me. I was cautioned not to go down on the audience floor—it might not be safe. But I scampered down anyway for which I have always been grateful. If I had not, I would have missed the most unique compliment of my life. Among the men who came to speak to me were two men arm in arm. One of them said, "My brother, he wants me to tell you that was the best speech he ever heard." I replied with my best smile, "Why doesn't your brother tell me himself?" to which he answered, "My brother, he don't speak and don't understand no English." Ah, well, a lot of truth in the old saying, "Pride goeth before a fall."

I was to return home to Cheyenne after the meeting, and my hosts had reserved a Pullman berth for me, no roomettes or bedrooms on that train. You young Readers are unaware that for some perverse reason Pullman reservations were always allocated so that women travelers were at the end of the train next to the men's lavatory and vice versa for the men travelers. By the time I was put on the train, I smiled bravely but knew without doubt that I was dying of food poisoning. I have never been so sick before or since. Even a goat would have been desperately ill.

When I packed for my overnight stint, I had proudly put in my beautiful new Christmas nightgown, which I had not yet worn and forgot to pack slippers. Because it was snowy, I had worn galoshes, which in those days were made with hollow high heels into which the heels of your dress pumps would fit. What a night! Well over a half-century ago, I recall it as though it occurred last night. I found out that my nightgown was about twelve inches too long, so it hung far beneath my muskrat coat and draped itself on the floor around my feet. Thus attired and bouncing up and down on the hollow heels of my galoshes, I dragged to and fro on the aisle all night to the far end of the train to the women's lavatory and return trip to my berth.

When I arrived in Cheyenne, I was walking from the station to my husband's office when I met a group of lawyers. They grabbed me by the arm to join them for breakfast at the lawyers' favorite restaurant, which had special pancakes that day. I could not escape, went with them, and ate the pancakes. Then I fled to my husband's office. When he saw me, he said, "What happened to you? You've been gone twenty-four hours and you look like you've been gone twenty-four years." And I felt older than I am now, when writing this—but I had a check for $500 in my purse.

The Trial Lawyer

EARLY CASES: JUSTICE OF THE PEACE AND POLICE COURTS

I EAGERLY accepted any small legal business that came my way. My only standards for representation were that nothing dishonest was involved and that the client would pay. In my time, law schools did not have practicum courses in which students are taught the actual mechanics of trying a lawsuit. I learned by doing, and my goal was that no client of mine would be prejudiced by my inexperience. So I spent many unbilled hours in the law library and at home studying and preparing for the smallest trial.

At the University of Colorado School of Law, I had a fine professor affectionately known as "Pop" Arthur. His private life was dedicated to making sure that no widow or orphan in the area would suffer harm for lack of money to retain a lawyer. He emphasized to his students that no legal problem was unimportant to the person who brought it to you for legal help. "If you don't think his case is really important, don't take it because you cannot do a good job." I would remember this as I toiled for free to make sure my client was adequately represented.

Way back in the 1940s, Justice of the Peace Courts in Wyoming were courts of more limited jurisdiction than the state's District Courts. Their jurisdiction in criminal cases was limited to misdemeanors and did not include offenses that carried sentences of more than one year. In civil suits, jurisdiction was limited to a $1,000 in controversy and later, as I recall, raised to $5,000. Now, Justice of the Peace Courts are no more and are replaced by counties' Circuit Courts, whose judges are required to be lawyers and their jurisdiction has been much expanded.

Police Court had the most limited jurisdiction of all. It heard no civil cases, and its jurisdiction was limited to hearing cases involving infractions of municipal ordinances. My police court practice was a great training ground for courtroom work in later large cases. I do not recall the ordinary cases that proceeded to an orderly conclusion. To my surprise, I do not even recall my early victories.

The Case of the Cafe with Too Many Waitresses

INSTEAD, I remember, for example, The Case of the Cafe with Too Many Waitresses. A minister of a local church came to see me in the early months of my practice to enlist my aid, with a paid fee, for a member of his church. He assured me that she was a fine woman who had been unjustly accused and was facing humiliating criminal charges in police court. Because I was the only woman lawyer in town, he and the hapless ewe of his flock thought I should represent her.

I did represent the woman. I found out that she was charged with running a "house of ill fame" as the city's ordinances described it. She assured me that this was a horrible lie. We went to court and under oath my fine client confirmed that her cafe had four small tables and twelve waitresses. We lost. I don't know what moral, if any, my client learned from this case. But I learned an important lesson never since forgotten or overlooked: get all the facts that you can from your client, even though sometimes extracting the facts is as hard as extracting an impacted wisdom tooth. And only with experience, unless you are blissfully endowed with sensitive antenna for the lying client, can you determine if you are getting the truth, the whole truth, and nothing but the truth.

Going "Blind" to Court

THE SIXTH Amendment to the Constitution of the United States, which is part of the Bill of Rights, declares that *in all criminal prosecutions the accused shall "be informed of the nature and cause of the accusation."* (My emphasis added.)

When I started to practice law, this guarantee was not always honored or perhaps even known by police officers. The first time when someone wanted to hire me ("retained" is hardly the appropriate term) to represent my first client in police court, I asked the man with what he was charged. "I don't know. The police won't tell me. And my hearing is this afternoon." I agreed to represent him. As soon as he left my office, I scampered to the police department to find out what the charges were against my client. When I asked the officer, he replied, "Who are you?" "His lawyer," I said. "You are his lawyer, aw come on. You're his girlfriend." Indignantly I pulled out my lawyer's registration card and asked, "What are the charges against my client?" His response was "Come to court at four o'clock this afternoon and find out." Which is what we did, and we justly won.

Now the accused is almost invariably informed of the nature of the charges. As the lawyer for the accused, I remember experiencing with my client a horrible feeling of uncertainty bordering on fright when we went into court without knowing either the charges or who would testify against my client.

Epilogue: The Inquisition Religious Trials 1570–1820

THE SIXTH Amendment also provides that the accused shall "*be confronted with the witnesses against him.*" (My emphasis added.) Many years after "The Surprise," which is the name by which I remember going "blind" to the police court with my client, I had a holiday in South America. In this book's Part Three: The Law is my discussion of the Bill of Rights: Sixth Amendment— Confrontation Clause, I tell you about an old Peruvian courtroom where from about 1570 to 1820 the Inquisition's religious trials had been held and its peephole for hiding witnesses. Of course, I then thought of that police court case so many years ago and gave thanks for the increasing awareness by police and judges of our Sixth Amendment rights.

FEDERAL DISTRICT COURT: EARLY CRIMINAL APPOINTMENTS

Selling Liquor to Indians: "They Don't Have No Whiskers"

WHEN I first started to practice law, the custom was for the federal judge to appoint the newest lawyers to represent the indigent. In 1946, our city did not yet have a Public Defender or Legal Aid Clinic. The federal appointments paid the lawyer absolutely nothing for the representation—nothing for any expenses and not a penny for fees. When I began, the most common appointment for the new lawyer was defense of a person charged with selling liquor to Indians. The evidence was always ample and plain that the defendant was guilty. Many of those charged with this offense had apparently been charged and convicted before of these sales, knew no defense was available, but seemed to enjoy having their "day in court."

My first appearance in federal court was in one of these "selling liquor to Indian cases." I was very proud to be going to federal court but scared because I did not know the procedure and no reference book or mentor was then available to me. I need not have worried because my "client" assigned by the court was an old hand at these proceedings in the same courtroom before the same judge. His face fell and he was obviously upset that I was his attorney. He was rudely incredulous but then the judge came in and ascended the bench, so the defendant just accepted his bad luck in assigned counsel. While the prosecution put on its case, however, my client sat unruffled as the evidence against him piled up. Then my client leaned over to me and whispered something that sounded like "Tell the judge he had whiskers." Several minutes later, my client leaned toward me again and whispered loudly "Tell the judge he had whiskers." I endured several more loud whisperings into my ear, but I always heard the same, to me, incomprehensible message.

The time came for me to put on the defense and a feeble effort it was. Not only was it my first time in federal court, but no facts and no law supported my assigned defense. This was not a jury case, and the judge unhesitatingly ruled, "Guilty." Even though the evidence against the defendant was insurmountable, I still dreaded to face my client. Worse was yet to come. When I turned to face him, he snarled, "Why didn't you tell the judge what I told you to tell him?" I responded, "What difference would that have made?" And sixty-plus years later, I remember his answer verbatim, "What kind of lawyer are you that you don't know that Indians don't have no whiskers?" With that he drained dry my scant half-cup of self-confidence, and I wondered how many more so-called facts of common knowledge in Wyoming that I didn't know. (This client was referring to an erroneous stereotype that Native Americans do not grow facial hair. As a result of various federal laws, selling alcohol to Native Americans was prohibited until repealed in 1953.)

Bank Robber: Get Rid of California's "Hold"

A MONTH or so later I was "promoted" by a federal court assignment to defend a career bank robber. He robbed banks in different states and told me that he preferred California banks in winter. This case brought me my first contact with an FBI agent. He specialized in bank robberies in the region, with his office in Denver. We had no FBI agents in Cheyenne at that time. I shall always remember this agent because he was so knowledgeable but always so fair. Over forty years later I met him again after I had moved to Denver, when his talented daughter worked for me as a legal intern, and he was still as I had remembered.

Back to my bank robbery case in Cheyenne, my client stated that he would plead guilty because "the Feds got all the evidence," and he'd been in the prison where he would be sent. He liked it, as prisons go, because he said that the food was very good and the recreation facilities excellent. But he added that he wanted me to get rid of the California "hold" on him. He mentioned this again to me several times. I didn't lie but promised "to look into it." I didn't know what he was talking about but had become very careful after my selling-liquor-to-Indians case. I will tell you this: a "hold" was not on the agenda in criminal law when I was in law school, and I don't know if it is today. So I later asked the United States Marshal, who explained it to me—but California would not release the "hold." For the Reader: as you probably accurately guessed, the jurisdiction with a hold on a wrongdoer has an outstanding warrant on that person so that when the sentence has been served in another state, the prisoner is not released from custody but sent to the state with the "hold" to serve the sentence there.

My early solo court appearances were bringing me much new information that had never come my way in law school. Although I was number one in my class, I felt that, instead of the hat I was required to wear in court, I should wear a dunce cap with a very tall peak.

"The Fair Sex" Criminal Defendants

OVER TIME, my trial practice was civil cases and, being now past the "junior" status, I was spared frequent federal court-appointed criminal cases for then no-fee legal services. But the federal court thought because a woman trial lawyer (me) was available, it was appropriate for a woman lawyer to represent a woman defendant. So, I still occasionally was appointed for no-fee legal services. Most of those woman defendants were not only guilty with plenty of evidence to prove guilt, but also some were truly scary. I remember one, who when I first visited her in the Cheyenne jail, said, "Fix it for me to see my boyfriend." "Where is he?" I asked. She replied, "In jail in Casper." When I accompanied her to court for her arraignment, she towered beside me at the podium. She was not only tall, she was big and muscular. When the judge read the charges against her, without warning my "client" started yelling vile expletives at the judge. Fortunately, the United States Marshal had seen the defendant I had in tow and had stayed in the courtroom. Shamefully, when he stepped forward to grab the defendant, I disappeared into the elevator to return to my office. The Marshal called me a short time later to ask what happened to me. I apologized and, dear man, he said that he didn't blame me and that it was the safer course. So much for representing "the fair sex."

FEDERAL DISTRICT COURT: LATER JURY TRIALS

Trust the Jury

I WOULD always choose trial by jury over trial by judge. I trust juries, and juries trusted me. I never lost a civil jury trial. Also, my personal theory is that the jury, as a whole, has a synergy.

For the *Colorado Lawyer*, a publication of the Colorado Bar Association, I authored three Profiles of Success articles, each with a distinguished lawyer. One was a water lawyer. The other two were litigators: an oil and gas lawyer and a corporate trial lawyer for major companies. I asked each to select one or two of the most memorable matters he had handled. I was interested, touched—and proud—that the two litigators selected as the most memorable trial one for which he had received no fee! They had undertaken the representation to protect against injustice. When my Profile of Success was being authored, I also recalled that one of my most memorable trials was one for which I had no received no fee. The reason: the federal judge appointed me to defend.

This following case shows why to trust the jury system.

A Weeping Jury

I DIGRESS and remind you that previously I have related several of my federal appointments when I was a very green young lawyer. And I also remind you that formerly a lawyer received no fee whatsoever for serving as appointed defense counsel in a criminal case. I had been seasoned with a few years of jury trials when the then federal judge, Ewing T. Kerr, appointed me to defend a woman charged with forging the endorsement on a Social Security check. By now my practice was doing very well, and I was not happy with the appointment—how could I fit it into my heavy, fee-paying schedule? But in all my years of practice, I never declined an appointment—it can cause trouble for the lawyer and, more importantly, is a deservedly wrong decision for a lawyer. A lawyer always wears two hats: an advocate for the client and an officer of the court. When wearing the latter hat, the lawyer is a key player in our legal system as envisioned in our federal Constitution. So I went to see my client in the jail.

Let me tell you about this client. She was in her late sixties, very small, gray, uneducated, inarticulate, and freely told me that she had forged the endorsement. But she refused to plead guilty, saying that this was because of her husband. When she told me this, I did not have a vision of a great defense but a waking nightmare: the defense of this woman before a jury. Nonetheless, I have always believed with all my heart the lawyer's ethical mandate: a lawyer owes undivided loyalty to and a zealous representation of the lawyer's client. And this woman was my client—not by choice—but my client. So I visited with her about her life, her husband, and why she forged the endorsement on the check. I gave her a hug when I left, told her not to worry, and walked back to my office with a heavy heart, but I was determined to get her probation. After all, she had no prior criminal record.

The trial day arrived, the twelve-person jury selected, and the government prosecutor presented his case. The Department of Justice had flown out two experts from Washington, DC, to testify; they were tall, well-dressed in dark suits, impressive, and they had brought with them twelve 8.5-by-11-inch prints showing an enlarged comparison of the forged endorsement with the defendant's poorly scrawled handwriting. Twelve pictures!—one to place in each juror's hand. Before the photographs could be admitted into evidence, they had to be shown to me as opposing counsel. I looked at one. Even a person in dim light with poor vision could see the writing matched.

The time came for the defense case. I had only one witness: the defendant. She would not let me call her husband as a witness, but he was in the courtroom. I had met him before the trial. He was also very small, gray, uneducated, inarticulate—and grieving. They obviously loved each other very much. So I put my defendant on the witness stand. I had told her before the trial to be always truthful, answer all my questions, and speak facing the jury, not me. The following is a summary of the evidence that the jury heard.

The defendant and her husband were brought up in Chicago and were from very poor families. They met in their teens at a big meat-packing plant, where they both worked cutting up beef carcasses. When they retired at age sixty-five, they followed their life-long dream of coming "Out West," where they could live on their Social Security payments. They lived in a rooming house in Cheyenne. All went well until an extra-cold winter when the husband's jacket wore thin. He was so cold, and the defendant wanted to buy him a warm jacket. She saw this Social Security envelope sticking out of a mailbox and forged the endorsement for money to buy her husband a warm jacket. It was a surprise—he did not know what she had done until she was arrested.

In closing arguments in a criminal case, the prosecution gets two arguments, opening and closing arguments. The defense argument is sandwiched in between. When I rose to address the jury, I was never more aware of my unimpressive stature and appearance. So at the outset I truthfully told the jury that I was no orator, but would simply summarize the defendant's testimony. I tried to paint a vivid picture for the jurors: this small woman, born into poverty, worked hard all her life at a humble job and retired in poverty. I described for them how physically demanding her job was for all those years—cutting up those big animals—and the revolting nature of her work. I reminded them that she had not stolen for herself; she had not stolen for them both to have some small luxury; she had not stolen to buy a big overcoat for her husband. She had stolen to buy him a warm jacket for this bitterly cold winter. Finally, I frankly told them that I entrusted her to their mercy. They were a kind and decent jury. I did not see, but the judge told me later that they all were in tears when they left the jury box.

The trial ended at 5:00 p.m., and the jury was sent out for an early dinner. They began deliberations at 6:30 p.m., with the twelve photographic exhibits going with the jury. I inwardly prayed they would be gone at least a half-hour, long enough for me to tell the defendant and her husband that this was long enough to help for the hoped-for probation. Seven o'clock—no jury. Eight o'clock—no jury. Nine o'clock—no jury, and one of the government witnesses came to me rather angrily. He said, "If this jury acquits, I am going to quit my job." Finally, at 10:30 p.m., the jury returned, teary-eyed. The judge asked: "Have you reached a verdict?" The foreman replied, with tears on her cheeks:

"Yes, guilty, but we all want you to assure us that the defendant won't go to jail and will get probation tonight as soon as this is over."

Bless that dear jury! And bless that dear judge. He didn't say "That's not the way we do it. We refer the matter to the probation department for investigation, which may take several or more weeks, and then have a sentencing hearing." No, instead the judge said, "Your verdict is received." Then he called the defendant and me to the podium, and then and there granted her probation. And the judge, jury, prosecutor, and his witnesses, and I all watched as the little defendant ran to her husband, they hugged each other, thanked me, and were the first ones out of the courthouse that night. For years, the judge would tell at conferences how I had made the jury cry and got mercy for the client. I would respectfully contradict him with the truth: I did not make the jury cry—the facts did.

So that is a memorable case for me. No fee? Yes, a fee so large that it's a treasure for life.

STATE DISTRICT COURT

Oops!

AFTER I had been practicing law for some years, a woman acquaintance of mine asked pleasantly, "Brooke, I have heard that you never seem afraid in court. How can you do it?" I gave her what I then thought was a truthful answer: "Because nothing is left to happen to me in court that has not already happened." Time proved me wrong. Let me share several of my embarrassments in court.

"Damn It, Sam, You Know Better Than That!"
Said My Very First Expert Witness to the Judge

MY FIRST ineradicable memory occurred early in my district court appearances. The state district court courtroom in Cheyenne, where I practiced many years, was large, with a very high ceiling in which there was a big, stained-glass skylight with a symbol of justice. The judge's bench, counsel tables, and chairs, and the jury's chairs, were all also large and of golden oak. The acoustics were poor, and no microphones were then in use. The lighting also was poor. So into this intimidating place I went to obtain a judgment in a non-contested, quiet title suit to obtain marketable title to my client's property.

The defendants were all long deceased or "unknown." As was then customary, notice of this type of quiet title suit was given by publication once a week for four weeks in a weekly newspaper published in a very small farming community east of Cheyenne. The basis for claiming ownership was by continuous and open "adverse possession" for a certain number of years. Although I had a "gap" in my chain of title, I was not worried because Wyoming had a curative statute removing such a gap as a title flaw after the lapse of many years. And my gap plainly qualified for this cure. But our Clerk of Court, W. A. "Billy" James, warned me that the judge "did not like the statute," and hence I could not rely on it. Billy James, always so kind to young lawyers, recommended that I call an expert witness to testify about occupancy during the gap, and said that Jack Wenandy, a well-known Cheyenne realtor, would be glad to help me.

I appeared for the hearing with my witness, Mr. Wenandy, and the statute book. Today, Wyoming statutes are in a multi-volume set. At the time of my early quiet title suit, all the statutes were in one very thick black leatherette volume. I opened the book to the pertinent statute's page, and addressing the court, stated its provisions. The judge smiled kindly and said, "The court is pleased to have a young lawyer look up the law." I was relieved but remembered the caution I had been given, so called my witness. I qualified him as an expert in the area of the real property involved, and then, without warning, the judge asked: "How does the court know that there were no squatters or trespassers on this property during that period?" Whereupon, my witness answered, "Damn it, Sam (the judge's first name), you know better than that." I clutched the podium; nothing in law school had prepared me for this! Then, I heard the judge say, "I guess you're right, Jack. Counsel, if you have your judgment ready, I'll sign it." I breathed once again.

A Dam Built How?

AN EMBARRASSING incident that I recall with pleasure occurred when I was an experienced trial lawyer. Among my favorite clients was a big man with a big voice who was a big rancher with a big ranch. He truly enjoyed an occasional bit of litigation, and I enjoyed his honesty and unshakable beliefs in what he believed to be right.

This particular trial involved among other matters a dispute over a dam. Before representing Wyoming ranchers, the only dam that I had ever seen was what is now called Hoover Dam. When I was first shown a dam on a ranch, I naively asked, "Where is it?" and was startled to have an inches-high dam pointed out as the block in a stream. Back to the trial, and the small dam that was involved. On cross-examination, opposing counsel apparently unfamiliar with these small dams, asked my client, "Are you trying to tell this jury that you built that dam with your hands?" And my client stood, turned his back to the jury, bent over so that his substantial rear-end was in their view, raised his very large hand to his rear and, waggling it, answered in his big baritone that echoed in that courtroom: "Did you think that I built it with my tail, like a beaver?" The jury thought this hilarious and opposing counsel looked to me for help. I uncharitably thought, "You did it. You fix it." And I daintily shrugged my shoulders.

Highway Patrolman's Fly

ANOTHER MEMORY that always remained vivid I am about to tell you. It occurred in a jury trial in a rural small town up north. The judge was a newly appointed judge under the recent readopted so-called "improved" method of a selection commission with interviews, certification to the governor, and eventually ending in a single political appointment. This judge was a lawyer of mediocre ability but was a tenacious lobbyist for the adoption of this new method of selection. And, sure enough, he was the first appointee. My jury trial with this new judge presiding was defense of a bad highway motor vehicle accident with serious injury. I was delighted when the young highway patrolman who had investigated the accident voluntarily came to see me and go over his diagrams that indicated my client, the defendant, was not the one at fault. He was young, tall, good-looking, and well spoken; ah, what a gift to the defense lawyer!

When I called him at trial and he took the witness stand, with the witness chair facing the jury, imagine my horror when I saw that the fly on his trousers was wide open. And, to deepen my horror, I quickly became aware that the jury of twelve had already noticed and was staring. So, I approached the bench, waived to plaintiff's counsel to join me as is customary, and asked for a short recess. This new judge, who seemed to think he was a king or emperor, said, "We had a recent recess. We're not going to grant this one." I said, "Your Honor, with all due respect, this is urgent." And I told him why. Whereupon his honor raised himself up on his elbows, craned his neck, and took a long

Figure 2.15. Brooke, then President of the Laramie County Bar Association, explains the art of testifying in court to a Wyoming highway patrol training session, in the mid-1960s.

stare at the huge opening that seemed to grow wider; so, he granted the short recess. (Flashing through my mind was the then current joke: how do you make an elephant fly; first, get a very long zipper.) When we got to the hall, I told my witness to fasten his trousers, which he did, and then he said: "I can't go back in there." I looked up at him and said, "You must. Justice cannot be done without your testimony." "I just can't go back in." And then a small voice within me gave an inspiring message: "The jury will be impressed by your courage if you go back in." "I'll do it." He did, and justice was done.

Default Divorce: "I Buried All of Mine!"

ANOTHER INCIDENT I recall, but not with pleasure, is a default divorce hearing I squeezed in before leaving for a conference I'd been invited to attend in Washington, DC—as the judge knew—and I was scheduled to leave about noon. My client was an older lady, scrawny, of uneven temperament, and her witness was a large, muscular woman. The little hearing took the usual routine short time, and I called the required one witness. I can still see her. She put her arms akimbo and said, "Well, I'll tell you what this husband was like.

But I buried all of mine!" This was a newer judge, well-liked by all of us, and he looked at me, having been a trial lawyer himself for many years, and said: "When do you leave for Washington? I'll sign your decree."

Can the Jury Hear?

THE THEN new courthouse in Rawlins, Wyoming, was built on a vacant lot south of the federal main east-west highway, then Lincoln Highway, now Interstate 80. This highway just north of the courthouse had a grade steep enough to require the big trucks to shift repeatedly. The noise in the courtroom was horrendous. I was representing the defendant company, and when I put my third defense witness on the stand, he spoke softly and seemed to lack both volume and resonance. "Please speak louder so the jury can hear you," I asked.

Finally, turning to the jury, I asked, "Can you hear this witness?" A juror in the back row replied, "Ma'am, you're the only one we've been able to hear the whole trial." I figured I would win their verdict, and did.

A Jury Free from Bias

MANY TIMES in the twenty years that I taught law in the evening law school, although irrelevant to my courses, I would mention that justice was the weakest argument that a lawyer could make in court. I still believe that. Justice is an intangible, indefinable, noble objective. I believe that a trial lawyer can best obtain a fair result by presenting the evidence competently and making an argument fairly that is persuasive because the evidence supports it. Sometimes obtaining a just result is a very difficult task for the lawyer because of the fact-finder's biases or prejudices. The fact finder may be a jury or, if a trial to the court only, a judge. As I write some of my memories of the trial courts, I recall one civil case that at first seemed a sure "loser," but I truly believed should be a victory for the defense because that result seemed fair. Or, if you prefer, justice should prevail. Let me tell you about it, briefly.

One day a woman telephoned me for an appointment about defending her son who had been sued. When she arrived, I met a woman in her late forties, ladylike in appearance and demeanor, who had a sad tale to tell. Her fifteen-year-old son had been sued for wrongful death of two persons in an automobile accident. Here is what the woman told me.

She and her husband, with their son, had moved to Wyoming several years previously. Apparently, they had suffered serious financial reverses in the East and had moved to Wyoming to start life anew. Further questioning disclosed that her husband was a recovering alcoholic, earnestly committed to staying sober. They had been living in a small, primitive house west of Cheyenne near a county road. Recently they had acquired a better place a little farther west also on the same county road and were in the process of moving to the new place. The mother had carefully packed the family heirloom china and other precious items for the move. The son had recently received his learner's license, which restricted him to driving only when an adult licensed operator was in the car with him.

On the day of the accident, the father was at work, and the mother did not drive. The son volunteered to take the breakable family heirlooms to the new place, which was not far distant, and assured his mother that he would be very careful. So she agreed, the car was packed, and the son drove away. On the way, the county road became very rough, the boy worried about the china and decided to go on the interstate highway for the short distance before he could turn off to their new place. The accident with another car occurred while he was driving on the highway: two men were killed and three were injured seriously. The boy, and his parents as natural guardians, had been sued.

The woman concluded with a blockbuster: the family had no insurance! I explained that I was a poor choice for defense counsel because I had represented defendants in a number of accident cases in which the defendants were insured, and people in my community were aware that I had represented insurance companies in these cases. The jury would assume, therefore, that these defendants were insured, and Wyoming law then did not allow me to tell the jury that they had no insurance. Nonetheless, the woman was insistent that she and her husband wanted me and became very upset. So I agreed to discuss the accident with her son and then decide if I would undertake the defense.

The son, a fine young boy with impressive sincerity, was understandably greatly disturbed by the fatal accident. We went over the details as he remembered them, and I probed repeatedly into all the circumstances. Finally, I decided that, in my opinion at least, the boy was not responsible for the accident, and I agreed to undertake the defense. I remember the trial well, because I conducted a far longer *voir dire* than was my custom. The purpose of *voir dire* is to select, by questioning prospective jurors, a fair and impartial jury. Here is a digression: in the state courts where I have practiced, the lawyers conduct the *voir dire* of the jury; in federal court, the judge usually conducts the *voir dire*, and theoretically will ask suitable questions that the lawyers submit to the judge. In the case that I am relating to you, I worked very hard for a jury free from any bias against teenage drivers—they were as prone to serious car accidents over a half-century ago as they are today. Finally, our jury was selected, and the trial began.

The trial was without unusual incident. The mother had been a concern to me because she drowned you with words. No matter how simple the question, she responded with a flood of words. When I called her to testify, I braced myself—but she was one of the best witnesses whom I had ever questioned. Her answers were clear, concise, and always audible. The cross-examination of the investigating highway patrolman also went better than I had expected because he did not stubbornly cling to a conclusion to which he should not have jumped. All the evidence (testimony and exhibits such as diagrams and photographs) was admitted by the court for the jury to hear and see.

When time came for the lawyers' closing arguments to the jury, plaintiffs' lawyer speaks first and, in this case, I thought that the plaintiffs' lawyer was excellent. I sat there thinking what an adverse verdict would mean for this young boy and for his parents' efforts to start anew and for their financial situation. When my turn came, I truly had my heart in my argument while I reviewed the evidence that had convinced me to undertake the defense. The jury returned a verdict "For the Defense" and again confirmed my faith in the jury system.

After all these many years, I remember what the young boy said to me after the jury verdict. I was still in the courtroom, packing my briefcase. His parents had already thanked me and were putting on their coats. The boy came up to me and in words almost identical to these, said: "You will never know what this verdict means to me. All my life I can remember that twelve grownups decided, based on all they learned at my trial, that the accident was not my fault, and I did not cause those deaths."

A Case Called *Miranda*, I Was a First

A 1966 United States Supreme Court opinion called *Miranda* is the source of the requirement that persons arrested or detained are advised of their rights, before being questioned. Every United States jurisdiction has its own regulations regarding what, precisely, must be said to a person arrested or placed in a custodial situation. The typical warning is similar to the following:

» You have the right to remain silent when questioned.
» Anything you say or do may be used against you in a court of law.
» You have the right to consult an attorney before speaking to the police and to have an attorney present during questioning now or in the future.
» If you cannot afford an attorney, one will be appointed for you before any questioning, if you wish.
» If you decide to answer any questions now, without an attorney present, you will still have the right to stop answering at any time until you talk to an attorney.
» Knowing and understanding your rights as I have explained them to you, are you willing to answer my questions without an attorney present?

I was one of the first lawyers to meet *Miranda* because the opinion was announced while I was in the middle of a trial. After I had established myself in Wyoming as an experienced, successful lawyer, I enjoyed being able to limit my trial and appellate practice to civil matters. For one of my last jury trials, however, I did voluntarily undertake one criminal case that is memorable for me and that I share briefly with you. The parents of a young woman, who had been charged with second-degree murder, retained me as defense counsel for their daughter's trial. The big problem for the defense: the daughter had confessed the killing to the sheriff and one of his deputies when they interviewed her. The prosecutor was like a cat with a bowl of cream because the sheriff had obtained that written confession. When I met my client, the daughter, I understood the horrifying extent of the parents' concern. The young woman was intellectually disabled. I am certain that she would have confessed as those two big lawmen urged her to say that she had done the killing. She would have been afraid and said what she was pressed into saying, and her interrogators would sincerely believe that she was guilty.

So what happened? You could never guess. The jury had been selected by Friday afternoon of the previous week, and Mondays were reserved for the court to hear motions in other cases. The trial was to begin on Tuesday. The trial was in a small community close enough to Cheyenne that I could leave my home very early Tuesday morning to be ready for the trial to start. Every Monday in those days, the leading law publisher's "advance sheets" were delivered. That Monday, the Advance Sheet for the United States Supreme Court had an opinion named *Miranda v. State of Arizona*, 384 U.S. 436

(1966). When I returned to court on Tuesday morning, I asked for a pretrial conference with the judge and prosecutor. I well remember that conference. I laid the Advance Sheet with its *Miranda* opinion before the judge, and with the prosecutor looking over his shoulder, the judge and he read the *Miranda* opinion.

I also well remember what the judge exclaimed: "The Court can't do that!"

I responded gently: "With due respect, Your Honor, the Court did do that. I ask this court to rule that the defendant's purported 'confession' is not admissible into evidence because she was not first warned of her rights." And so ended the prosecution and the trial—because what the defendant had said under pressure from the two lawmen was the only evidence of defendant's alleged guilt. Was she guilty of the killing? I don't know, but I shall always believe that a forced confession, without a *Miranda* warning, is not sufficient to establish guilt beyond a reasonable doubt.

I also believe this to be one of the earliest cases where the *Miranda* opinion changed the course of a criminal proceeding.

Now, based on alleged violations of *Miranda*, criminal trials are flooded with motions to suppress evidence. Indeed, sometimes such a motion is filed even if it does not apply to the facts of the case. When many years later I was Denver's Chief Appellate Deputy District Attorney, I remember arguing an appeal before the state supreme court when a justice asked defense counsel, "Why did you file a motion to suppress evidence (a *Miranda* motion) when there was no questioning until after a formal arrest and advisement of the suspect?" The response is unforgettable: "I always file this motion when defending a criminal case." So, this is an example of how courts are flooded with superfluous paper.

Never Again!
Once Was Enough!

I remind the Reader that these are not remembrances of a lawyer who began practicing law as the son of a valued client in a large, prestigious law firm in a major city. Instead, I was one of the majority of young lawyers who start the practice of law slightly below the bottom in a small or medium-size town. I was in Cheyenne, Wyoming. Add to that less than auspicious beginning being a solo woman lawyer in the 1940s, and then you understand why I could not start out being selective in my clients. All I asked was that the client be honest and able to pay my fee. Oh, my joy when my practice grew so that I could be selective in what legal matters I would undertake. In my early days, however, I had suffered through representations which, when over, I swore that I would never again undertake a similar one—a promise to myself that was easy to keep. Here are several miserable "once only" experiences.

THE DOG BITE CASE

I HANDLED one dog bite case. I represented the plaintiff, who had been severely bitten, followed by hospitalization and rabies shots. The defense lawyer was an experienced, excellent trial lawyer; I was very new. Hence, the defense lawyer had no interest whatsoever in settlement because he was confident of an easy win against me. The judge set the trial for 8:30 a.m., which was surprising because he usually never showed up in the courthouse before 9:00 or 9:15 a.m.

The inflexible rule is that the lawyer must be in court ready to begin at the scheduled time. There I was with my client, a nice but timid woman. Defense counsel showed up with his client, the dog owner—and the dog on a leash. I have always been a dog lover, but not all dogs are nice. This one was a large, hairy beast with a malevolent eye. By 8:45 a.m., the judge had not yet arrived. The dog became impatient and started to growl. The growl began with a sort of low rumble like the beginning of a thunderstorm. The rumble increased in volume until it was a very loud, angry growl. When the dog bared his big fangs while emitting angry growls, opposing counsel shouted to me: "Brooke, I can't hold this brute much longer. How much to settle?" No judge yet, my client trembling behind me (and believe me, I was no protector at just over a hundred pounds), I said: "No settlement, that is what you have always told me. Wait until the judge sees and hears this dog. Hold tight, please." We settled for a good, tidy—and justified—sum. And I decided at the moment of settlement never to take another dog bite case—it was too dangerous!

CHEMISTRY AND "LEMON MERINGUE PIE"

I WAS delighted with my growing practice but had yet to learn to be more careful in screening what matters I undertook. One day, still a "junior" lawyer, I received a telephone call from a man in Denver who wanted me to represent him and his company in a matter involving the federal Food and Drug Administration (FDA). I foolishly flattered myself into thinking that my legal prowess was becoming more known in the Denver business community, which had already availed itself of my services. So, I made an appointment to discuss the matter.

At the appointed time, two men showed up, and pardon me for referring to former clients thus, but they immediately reminded me of two weasels. My inner voice was saying: "Watch out! No, no!" But, be honest, we don't always listen to our inner voice, do we? And I didn't.

The FDA wanted to prosecute them for their "purported food" product. *The product was horrifying: lemon meringue pie with a guaranteed shelf life of two years!* The men's description of their product was sickening.

I digress. My mother made the most delicious lemon meringue pie ever made: very light crust, tart lemon filling, with fluffy fresh meringue. Also, I had hated high school chemistry where all we learned was memorized valences for chemicals.

Back to the FDA versus my clients. The ingredients in their alleged "lemon meringue pie" were more advanced chemicals than I was taught about in high school. I resolved their problem to the clients' satisfaction: a consent decree that relieved them from both FDA prosecution and penalty in return for my clients' never again making their alleged "lemon meringue pie." I promised myself never to represent manufacturers of dubious food products again—and I have never since been able to eat a piece of real lemon meringue pie. As to being more careful about selecting clients whom you will represent, I guarantee young lawyers that you will become more accurate but will never attain a goal of 100 percent.

CONTESTED PROBATE

HERE IS a third area that I vowed never again to undertake: trial lawyer in a contested family probate matter. The cliché is a perfect fit: "words are not adequate." The greed, malice, lies, anger, and violent emotions involved in a family fight over estate assets are horrifying beyond description. I tried one such case, a major one, and worked incredibly hard to obtain a victory. But the victory brought no good feeling to me, and I realized that if I had been on the other side and won, I would have felt the same way. The ugliest aspects of human nature erupt in full force in family litigation over wealth. I chose never to handle this type of case again. Many years later a lawyer friend of mine, an excellent and experienced trial lawyer, told me of his upcoming trial of a family feud over an estate, his first such case. I told him of my experience and refusal to handle more of this type of case. After his trial he called me to say that he had made the same promise to himself as I had: never again.

IMMIGRATION

AS I have been writing these small memories of my mistakes in agreeing to undertake certain legal matters, I realize that although I must have made more mistakes, one more is enough to write about. This is, "Twice was enough. Never again." And the area of representation was immigration. The first one I undertook had a very happy ending. A local Latvian woman asked me to be her lawyer to obtain permission for her mother in Latvia to come live with her. The mother was alone in the world except for this daughter, who loved her very much. I told the woman that I had never handled an immigration matter, but she wanted me. The only problems were people. The USSR government, which then controlled Latvia, insisted that the mother apply to a government office where only Russian was spoken, and the mother spoke no Russian. Then the American authorities in Moscow proved uncooperative. Finally, we got her to New York, where the language barrier was impossible, and she was treated cruelly. I got her to Canada, where the authorities were wonderful and from thence to Wyoming and her daughter.

My first immigration matter left me with a warm glow of having accomplished some good, and I decided that an occasional such matter would be worth doing.

Then came my second—and last—immigration matter. The person in charge of a local church, which I so describe to avoid disclosing which church, came to see me about representing a member of his flock, who I shall here call John Doe. He told me that Mr. Doe had been a faithful member of his church for the past five years, was a quiet man, retired, had never married, and lived alone. He said that Mr. Doe wanted very much to become a citizen of the United States of America, but he had "jumped ship" illegally in New York about thirty years previously.

I checked the statute books and found a federal law that provided a "window" permitting naturalization despite illegal entry when the entry occurred in a specific long-ago window of time that applied to Mr. Doe. When I met with Mr. Doe, I pressed him to tell me about any arrests and any convictions he may have had since coming to the United States, informing him that the government would make diligent search to check his criminal record. He assured me that he had only been arrested once: the day he arrived in the United States, which was July 4. He saw the parade in New York City and was so excited by the celebration that he drank too much alcohol and was arrested for being drunk and disorderly but was later released. That was all he had to report? Yes, he assured me. So I undertook to represent him.

I prepared all the necessary paperwork and submitted the application to the federal Immigration and Naturalization Agency in Denver, Colorado, because that agency then had no office in Wyoming. A few days later, I received a letter from the Denver office informing me that I would need to come to Denver to consult personally with the head of the Denver office about the Doe application. I failed to understand why any concerns could not be handled by mail (a very long time before e-mail!) or by telephone, but I called and made an appointment.

After driving the hundred miles from Cheyenne to Denver, I arrived at the immigration office and was shown into the chief's office—and was shocked!

The man behind the desk was dressed weirdly, needed a shave and a haircut, and was a scary sight. My shock obviously showed because the man said, "I am working undercover and just came into the office to meet with you." Being thus reassured of my personal safety, I asked him if the application papers I had submitted posed a problem. He said "No," the problem was my client. So, I told him his reputation in the church he faithfully attended and his assurance of his one arrest for celebrating our Fourth of July holiday on the day he jumped ship. The man then said to me, "You really don't know who your client is, do you?" He asked this in such a grave and grim manner that I realized something was badly amiss. I replied, "No. Who is he that I don't know about?" The man replied, "We were never able to get admissible evidence to arrest him, much less convict him, but he was well-known to law enforcement officials, especially gangster units, as the head of Al Capone's rum-and-gun-running fleet. We also knew that he was involved in some murders and disposal of cement-loaded bodies in the Great Lakes." But he added that the authorities could not prosecute him or block his naturalization.

I gave a frank response to this startling disclosure about my client: I did not yet know if I would be brave enough to tell Mr. Doe to go away. Maybe the safest course for all would be just to let him become naturalized? We looked at each other. Then I said that I would think about what to do during the hundred-mile drive back home. And I did think, very hard. Should I tell my husband? We were very close; he would be frightened for me and tell me to drop the matter immediately. Answer: no; I won't tell my husband. Will you mention the matter to anyone? No; especially not the client because I was afraid that he might have a negative reaction. I had no experience whatsoever in dealing with anyone who had lived a life of violent crime. Notify the federal agent of my decision to let the naturalization proceed? All indications were that Mr. Doe would continue to live quietly in our community, which he did. But I never handled another immigration matter.

Appeals and business law (now called transaction law) became my bread and butter, with enough jury trials as jam, to be my comfortable law practice in Wyoming.

The Appellate Lawyer

MY FIRST APPEAL: MAKING HISTORY
IN MY STOCKING FEET

ALTHOUGH I had long dreamed of participating in the legal world of appeals, that was not realistic for a young lawyer and for a young woman lawyer in Wyoming in the 1940s, "Forget it." My practice had grown comfortably, and trial victories continued, but I never forgot my dream. One day after only a few years of practice, the clerk of the Wyoming Supreme Court telephoned me to say that then Chief Justice Fred H. Blume wanted to see me in his chambers at my earliest convenience. The Supreme Court building was only a few blocks from my office, and I arrived there soon after my call.

The chief justice greeted me graciously and proceeded immediately to why he wanted to see me. He and the other two justices of the court wanted to appoint me to represent a young indigent woman in her appeal from a conviction in Casper, Wyoming of "infanticide," killing her newborn child. The three justices thought that the defendant had been represented by incompetent trial counsel. Chief Justice Blume said that no statute authorized such an appellate court appointment and jokingly added that they might all go to jail for it. He and the other two justices were all in their middle to late sixties—which I then thought incredibly old. The prospect of sharing a jail term with them was not alluring. Most important to me was that I could actually do an appeal by appointment from the Wyoming Supreme Court. The chief justice directed me to go to the clerk's office to pick up the record.

The record in an appeal is a verbatim transcript of every word (including murmurings such as "hm-m-m") at a trial, every recess time, and all other trial interruptions. The record also includes all exhibits (unless you obtain the court's permission to file a photograph of an outsize exhibit to be lodged on the court's premises). Also, some appellate courts provide for summaries of the record, or permit the appealing lawyer to file selected portions, to which the non-appealing lawyer may add. But over a half-century ago the record was everything—every word and every exhibit.

The record for my first appeal is memorable: it was monstrous. The 8.5-by-14-inch pages of transcript were bound into long black covers, with about four inches of pages for each volume. My first appeal had twenty-eight volumes of record! As the always kind Clerk of the Supreme Court, Fred S. Fobes, sadly kept piling stacks of the record, I knew that I could not move it. So I called my husband, a tall, strong—and loyal—man, to come help me, which he did. I read every page of that record, as I later always did in my numerous appeals. Next I researched carefully the law applicable to this case. I was busy at my office with my paying practice, so on Saturday afternoons while my husband played golf, and our daughter played with neighboring friends, I went to the state law library and buried myself in the research for my opening brief.

At last, I prepared my opening brief. "Brief" is an amusing misnomer in the legal profession. At the time of my first appeal, the page limit for each of the opening and answer briefs was fifty pages. Now the more common limit is twenty-five or thirty pages. I never wrote long briefs, and I believe that my first one was only about thirty of the fifty allowable pages. And, what a horrid job for the poor legal secretary to type. No copy machines yet. The minimum number of copies required was six—five sheets of carbon paper! A typo was a dread occurrence. I told my secretary that if the typo could be made into another word to call me and I would try to rewrite it so that "other" word could be used.

Finally, all briefs filed, the appeal was ready to be scheduled for oral argument, which was a half-hour for each side, far different from now. I had never heard an appellate argument and wanted to listen to one before I did mine. I asked the clerk of court please to let me know when a good one was scheduled. When he called, I shuffled matters at my office so I could attend. The appellant's lawyer was a senior lawyer in Casper, known for his skill in natural resource and business law. The case on appeal was unusual for him: a murder case. The defendant had killed her husband, and both had been very prominent in the community, socially and financially. I went to hear the argument and how this able lawyer would persuade the high court to reverse his client's conviction. I have an unforgettable memory of that argument. After describing in detail the husband's severe maltreatment of his wife, the lawyer said: "So she went downstairs to the kitchen where her husband was eating breakfast and shot him in the middle of his shredded wheat." "Well," I said to myself, "I can do better than that."

In the evenings after working in my office all day, fixing our dinner and tidying up, and checking on our daughter and her homework, I would go into our guest bedroom, stand before a mirror, and practice my argument, which I had carefully outlined but never wrote out.

The great day came: mine was the second argument of the morning, and so I waited in what was then the lawyers' waiting room. Looking out the window, I could see the snow falling heavily. Even now I can close my eyes and see the pictures that hung on the walls of that sparsely furnished little waiting room. The walls were lined with enlarged old-fashioned photographs of long-deceased justices of the court. They all had white hair and then fashionable white beards! I looked at those pictures and then at the dismal snowstorm outside and thought: "What am I doing here?" I answered honestly, "This is your dream coming true."

At last I stood before the Wyoming Supreme Court for the first of many times to come and said: "May it please the court." Then I presented my argument with a fervent belief in my client's innocence to inspire me. Result: conviction reversed.

This was a different judicial era. When the argument of the case was concluded, the chief justice announced: "The case stands submitted." Then counsel stood at their respective counsel tables as the justices came down from the bench for each to shake the hand of the lawyers and say thank you. All was so courteous and attentive that as a lawyer I felt that my client had received a hearing in a court of justice. Today appellate argument is a sadly different story as I relate in Part Three's "Inside a Civil Jury Trial," About Appeals section.

Back to my first appeal: when the justices had departed, a spectator in the courtroom came up to me and congratulated me on my oral argument.

I was flattered because he was a well-known and successful trial lawyer in Cheyenne. After thanking him, I asked what I could do better next time, and he evaded a direct answer. Then he offered me a partnership with him! I was thrilled—a lawyer willing to be a law partner of Wyoming's first woman trial lawyer! I accepted on the spot, and we were partners for fourteen years until my husband and I moved to Denver, and my partner also moved to another state to practice law.

After my quick acceptance of his offer, I pressed him to help by telling what I could do better in my next appearance before the state's supreme court. His response: "After you said, 'May it please the court,' you stepped out of your shoes and never put them back on until after you finished your argument. Next time, keep your shoes on." I was horrified and knew how it happened. I had practiced my argument at night after a long, busy day, and so would slip out of my shoes as I practiced in front of a mirror at home. In later years, with several new justices replacing a deceased and a retired justice, my shoeless argument remained part of court lore. The justices would tell aspiring appellate lawyers to listen to one of my arguments as a role model. They apparently always concluded this advice, so flattering to me, with a caution not to argue in their stocking feet as I had done in my first appellate argument.

PS: The Real End of My First Appeal

MANY YEARS after the appellate reversal of my client's conviction and when I had been practicing in Denver for some years, I received a heartwarming telephone call. When I answered the telephone, a woman's voice said, "You may not remember me." Not a promising beginning. Then she told me her maiden name, and of course I remembered her. She was the defendant whose conviction for killing her baby I had caused the Wyoming Supreme Court to reverse. She said, "I live in Denver and saw your name in the newspaper and decided to call you." I assured her that I did remember her. She said that she wanted to let me know she had been happily married for many years and had three fine sons, now all college graduates.

Then she said, "I shall always be grateful to you for believing me and the truth: that poor little baby was stillborn. I owe you my life, pray for you, and shall always be grateful." My grim memory of reading through twenty-eight volumes of record suddenly became a good memory of worthy endeavor. A warm feeling of "justice served" suffused me.

Figure 2.16. Brooke and her mother visit with United States Senators at the Capitol in April 1958, when Brooke was admitted to the Bar of the United States Supreme Court.

PRIME PRACTICE IN
WYOMING—CONSTITUTIONALITY?

IN THE time about which I now write, Justice of the Peace Court and Police Court cases were behind me, but I owe them much for my on-the-job training. Now I practiced in the more rarefied atmosphere of business law with a wide variety of areas, my trials were in state and federal district courts, and appeals were in the Wyoming Supreme Court and the United States Court of Appeals for the Tenth Circuit, and I was honored to be admitted to the Bar of the United States Supreme Court.

Enjoying the prime of my Wyoming practice, I happily established corporate entities for clients for whom I may have established partnerships years previous and that had grown into prosperous corporations. I found oil and gas law interesting to practice as well as "hard mining" law and real estate and tax matters. We lawyers in smaller communities did not then specialize. I, as well as other Wyoming lawyers, drew the wills for our clients and handled probate and a host of other areas. You were "The Lawyer" for your client, who felt free to call you

Figure 2.17. Brooke, with a group, touring the United States Capitol Building during her April 1958 trip.

at home on holidays about any little potential legal worry. Nonetheless, I probably unjustifiably criticize that today's legal super-specialists confirm Edmund Burke's statement that "Law sharpens the mind by narrowing it."

My years of prime practice in Wyoming were made memorably happy by some very interesting appeals. These appeals kept alive my dream of one day serving as an appellate judge. In researching for my appellate briefs, I tried to read each opinion to determine if it were well structured so that its reasoning supported the opinion given. I, of course, expected the appellate court's opinion to be well written so that its proper usage of our language would avoid ambiguity in the opinion.

WYOMING FAIR TRADE ACT

ONE DAY I received a telephone call from New York—not common in Wyoming in those days. The caller was an executive with a large corporation who wanted to retain me to handle an appeal on a constitutional issue. He said that he was flying from New York to meet with me and made an appointment. I was understandably excited: a woman "country lawyer" sought out by this big corporation to test a constitutional issue. I cannot describe how "non-picky" I was as to what might be involved. As it turned out, the matter was a respectable constitutional issue involving a commercial statute that had recently become popular with some of the states—the so-called Fair Trade Laws. These acts were passed in forty-six states; in seventeen states they were upheld as constitutional; in twenty states they were held unconstitutional. I was retained to attack the constitutionality of the Wyoming Fair Trade Act. The impetus for these laws had been the claim that they would protect small businesses from big chain stores that were proliferating—but they did not provide the anticipated protection.

When my client's representative met with me in Cheyenne, he was plain-spoken. He said: "We want you to attack the constitutionality of the Wyoming Fair Trade Act. We want you to *Win*! Get any materials you want and any help you think you need. We'll pay you very well (this was before today's prevalent hourly rate). We are aware of your appellate successes, and I stress that we'll pay you very well. We expect to *win*." (My emphasis added.) I realized that it did not matter to my new, big client that I was a woman lawyer. It would not have mattered if I had two heads and a long furry tail—the company had checked my record, wanted to *win*, and expected me to *win*. That was all fine with me, and I undertook the representation.

First came a mini-trial to lay out the constitutional issues; I prevailed with the trial court adjudging unconstitutionality. Good! It's always easier to argue for an affirmance than for a reversal of a lower court, subject to the exception of the trial judge's having a poor record, of often being incorrect.

The Wyoming Fair Trade Act was considered by many to serve as a protection for small business because it allowed the manufacturer to set a minimum price for its product. This had proved, however, not to be the case. I believed strongly that the act unconstitutionally delegated the legislative power to private parties.

The Wyoming Supreme Court agreed that the statute was unconstitutional, based on a lack of due process and being beyond the state's police power. The court's opinion is lengthy in *Bulova Watch Co. v. Zale Jewelry Co.*, 371 P.2d 409 (Wyo. 1962), but I think brilliant and received professional praise. Of particular interest is the court's statement of the scope and limitations on the judicial function—a heartwarming read, today. For example,

We will not and we do not substitute our opinions . . . for the considered judgment of our lawmakers. Yet, we ourselves have a function to perform, a constitutional right, and the paramount duty to insist that the legislature not renounce its legislative power by any such attempt to delegate it away.

The author of the opinion was Justice Harry S. Harnsberger, and many of his opinions received national recognition. He also became our close personal friend.

Back we go now to my victory in assailing the constitutionality of the Wyoming Fair Trade Act. My client was very pleased with the victory and did pay me very well. I had a memorable incident during the oral argument of the appeal. Having won in the trial court, I was the appellee and spoke once during the appeal. The appellant had both the opening argument and the closing argument—the precious last word. In the argument of the Wyoming Fair Trade Act, opposing counsel in closing argument stated that I had "seriously misrepresented the case to the court." I was furious, but then to my delighted relief, the court intervened. The chief justice told appellant's counsel: "The court knows Brooke Wunnicke, who has appeared before the court many times, and is confident that she would not misrepresent to us." The court then gave my accuser ten days within which to file a statement with the court stating "specifically" the alleged misrepresentations to the court. I was proud of this public endorsement of my professional integrity, announced by the highest state judiciary. When I left the courtroom after the oral argument, the offending opposing counsel was waiting for me. He said, "Brooke, you're not going to make me file that statement, are you? I don't have anything to put in it." I replied, "No, I'm not going to make you do it. The court is." Then, he said, "But I don't know what to say because I was just arguing." I have always tried to help another lawyer in need, so I snapped, "Try a retraction and an apology."

PUBLIC BOND STATUTE: ADVANCE
ESCROW-TYPE REFUNDING STATUTE

SO MANY appeals and so many issues and so much that I would like to share. Instead, I have prudently chosen just two more from Wyoming to share that were especially important for Wyoming and enjoyable for me. They both involved testing the constitutionality of new public bond statutes for my client, Denver bond counsel. Doesn't seem interesting? I think that you will change your mind.

The first one I chose involved testing the constitutionality of the "advance escrow-type refunding statute"—yes, that was really its name. It was an ingenious statute, and I heard years later that it had been used to good advantage in Wyoming by educational institutions. It was complex, and when the case was set for oral argument in the Wyoming Supreme Court, with opposing counsel's consent, I applied to the court to sully the previously unused courtroom's blackboard. It was elegantly framed in myrtle wood from Oregon, the same wood used for the justices' bench and in the courtroom—all beautiful, and now all replaced in a government "modernization."

Now, when appellate courts can barely deign to hear oral arguments of fifteen minutes—yes, only fifteen minutes per side—this is going to seem incredible. The Wyoming Supreme Court allotted the afternoon to this case, with two hours per side for argument! For two hours I carefully said, "advance escrow-type refunding bonds," with longing for Shakespeare's "trippingly on the tongue." I filled the court's blackboard with several sets of computations under the statute to show well its provisions all dovetailed for the happiness of all involved. One of the justices, Norman Gray, had been a star University of Nebraska football player and physically looked the part. A kind and gentle person, he had an incisive legal mind but usually asked little during oral argument; but when he did, it was always to the point. Near the end of my presentation, Justice Gray asked, "Counsel, isn't this statute really a form of arbitrage?" Of course it was, but arbitrage does not have a wholesome connotation when applied to public finance. And I had been so careful to use the statute's unwieldy title! I am pleased to report that the court affirmed the constitutionality of the statute in *Rodin v. State*, 417 P.2d 180 (Wyo. 1966). The victory in *Rodin* made possible a $25-million issue of refunding bonds by the University of Wyoming to replace other outstanding bonds and pay for construction of facilities for the university. And, for long after that, the advance escrow-type refunding bonds proved useful in public financings.

PUBLIC BOND STATUTES: INDUSTRIAL DEVELOPMENT REVENUE BONDS

IN THE 1960s, many states, including Wyoming, enacted Industrial Development Revenue Bond Statutes (IDRBs or IRBs). As originally enacted, no dollar

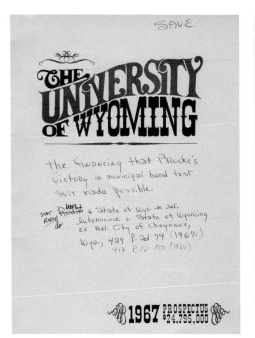
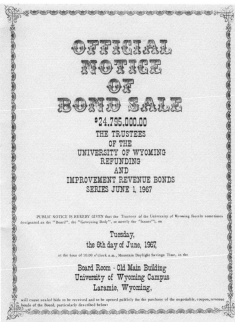

Figure 2.18. Colorful two pages from the 1967 prospectus for the University of Wyoming refunding bonds of $24,795,000. This financing was made possible by Brooke's victory in the *Rodin* test case at the Wyoming Supreme Court for constitutionality in Wyoming of this type of public revenue bonds. (The gold-toned paper with bright red lettering and decorative borders perhaps indicates the enthusiasm of the university.)

"cap" was included, but I am pleased to report that the court upheld the validity of the statute. For "small issue IRBs," the Internal Revenue Code enacted a $1 million cap, which cooled the early eager use of these bonds, and since then I believe for certain situations, the cap was raised to $10 million. (IRBs now come in many "flavors;" for examples, tax-exempt facility IRBs, non-tax-exempt IRBs, and IRBs issued on behalf of non-profit corporations, 501(c)(3) bonds.) The Wyoming statute was for bonds issued on behalf of a state or local government which guaranteed their repayment, but the proceeds from the bond sale were to go directly to a private for-profit business. The bond interest and principal are paid from the revenues of that business. This financing "gimmick," as some called it, was used to attract a new business to a state by offering a big free initial ride.

I am pleased to report *Victory*—the constitutionality of the industrial development revenue bonds statute was upheld, and an excellent court opinion, again authored by Justice Harnsberger, provided useful precedent in the

PRELIMINARY OFFICIAL STATEMENT Dated   , 1967

NEW ISSUE

The Internal Revenue Service has ruled that the interest on the Bonds is exempt from present Federal income taxation. In the opinion of Bond Counsel for the City, interest on the Bonds is exempt from all present Federal income taxes, and in the opinion of Special Counsel to the City, principal and interest are exempt from all present Wyoming state and local taxes.

[handwritten: Brooks Wunnicke / Enabled by Victory / In Industrial Rev. Bond) / Uhl v. Wyo / 429 P. 2d 74 (1967)]

OFFICIAL STATEMENT

$20,000,000

CITY OF CHEYENNE, WYOM

Industrial Development Revenue Bonds
(Wycon Chemical Company)

Payable solely from and secured by a pledge of revenues and rental income from or in connection with the Project, including amounts to be received under a Lease Agreement with Wycon Chemical Company guaranteed unconditionally by Colorado Interstate Corporation.

Dated: July 1, 1967   Due: July 1, 1968-1976, inclusive and July 1, 1987

Principal and semi-annual interest January 1 and July 1, (first coupon due January 1, 1968) payable at the principal office of   in the City of   , Trustee, or at the option of the holder at the principal office of   in the City of   , Paying Agent. Coupon Bonds in the denomination of $5,000 each are registrable as to principal only, or as to both principal and interest, reconvertible. The Bonds are subject to redemption prior to maturity as more fully described herein.

MATURITY SCHEDULE
$ Serial Bonds

Amount	Maturity	Coupon	Price	Amount	Maturity	Coupon	Price
	1968				1972		
	1969				1973		
	1970				1974		
	1971				1975		
					1976		

$.........% Term Bonds
Due July 1, 1987

Price 100%
(Accrued Interest to be added)

These Bonds are offered when, as and if issued and received by us, subject to the approval of legality by Messrs. Chapman and Cutler of Chicago, Illinois, and certain other conditions.

EASTMAN DILLON, UNION SECURITIES & CO.
Members New York Stock Exchange

Main Office: One Chase Manhattan Plaza, New York 10005, Telephone 770-8000

ALEXANDRIA	CARLISLE	ESCONDIDO	LOS ANGELES	PHILADELPHIA	SAN JOSE
BALTIMORE	CHICAGO	HARTFORD	MINNEAPOLIS	READING	SAN JUAN
BOSTON	CLEVELAND	HOUSTON	NEWARK	RIVERSIDE	SAN MARINO
BRIDGEPORT	DALLAS	LAS VEGAS	NEW HAVEN	SAN DIEGO	VENTURA
	EASTON	LONG BEACH	PATERSON	SAN FRANCISCO	

Dated ...., 1967

(vertical left margin text): This preliminary Official Statement and the Information contained herein are subject to completion or amendment. These securities may not be sold nor may offers to buy be accepted prior to the time the Official Statement is delivered in final form. Under no circumstances shall this preliminary Official Statement constitute an offer to sell or the solicitation of an offer to buy nor shall there be any sale of these securities in any State in which such offer, solicitation or sale would be unlawful prior to registration or qualification under the securities laws of any such State.

Figure 2.19. Prospectus dated July 1, 1967, first page, for the City of Cheyenne, Wyoming $20,000,000 Industrial Development Revenue Bonds for the Wycon Chemical Company. This financing was made possible by Brooke's victory in the *Uhls* test case at the Wyoming Supreme Court for constitutionality in Wyoming of industrial development revenue bonds.

area of constitutional law. *Uhls v. State*, 429 P.2d 74 (Wyo. 1967). The statute for industrial development revenue bonds being declared constitutional resulted in an important $20 million financing for expansion of an industrial plant in Cheyenne.

The lawsuit arose out of an attack on the industrial revenue bonds by alleging that their authorization was unconstitutional. The repayment of the bonds was to be made from the industry receiving the bond money as it engaged in its business. These were quite popular in that era, and in other states they had been made available by statute to lure out-of-state companies to come to their state because they could get these bonds. In the appeal that I argued for the constitutionality of our statute, I made no secret of the fact that we already had this particular industry, a local refinery. I was active in our local Chamber of Commerce (the first woman elected to its board). Our local refinery needed the money to modernize and upgrade its facility; and the refinery is still in operation.

After the victory upholding the constitutionality of the Wyoming Industrial Development Revenue Bond Act, I received a telephone call promptly from the Bond Dealers Association in New York. After congratulating me, the caller said that they had heard we did not use the bond to attract a new business to Cheyenne, but instead the bond proceeds were to go to a business already here. When I confirmed that what they had heard was true, he was astonished. Why? The answer was simple: the beneficiary of the revenue bond issue had long been a good employer and good corporate citizen of the community. Who deserved the economic boost more—that company or a stranger? I could sense that my caller thought we people Out West were a strange people indeed. I was proud to live in a community that accepted and acted with loyalty.

MY FIRST AND OTHER MEMORABLE FEDERAL APPELLATE ARGUMENTS

RECENTLY, I had lunch with a young lawyer friend who asked if I remembered my first argument in the United States Court of Appeals for the Tenth Circuit, to which I could quickly reply "Yes." As the Reader may remember from high school civics class (I don't know the modern name for this course), the federal circuit courts are the next highest to the United States Supreme Court. The federal judicial hierarchy has three main levels: district court, which is the trial court; the court of appeals, to which district court decisions may be appealed; and the Supreme Court (see Part Three: "What the Law Means for Us," about The Judiciary, What It Means for You, where I discuss the Supreme Court's jurisdictions and *writ of certiorari*).

For a young lawyer, the first appellate argument before a federal circuit court of appeals is comparable to a rookie's first participation in an

NFL game. Each circuit has a group of states within its jurisdiction. The two states where I practice, Colorado and Wyoming, are both in the Tenth Circuit. So a long time ago, in the 1940s, I had the opportunity to appear before the Tenth Circuit. I prepared, prepared, and then prepared some more. When my big day arrived, I was up early to drive to Denver from Cheyenne (a little over a hundred miles) because the Tenth Circuit court did not "sit" in Wyoming.

How the Court Appearance "Worked"

NOW, I digress to tell you a bit about how the court appearance "worked." The lawyer received a written notice of the date and time of appearance, for example, May 19, 1948, at 11:00 a.m. Each oral argument was allotted one hour—a half-hour per side. If the 9:00 a.m. argument only took forty minutes and the 10:00 a.m. took fifty minutes, your 11:00 a.m. argument still began at 11:00 a.m. This was a predictable and dignified procedure.

After a few years, the procedure changed. If you were scheduled for 11:00 a.m., and the first argument of the day was for 9:00 a.m., you were safe only if you were in the courtroom ready to argue by 9:00 a.m. The reason: the earlier scheduled arguments might not take the full time—whenever the earlier arguments ended, you were required to begin. Meanwhile, you might sit in the courtroom for up to two hours—having to wait at your client's expense.

Formerly, when argument in your case ended, the court would intone: "the case stands submitted"; all the judges would rise and leave. Then, you would pack up your files and leave.

That also changed. The court still intoned "the case stands submitted"—but then immediately called the next case, while you were still packing your briefcase. And I thought that I might get trampled as counsel for the next case rushed past me and started unpacking their briefcases and files. Well—quite a digression, wasn't it? But as I was writing this, memories came back very vividly of my unseemly dashes to rush out after my oral arguments, with my briefcase partly packed and files and loose papers under my arm.

My First Argument before the Tenth Circuit Court of Appeals

NOW, AT last, I go to my first argument before the Tenth Circuit. The old courthouse had two courtrooms, both elegant. The main one, where I argued, had marble and in back of the bench where the judges sat were full-length purple velvet draperies. At the hour appointed for my argument, the draperies were parted enough for the judges to come forth, attired in their long black robes, and take their places in their large, impressive chairs behind the high bench. As I approached the podium, attired in my black suit and white blouse with my polished plain black shoes, I looked up, and on the marble proscenium over the bench was inscribed an "inspiring phrase" about justice. Based on my trial experience to keep a vigilant eye on judge, jury, witness, and opposing counsel (with periodic glances at spectators to catch any signals), I glanced at the court—and every judge was grimacing. Aha! The poor judges had heard that "inspiring phrase" read to them intolerably numerous times! So I smiled at them, shook my head gently, and began my argument. I was pleased to see that I had attained immediate—and hopefully a friendly—attention. Both the argument and the decision, rendered weeks later as usual with a written opinion, went well.

"Your Honor, I Don't Think Your Question Is Relevant." Appellant's Counsel Loses

I DO not recall the specifics of those appellate court arguments where all went well without unusual events, although often with complex fact patterns and various principles of law. Instead, only the unusual incidents come to mind as I write this. I remember the time when I had gloried in a favorable jury verdict in the federal district court in Wyoming, and the loser appealed to the Tenth Circuit. When the trial judge had called me to his chambers after the verdict, I thought he was going to congratulate me on winning a tough case. To the contrary, he said that my jury verdict was "the worst miscarriage of justice" over which he had ever presided. He was an excellent judge, so I was gloomy about my prospects in the appellate court. The lawyer on the other side was able, tall, and distinguished looking. Also, he had the facts and the law on his side. As counsel for the appellant (the one who takes the appeal), he argued first. In the course of his argument, the presiding judge asked appellant's counsel a question. In response, my opponent said—and I quote verbatim after all these years: "Your Honor, I don't think your question is relevant." It took all my willpower not to show my joy!

One of the basic rules of appellate argument is when the court asks you a question, answer it—then. You don't say—as I have often heard—"Your

Honor, I shall get to that later"—or, worst of all, "I don't think that your question is relevant." The presiding judge, before whom I had appeared several times, although able, had a "short fuse" and when it was lit, he would stand with his hands on the bench and lean forward as though he would vault over it to reach the offending lawyer. In my case, when the opposing lawyer said "not relevant" instead of answering the question, the judge literally rose to the occasion. The court affirmed the judgment on the jury's verdict, but I don't think that I won the appeal—I'm confident that appellant's counsel lost it.

One Judge Educates the Panel—A Cherished Victory

I CLOSE here with one last Tenth Circuit memory, not colorful or amusing, but cherished—as any lawyer reading this would also feel. The key issue in the appeal was whether the doctrine of collateral estoppel applied to bar the plaintiff's claim. Collateral estoppel is a sort of "poor relation" of the ancient-but-still-very alive doctrine of *res judicata*. *Res judicata* means that the same "thing" has already been judicially decided between the same parties. The party who tries to bring the "thing" or matter again before a court does not get two bites of the apple. *Res judicata* will bar a second adjudication *only if* the four requirements for the doctrine to apply are all met: identity of thing sued for, of cause of action, of parties, and of "quality" in persons for or against whom judgment is made. The doctrine's humble relative is collateral estoppel, which only requires that a particular question has been decided in a prior lawsuit over which the adjudicating court had general jurisdiction. Stated otherwise, the lawyer's burden for *res judicata* to apply is to establish the presence of the required fourfold identity. Ah, but for collateral estoppel to apply, the lawyer has a much smaller load—proof that a particular issue has already been decided in another suit involving the same general matter.

Well, after that short digression for two legal doctrines, there I was before the Tenth Circuit with only a single dispositive issue: collateral estoppel. I was confident that I was on solid ground with the record in my case. An old saying among cynical lawyers was that a judge's decision depended on what the judge had for breakfast that day. If that saying were true, then all the judges before whom I appeared that day—except one—had eaten a very bad breakfast. The judges—all but one—continually interrupted me to complain that *res judicata* could not apply because I lacked the requisite fourfold identity. As the judges became increasingly impatient, I became increasingly grateful that they could not know what I was thinking about them. The kindest adjective that I can use here and still be respectful is that they were being unbelievably "obtuse"—but that was not the kind of word that I was thinking. One judge, however, did not join in this miserable questioning. I remember him fondly, and he deserves mention by name: Orie L. Phillips. Judge Phillips was always courteous to counsel and was exceedingly competent. Soon after he went on senior status, he assisted circuit courts throughout the country in catching up on their dockets, including writing more opinions in one year than any other circuit court judge. Back to Judge Phillips as my savior in this argument, which was becoming more unsavory by the minute. He waved his hand at me and said, "Counsel, please let me interrupt you to speak to my colleagues." Then, he turned to the other judges and instructed them on the difference between *res judicata* and collateral estoppel. He concluded by emphatically telling them that this was a collateral estoppel case. An eerie silence ensued, and I deemed it prudent to say nothing. Finally, the presiding judge said, "The case stands submitted." And well it should have. And I can happily report that the court decided in my favor based on the doctrine of—guess which?—collateral estoppel.

Part Three's "The Law," about Inside a Civil Jury Trial, is more detailed for you. But next—in The General Practitioner—I hope that you will enjoy continuing "inside" my being a lawyer in Wyoming.

The General Practitioner

I WELL remember my first business client. I was surprised when he called for an appointment and told me the nature of the legal assistance he wanted. Needless to write, I exerted every possible effort to accomplish what my new client wanted and needed. He was pleased with what I accomplished and paid me promptly.

My First Business Client Pointed at Me
as If I Were a French Pastry

A SHORT time later, my first business client telephoned again to make an appointment for a friend. When the two men arrived and were shown into my office, my first business client pointed at me as if I were a French Pastry. I still remember verbatim after many years what he said: "There she is. Even though she's a woman, she is a really good lawyer."

Was I offended? No. I appreciated the compliment, wanted the new client, his business matter, and his fee. All went well, and thus my business law practice began and soon did very well.

I ask the Reader to bear with me for this boastful paragraph. I had a Cheyenne store owner whom I enjoyed as a client. I handled all his legal matters, including tax, involving his store. He and his nice family lived in the same block as we did. His little daughter was the same age as our daughter;

they played together, and I always liked our daughter's little friend. While I was writing about this, that client's daughter, now a retired adult also living in Denver, sent a note, which I paraphrase, in part, and quote:

> When she was in grammar school, she went to downtown Cheyenne after school on an errand and then to her father's store to ride home with him. When she arrived at the store, he was in the back room visiting with three of his friends. She heard one of them ask her father, and her note quoted:
> "We hear that you are going to the woman lawyer. How come?" And her father replied, "Because she is the best god-damned lawyer in Cheyenne."

That's now a cherished memory of my business law practice in Wyoming.

"Win! Win!" for Big Corporate Clients

OBVIOUSLY, I enjoyed the practice of business law, both its transactional and litigation areas. My major in college had been economics with sub-majors in accounting and statistics, and with excellent business courses. I liked the seemingly endless variety of legal problems and complexities of business law. And, yes, I always liked to *"Win!"*

After a few years representing local businesses, I was contacted by a New York corporation to represent it in a business dispute with a Wyoming company. I was delighted at the prospect. I can still recall the look of disappointment on the face of the New York executive who came to discuss the matter with me. I have always been aware that I lacked physical "presence" because of my size, or lack thereof. Nonetheless, we soon were getting along fine with our discussion of the lawsuit that I was being retained to defend. I had already learned that being a woman and small did not matter if you could *win*, whether a lawsuit or in negotiation. I believed that if I had two heads and a long, furry tail, my appearance would not suffer—if I could *win*.

It was a different past world about which I am now writing. At the present time, large corporations, and especially insurance companies, often keep their outside counsel on a tight leash as to fees and expenses. My first big corporate client informed me to spend all the time I needed and spare no expense, but *"Win, win!"* I was in Lawyer Paradise, and *"Win!"* I did.

My first big eastern corporate client having been content with my services led to other major corporate clients—and a major learning challenge for me. I recall being asked to review, to ascertain, its compliance with Wyoming law, a complex, wraparound mortgage sent to me by a New York bank for my client to sign. When the mortgage arrived, it was in a bound cover and was 125 pages long. I had not known before that a mortgage could be that lengthy, but I dutifully plowed through its copious verbiage. I found it impressive more for its length than for its content, a situation I have found is not as rare as it should be in legal documents.

Jackson, Wyoming: "Be Sure and Flush. Idaho Needs the Water."

JACKSON, WYOMING, is now known as a fashionable resort with many estates built by multi-millionaires. This was not the Jackson that I knew and where I had some early experiences as a lawyer. One thing has always been true: Jackson and its locale are memorably beautiful. When I later saw the Swiss and Italian Alps, I thought them beautiful also, but to me they still could not compare to the Grand Tetons and the way Jackson is located with respect to them. When I first started to practice law, no commercial service or even a train went from southern Wyoming to Jackson.

I had a rather tasty case I was handling for a large New York company, and the state court judge had set a number of motions for hearing in Jackson. I was not yet used to large clients who spent money so freely for their defense and was thrilled when my client told me to go to Jackson by chartered plane. The only one available was flown by our then state director of aeronautics. When I arrived early in the morning at the airfield in Cheyenne, I was surprised when I saw the plane, because it was an eight-passenger plane. I said, "George, there's only me, and you flying the plane." George had been a pilot in the Pacific Theatre during World War II and had flown the Burma Hump. I recall his saying that no smaller plane was safe, in his opinion, to fly from Cheyenne to Jackson because you flew close to mountains, and he said that there could be sudden, unanticipated downdrafts and other hazards. So, away we flew, but I have often thought of what he told me when I read year after year of tragic losses of small private planes flying in the rugged country of the Rockies.

When I arrived in Jackson, the hearing was held in the then courthouse, since replaced several times. The judge was an excellent and highly respected judge, whose district included three or four large counties. The courtroom was small with a large, old-fashioned, potbelly stove in one corner because it can get very cold in Jackson. When lunchtime came, the judge and opposing counsel, who lived in Jackson, agreed that the three of us would have lunch together. As was true in several other old courthouses where I practiced in the early days of my career, there was only one lavatory, and so it was with this old little courthouse. It was down a steep flight of stairs, illuminated by what at most could have been a forty-watt light bulb hanging on a bare cord. I also remember the sign that was posted: "Be sure and flush. Idaho needs the water." When I had finished, I saw the judge and opposing counsel waiting at the top of the stairs for me, climbed up, and joined them, and they took turns visiting downstairs. Then the three of us went to lunch. We did not discuss the case but instead had a pleasant time discussing other matters.

George had warned me that we had to leave not later than four o'clock in the afternoon, and we finished our legal arguments and the judge's excellent rulings by 3:30. They, together, drove me to the airport where my plane and George were waiting, and we returned to Cheyenne without incident.

The next time that I recall going to Jackson was when I had a jury trial there. By the time of this particular memory, Wyoming had just acquired air service from Cheyenne and several other towns in southern Wyoming north to Jackson. This was a development not pleasing to an old rancher, part of whose ranch abutted the landing strip of the Jackson airfield. So, it was his custom to show his displeasure by shooting his rifle at the plane as it came in for landing. He was a crack shot and never hit a plane, but he surely scared a lot of people flying there, including me, and I could see and hear bullets whizzing by the wing outside my window.

There were other memorable trips to Jackson, but all of that has long changed and now Jackson is elegantly modern. I, however, shall always cherish my memories of when I was there in the late 1940s and early 1950s, and the people were always friendly and good to know.

Enough about my practicing business law in Wyoming. Please remember that in the 1940s and 1950s most lawyers in Wyoming did not specialize in only one area of the law. So I'll now take you to another legal area.

WILLS AND PROBATE

SOMETIMES IN my early days of practice I would think, "We do everything for our clients except bury them." We planned their estates, drew their wills, and handled the probates of their estates. Some lawyers named themselves as executors in the wills they drew or as lawyers for the probate. So the heirs would have to contact them, some lawyers also kept the original executed will in their offices and viewed future probate matters as a sort of old-age annuity. These practices are banned in some states as unethical but were long ago permitted in Wyoming. I never named myself in a client's will, or kept the original executed will in my files, because I believe these practices are unethical.

My First Probate: He's Dying with a Leftover Common Law Wife?

THE LAWYER who handled the estate was expected to attend the funeral of the decedent. For my first probate, the decedent had three funerals! And I attended all of them: church, Masonic, and a men's service organization previously unknown to me. The widow gave me special thanks.

The decedent and his widow had been among my very first clients. They were a devoted couple, and both engaged in community services. He had prospered in business and investments, and I was pleased to prepare his will. About a year later, the wife came to see me and said that her husband was in the hospital after a nearly fatal heart attack. They had decided that she must tell me of their problem: they were not married to each other!

The husband had a common law wife in Colorado, then one of only two states left that recognized common law marriages. These were formed when a man and woman lived openly together and held themselves out as husband and wife, which my client had done for some years. The only way to dissolve a common law marriage was by a divorce, which my client had never obtained.

I was shocked and asked the about-to-be-widow—his condition was critical—to give me until the next day to try to find a solution. Otherwise, the common law wife would be entitled to receive one-half of the man's estate. Then a wonderful solution! I found a Wyoming Supreme Court case that held Colorado's purported common law marriages were a "meretricious relationship" and were denied full faith and credit in Wyoming. Hence, such marriages were of no legal effect whatsoever in Wyoming! I telephoned the about-to-be-widow and told her to have their minister meet her at the hospital at the bedside of her dying mate to "renew" their marriage vows. This marriage would have full legal status in Wyoming. Thus ended the inauspicious beginning of my first probate, but with a good end for good people.

A "Small Estate" in 1950s Wyoming, $5 to $10 Million?

WE HANDLED every aspect of the probate, including preparation of the federal estate tax return when applicable. Our clients would have been shocked if we had sent them to an "expert" in Denver for preparation of their federal estate tax returns.

I remember when the coauthor of a multi-volume text on federal tax laws came to Wyoming to present a lecture to us on administration of decedents' estates and federal tax laws. He was a pleasant, sincere man who prefaced his lecture by stating that he had limited his remarks to discussion of "small estates between five and ten million dollars." This was long before many of Wyoming's wilderness areas, where I had gone trout fishing with my husband, were invaded by eastern multimillionaires' properties. Five to ten million dollars? I suddenly found my shoes of interest, and as I bent down, I met the eyes of my colleagues. So we all sat up and gave polite ear to the excellent lecture about these, to us, large estates.

Judge Adorns Papers with Ink Spots

ONE LAST recollection of my estate practice is an unpleasant one. The lawyer's fee for estate administration was fixed by statute with a sliding downward percentage scale for increasingly large brackets of amounts. I had completed administration of an estate with a sizable fee because of its size. The sole heirs, two sisters in their fifties, were pleased with the expeditious handling of their father's estate, and we had enjoyed a comfortably pleasant attorney-client relationship. I took the Final Report to the courthouse for filing together with the Final Order and Award of Fees for the judge's signature.

The judge looked at the papers and picked up his pen to sign the Final Order. A digression now comes for the judge's pen. Back then, the downtown Cheyenne Post Office had small stand-up desks with ink bottles and a "stick pen" with nib of two parts that closed to write. When the pen got old, the two pieces of the nib pushed apart as the pen was used, causing a splatter of ink and messy signature. The judge, frugal, had the post office save these used pens for him rather than throwing them out. You should have seen the papers he signed, adorned with ink spots!

Anyway, on this occasion, he dipped one of these old post office pens into his ink bottle, held it over the Final Order and Award of Fees, but did not sign it. He did this several times, the pen drizzling ink. Finally, he said: "My son (who was a Cheyenne lawyer) could have well used this large fee. He has a wife and two children to support. You have a husband to support you."

Taken aback, I tactlessly replied by saying what I was thinking: "With all due respect, Your Honor, if the heirs had wanted your son to be the attorney for their father's estate, they would have retained him. They chose me, and I have handled the estate to their satisfaction, and am now entitled to my statutory fee." His Honor still held a wavering pen, and I spoke again: "Your Honor, I respectfully tell you that I would appreciate your prompt signature because I promised my daughter that I would be at the school this afternoon to hear her sing in the Christmas program." His Honor: "Oh, is she singing a solo?" The judge had seen me downtown the previous Saturday with my little girl, then age seven. I answered, "No. Her second-grade class is singing a Christmas carol, and I promised her that I would be there. I never break my promise to her." He promptly signed.

I am pleased to report that this small contretemps was the last time that anything involving my gender arose with this judge. To the contrary, he thereafter was fair to me, and I became the unfortunate attorney whom he trusted to compute the interest due on judgments that he needed to sign.

OIL AND GAS LAW

THIS WAS an area of law practice that I liked very much, and it could be said that I backed into it, in reverse gear. Although I later came to know many fine, honest persons who signed up ranchers and farmers as oil and gas lessors, my initial exposure was to a pair of scalawags who had, as independents, signed up some farmers near Cheyenne on patently bad leases. Having been successful in representing these farmers with respect to these leases, I was contacted by several oil and gas companies, whom I was proud to represent.

I handled a variety of oil and gas matters, including drafting farmout agreements and joint operating agreements—before standard forms were available. I have many good memories of practicing oil and gas law in Wyoming. And I continued to be active in that legal area after moving to Colorado, as I write about in my Colorado practice and teaching at the law school in Denver. See Adjunct Professor of Law (1977–1997) in the discussion about me in Part Two's "The Colorado Lawyer."

BLM AND WYOMING RANCHERS

I BRIEFLY reminisce with a memorable small event. The Bureau of Land Management (BLM) administers many acres of public land in Wyoming, and many ranchers depend on grazing leases on federal land. The BLM had sent an official out from Washington, DC, to Wyoming to hear and resolve a dispute between two ranchers, one of whom was my client. The hearing was held in a school on one of the ranches and was attended by interested adjacent ranchers. All went routinely until one of the audience, a small, wizened woman who ran a ranch homesteaded by her grandfather, stood up, disagreed with something my client had said, and then said, "And your pappy said that you couldn't even dig a proper fence hole." My client, a tall, burly man with a booming voice, stood up and, wounded, boomed, "My pappy never said any such thing." Then everyone seemed to get drawn into whether my client could dig a proper fence hole, tempers flared, and I looked at the BLM official from DC. He looked at me for help. I shrugged my shoulders because I knew better than to intervene. He then buried his head in his shoulders on the table serving as his administrative judicial bench, and I returned to witness the fray.

MINING LAW

ALTHOUGH I did a minimal amount of practice in hard rock mining law while in Wyoming, I enjoyed it very much. The basic law for what is often called "hard rock mining" is the General Mining Law of 1872. I once counted the words in this statute and confess not re-counting them for this book. My recollection is that one paragraph of the statute had one hundred and three (103) words. In recent times, efforts are made each year for Congress to amend this 1872 statute or write a new general mining law. I am among many professionals who are opposed to any change and share the same reason for our opposition. We look at the many thousands of words in the many new statutes that Congress enacts. You can well imagine—sharing our dread—the thousands of pages Congress would fill with a new general mining law. I admit that the 1872 Act has flaws, but then so do many of our statutes, including lengthy ones. So I am quite content to have hard rock mining continue under the brief statute that has served the country for about 140 years.

One reason that hard rock mining law is fascinating for me is that it is indigenous common law of the United States of America. The basic hard rock mining law in our country was developed by miners at their monthly district meetings, based on their experiences—the same basis as that of the English common law which we have adopted for other legal areas. For example, the early miners in the 1849 California Gold Rush developed the foundation of American mining law at their monthly district meetings. These miners sometimes set up their own governments, my favorite being the Republic of the Rough and Ready, which sometimes sounds tempting today.

When a miner makes a potentially valuable mineral discovery on open public land, the miner wants to "locate" (specifically describe its location) and file a claim as prerequisites to getting a "patent" from the federal government (obtain ownership of the land), including the mineral discovery. Although the parenthetical descriptions in the preceding sentence are obviously oversimplifications of the procedure for acquiring mineral interests in public lands, they nonetheless provide an accurate hint of what that procedure involves. This is the nub of the tale here to be told: there are two types of mining claims that may be filed, *lode* and *placer* (pronounced "plasser"). A lode is a deposit of ore that is embedded in hard rock. When the ore is found between layers of rock, the term "veins" or "lodes" may be used. Examples of ore deposits subject to lode claims are gold and other metallic substances. A placer is a deposit of minerals in loose material such as sand or gravel. Some minerals are found in both lode and placer deposits.

Uranium and Me

I HAD never intended to include this incident among memorable events of my practice, but here it is by request of friends. Several years ago I was invited to tell the incident at the lunch meeting of the Uranium Institute sponsored by the prestigious Rocky Mountain Mineral Law Foundation. To my surprise, when I had finished my short report about "uranium and me," the large roomful of attendees stood to applaud. Then I again forgot about the uranium incident until recently I recounted it, apropos of the conversation, to visiting friends. My tale was greeted with exclamations of "Oh, you must include that in your book of memories!"

One day my secretary told me that a man came in who wanted to see me. He had no appointment, and my secretary warned, "He looks very rough." I said to show him in, and indeed he was no elegant figure.

My new arrival told me that he was an independent miner and wanted to hire me for legal advice on filing a new claim. I guessed that he had already been to many male lawyers, who had rejected giving him legal advice, and guessed that something must be wrong. I asked: "What is the nature of your strike?" His reply was, "Uranium." Uranium was then a new word in most Americans' vocabulary. We knew that it was some kind of mineral that had some link to a nuclear weapon that we had heard was called an atom bomb. My would-be client added that he had made a "good strike," wanted to file a claim, but didn't know whether to file lode or placer. I did not know either, told him so, and asked him to give me until the next day to see what I could find out in the law books.

Here I digress again, but I think it important to do so. During my years as an evening adjunct law professor, no matter what course I was teaching, I always made sure to warn my students: "There's no shame in saying, 'I don't know.' The shame is in not saying 'I don't know,' when you don't know and when you know that you don't know. And the worst shame of all is not knowing when you don't know."

The man agreed to return the next day, and that evening after dinner, with everyone fed and all settled at home, I went to the state law library. Different times then indeed! Local lawyers had keys to this law library so we could use it after regular hours, weekends, and holidays. Well, I checked and researched but found nothing—uranium was still so new for general knowledge that the law so far had not considered it.

I guessed the miner would not return the next day, but he did. I told him of my diligent inquiry and negative result. Then I said, "If I tell you what I would do to protect my strike, would you pay me a fee?" His reply, "Yes." My answer: "I would file both a lode and a placer claim, which is legally permissible." He thanked me and paid me and left.

My uranium story is not yet ended. Every Friday in Cheyenne, the lawyers and judges who could met for lunch at a convenient restaurant with good food in a room reserved for us, named Terrace Gardens, with its three potted plants.

Five years after my uranium client, I was at one of these Friday lunches at which one of the state Supreme Court justices had joined us. He said that the court had issued four opinions that day, and one was a "first" on the issue: What was the proper way to file a uranium claim? The justice said that the court could not find any law yet applicable to this question, so the effect of the court's ruling was that perhaps a safe procedure was filing both lode and placer claims. (On this this topic, the Reader may be interested in *Globe*

Mining Co. v. Anderson, 318 P.2d 373, 78 Wyo. 17 (1957).) I forgot judicial respect and overcome with joyful relief, I pointed at the justice, and said: "The court was right." Decades later, after being an honored guest and telling my uranium tale, that dear audience all standing to applaud was a pleasing end for me of this legal area.

EVERYTHING EXCEPT BURY THEM

DURING MY years as a Wyoming lawyer, we general practitioners did not have special areas of practice as had already become common in Denver, Colorado. So, for example, we all handled divorce cases. Nevada had the shortest residency requirement, six weeks, for becoming eligible to file for divorce, and far less well-known was Wyoming's second shortest residency requirement of sixty days—just eighteen days more than that in Nevada.

I also handled business bankruptcies, estates, tax appeals to the Denver lower tax appeals division (which I disliked), and most often contracts, contracts, and more contracts of every type and description.

Looking back, I guess maybe the joke in our Bar was true: we general practitioners in Wyoming did everything for our clients except bury them. I know that we tried to serve them loyally, to the best of our ability, and with integrity.

Wyoming Wind and Casper's Jinxed Hotel?

asper, in northeast Wyoming, was one of the five towns when I was a lawyer in the early years that had populations as large as 5,000. Casper was the residence of lawyers who practiced oil and gas law because Casper, in Natrona County, was nearby successful exploration and production developments. My trips to Casper were often memorable.

My first airplane trip to Casper—in a small plane on Challenger Airlines, which was later bought by the old Frontier Airlines—was memorable. In those days, planes landed on the tarmac, and little stairs led down to it from the plane. I stepped out and thought I would blow off that top step. I could not believe the wind. I started calling out, "I can't make it! I can't make it!" They finally got me safely down the steps.

In those days, Casper had three rather large hotels (for Wyoming) that were on three corners of a downtown intersection. The oldest and of historic interest was the Hotel Henning, which took an instant dislike to me. The first time I stayed there, the shower didn't work, so I took a bath, and the whole stopper—huge—came out in my hands; then, I left it in the bathtub and told the clerk as I checked out on my way to the courthouse. The next time I was in Casper, back I went to the Henning, which was supposed to be a safe place for me. There was a sign on the desk that for a small extra sum you could have a room with a vibrating bed. I have always been a sound sleeper, and the prospect of a strange vibrating bed was not pleasing. So I told the clerk that I did not want a room with a vibrating bed. Well, my bed shook and shivered all night long. When I checked out the next morning to go to court, I said to the clerk, "I told you I did not want a room with a vibrating bed." He looked at my key and my registration and said, "That room does not have one." I replied, "You had better check that bedstead." The next time I went to the Henning, friends had informed me before I left Cheyenne that the hotel's dining room was serving baked potatoes in silver paper, and they were very good. I felt quite sophisticated when with my dinner I was served my first baked potato in foil. And that was a peaceful night at the Henning. The next time I went was for a legal conference, and I drove up with our federal judge and his wife. I was given a room right across from theirs. The bellboy opened their room and stopped in the threshold to make sure I was all right. He opened my room, and water rushed out—the whole room had water about two feet deep!

One more story of my doomed stays at that hotel. It is a sad story of the first and last time I was ever asked to be a chaperone. The Miss Wyoming contest was forthcoming and would be decided at a movie theater in Casper. I was asked to chaperone Miss Cheyenne if I were going to Casper because the ladies knew that I had been going to Casper on business. So, up we went, with me driving. She was not an easy one for me to chaperone or maybe I just did not know how. In our room, she's down to her underwear before changing to go downstairs in the hotel. And there's a fire escape outside our room. Miss Cheyenne says, "Oh, look, I'm just going to step out the window here because you can really see to the West." I said, "No, no, you don't have clothes on, just a bra and panties, don't step out." So, of course she did; I stepped out after her; the window slammed down shut, and we couldn't get it back up. The back of the hotel overlooked one of Casper's notorious streets of the Wild West—and it didn't look too tame to me then. Wouldn't you know! Some of the drunks down there looked up and saw Miss Cheyenne and responded with catcalls and whistles and, as you can imagine, she became hysterical. And the window would not open. It was horrible. Finally, someone from the hotel came into the alley and saw us and we were rescued. Handling the next day's trial and arguing difficult motions were my ill-luck, especially when the prior night's sleeping accommodations—and chaperonage—were not amusing (an understatement).

Other fond memories of Casper. When you fly in, you fly past Casper Mountain. I guess it's different now with larger planes, but in the old days it was so rough you thought your plane was going to crash. And I remember one trip with a photographer and reporter from some big newspaper—not in Wyoming—and they had wanted the front seats but could not because the seats were filled with boxes of baby chicks. When we flew past Casper Mountain, both men became air sick. "We've flown all over the world and never been airsick—argh." Travel, back then, was not for the weak. When they said that, I was reminded of traveling back East when the stewardess announced that we were entering a period of turbulence and so dinner would be delayed. Time passed, no food, and so finally I rang for the stewardess, and then asked, "When will we get dinner?" She replied, "We are still in the period of turbulence." Me: "We are?" Didn't seem turbulent to me so I said, "Could I have a cup of coffee please." To this day, I cannot break the habit of automatically raising and lowering the cup when drinking coffee on an airplane as I did in the early days in Wyoming, and nary a drop has ever been spilled.

I had other flying experiences in Wyoming. I flew to Rawlins for a trial the next day, and the weather turned terrible, and we couldn't land, so the plane returned to Cheyenne. In those days, the airlines hired veteran pilots who had flown during World War II, including the Burma Hump. I read in the newspaper the next day that a B-47, the *Flying Fortress*, had hit this rough weather, and two of its crew had suffered broken bones from being tossed about. Nothing happened to any of us with our veteran pilot. But I was glad to be home and called the court early the next morning to explain what had happened. It was a trial to the court and not a jury, so it was easily rescheduled. Judicial personnel were understanding of emergencies caused by Wyoming winds and weather.

Happy Decades as a Wyoming Lawyer (1946–1969)

rom May 1946 to May 1969, I practiced law in Wyoming. Then, I practiced law in Colorado for over thirty years and became fond of the Colorado State Bar and in general, its judiciary. Nonetheless, Wyoming remains my "home Bar," where I first was admitted to practice and gradually—despite being the first woman trial lawyer in that state—became a successful trial and appellate lawyer.

I shared with you some of my early stumbling, humbling steps as a trial lawyer. Here, I would like to record a summary of my successes. Boastful? Yes. Forgivable? I hope so. And I hope that my public sharing of travails and travels to success will serve to foster perseverance and encouragement to young professionals, whether in law or medicine or the sciences or in any endeavor.

As the years went by, I tried many jury trials, traveling throughout the state. I never lost a civil jury trial (100% victory rate). During my trial era, I didn't pay any attention to lawyers' adages about selecting jurors or news reports about the mix of people on juries. My guidance came from the prospective jurors themselves. I depended solely on my person-to-person relationship when I questioned each one. I cared about only one attribute: Would the person be a fair and impartial juror? l believe this is the best way to select a jury, and I still believe that the average American when serving as a juror wants to reach a verdict based on the evidence and the law, helped by fair argument. I dare to offer an old proverb: "The proof of the pudding is in the eating"—and I never lost even one of my many civil jury trials. I came to believe that generally

Americans are fair-minded and want to do the "right thing"—for their families, employers or employees, as citizens, whether as voters or jurors.

Because of my law practice, and being active in the Cheyenne business community, discrimination against ethnic groups came to my personal attention. In the 1960s, I was pleased to be invited as the as the guest speaker at the first chapter meeting with banquet of the National Association for the Advancement of Colored People (the NAACP) in Cheyenne. And I was the guest speaker at the first meeting of a Mexican American business group in Wyoming (now the Wyoming Hispanic Chamber of Commerce).

EDITOR'S NOTE: After World War II, in Cheyenne, the very large adjacent military base caused constant rotation of people from all over the country in and out of the Cheyenne community and its schools. The Union Pacific Railroad was then a major employer, with a hub for its huge main yards and with a rotation of mechanics and crews for freight and passenger trains. Thus, the town's small businesses were diverse, too.

During these happy days of Wyoming practice, I handled many appeals to our Wyoming Supreme Court. I enjoyed these tremendously: studying the trial verbatim record, researching and writing the appellate briefs, then presenting the oral argument. I enjoyed a variety of cases: business disputes, constitutionality of public bond issues, tort cases for insurance companies, and two appeals in criminal cases. I had a better than 90 percent appellate victory rate, and this is where my heart was—in the law. As a result, I received referrals from other lawyers to handle appeals in their cases. The presentation of arguments to the Wyoming Supreme Court was a pleasant and well-ordered affair.

One of my last scheduled arguments before the Wyoming Supreme Court was different. The court, with approval of opposing counsel, requested that, instead of presenting an appellate argument, I give a closing argument as at trial. The court had apparently learned of my reputation in making closing arguments. So, I complied and had a wonderful time giving my presentation.

When the court learned that I was indeed moving to Denver, Colorado, its justices each asked to write a letter about me. I am nostalgic and proud to discuss more in my Part Two's "The Colorado Lawyer (1969–Retired 2011)," about Starting Over in Colorado. After moving to Colorado, I had reason to argue my last appearance before the Wyoming Supreme Court. When we were finished, as is their custom, the justices shook the hand of counsel for the appellant and, when they came to me, they each hugged me.

In 2006 at the Wyoming State Bar Association's annual meeting, I was honored for my sixty years as an active practicing lawyer. Sixty years since my admission on May 7, 1946, to the Wyoming State Bar! (see figure 2.3). It was a fine occasion. I had also agreed to be on the program for a lecture, which was attended by all five Wyoming Supreme Court justices. To my surprise and pride, they all stood to applaud my remarks.

Wyoming is my "home Bar." I practiced there for twenty-three years. I have been practicing in Colorado since 1969, where the Bar is equally warm in my memory.

This book would not speak accurately about me if I did not tell you: the Wyoming State Bar and my years of practice there, with so many memories including my many fine colleagues—both lawyers and judges—will always have a special place in my heart.

Figure 2.20. Brooke with the Honorable Ewing T. Kerr, United States District Court Judge for the District of Wyoming (1955–1992). [COMPILER'S NOTE: undated photo about 1957–1960.] Judge Kerr was a friend from 1947 for many years to "Brooke at the Bar," including letters of recommendation and the foreword to her first book. Renamed in his honor is the Ewing T. Kerr Federal Building and U.S. Courthouse in Casper, Wyoming.

[*COMPILER'S NOTE: Here are brief excerpts from Judge Kerr's letters on the letterhead of the United States District Court in Cheyenne from his foreword.*]

December 15, 1978: "I have known Brooke for well over thirty years. . . . She was an outstanding trial lawyer . . . an outstanding student. . . . In short, was recognized as an outstanding leader in this community. As a writer, she has superb ability and I say this from personal observation in the examination of many of her briefs filed in this court."

1987: In his foreword to *Ethics Compliance for Business Lawyers*: "I met Brooke Wunnicke many years ago when she first arrived in Cheyenne, Wyoming. Within a short time she was widely recognized for her keen intellect."

1989: Note: "You are indeed a scholar. You always have been and time doesn't seem to affect your writing."

⠿DRI

1999 Annual Meeting
Awards Luncheon
Hilton New York & Towers
October 8, 1999

Louis B. Potter Lifetime Professional Service Award

Brooke Wunnicke
Denver, Colorado

Community Service Award

William T. Birmingham
Phoenix, Arizona

G. Duffield Smith Award

Forrest S. Latta
Mobile, Alabama

Figure 2.21. National award presentation event: Lifetime Professional Service Award for Brooke, luncheon invitation, October 8, 1999, New York City Hilton Hotel. The Defense Research Institute (DRI) is "the largest international membership organization of attorneys defending the interests of businesses and individuals in civil litigation. Julian Bond, then Chairman of the NAACP, was the keynote speaker and Brooke enjoyed meeting him at their luncheon table.

The Colorado Lawyer
(1969–Retired 2011)

"Behold it is the privilege of mine Honours, My oath and my profession."
William Shakespeare, King Lear, *Act 5, Sc. 3*

Figure 2.22.
Brooke's special
invitation for the
private dinner
party, with
beautiful views
of New York City
from the top
floor of the World
Trade Center, on
October 8, 1999,
two years before
the 9/11 (2001)
tragedies and
destruction of the
building.

Lloyd and Sheila Milliken
Request the pleasure of your company
at a dinner honoring
Special Friends of DRI
at the Windows of the World
atop the World Trade Center
Friday, October 8, 1999
Eight O'Clock

Defense Research Institute

150 North Michigan Avenue ▪ Suite 300 ▪ Chicago, Illinois 60601
(312) 795-1101 ▪ Fax: (312) 795-0747 ▪ E-Mail: dri@mcs.net ▪ Web site: http://www.dri.org

August 16, 1999

RECEIVED AUG 2 3 1999

Brooke Wunnicke
Hall & Evans
1200 17th Street, Ste. 1700
Denver, CO 80202-5817

RE: Louis B. Potter Award

Dear Brooke:

It is my great pleasure to inform you that you have been selected as this year's recipient of the Louis B. Potter Lifetime Professional Service Award. As you know, the award honors an individual who exemplifies both professionalism and professional service with professionalism defined as follows:

> "Professionalism goes beyond observation of the legal profession's ethical rules and serves the best interests of clients and the public in general; professionalism requires that lawyers conduct themselves before the Court and with opposing counsel in a manner which demonstrates respect for the law and preserves the decorum and integrity of the judicial process; it preserves and enhances the image of the legal profession in the eyes of the public; it supports programs and activities to educate the public about the law and the American legal system; and if fosters respect and trust among lawyer and between lawyers"

The award will be presented at the Friday, October 8, Awards Luncheon at the 1999 DRI Annual Meeting in New York City. The luncheon will feature Julian Bond, Chairman of the Board of Directors of the NAACP, as the keynote speaker. I hope you will be able to attend.

Congratulations on this honor. I look forward to seeing you in New York.

Sincerely yours,

Lloyd H. Milliken, Jr.
DRI President

Figure 2.23. Award letter for national Professional Service Award from president of the Defense Research Institute (DRI), dated August 16, 1999, to Brooke with invitation for its October 8, 1999, presentation in New York City.

Figure 2.24. Brooke in their library, photograph by Jim Wunnicke, before they moved to Denver.

Starting Over in Colorado

[COMPILER'S NOTE: *From her family library, Brooke sourced her scholarly quotations for her widely well-received speeches and writings. Brooke wrote: "I suggest that history, the arts, music, drama, poetry, philosophy and all the now called liberal arts provide breadth and depth to the lawyer's ability and character." She also often commented that "the library nestles in my heart, next to the law." In 2014, the University of Colorado (CU) and Brooke arranged for the family library (which has no law books) to be placed in the James, Brooke, and Diane Wunnicke Library Room at the Auraria Library which serves CU Denver and Metro State University and Community College of Denver on the central Denver campus of the Auraria Higher Education Center; most of the students are working their way through school, as did Brooke. When and as books are digitized, the fragile books and their illustrations, images, and maps will be protected while their contents become accessible to students and faculty.]*

THE OLD DAYS: BAR ADMISSION FOR A MARRIED WOMAN COLORADO LAW SCHOOL GRADUATE

When my husband retired from business and wanted to move to Denver, Colorado, we agreed that I should not retire from the practice of law. He had interests and athletic pursuits, such as golf, that I had never shared, and he was content with my devotion to law as both vocation and avocation.

The first professional need for me was to obtain my admission to the Colorado State Bar. This would pose no problem because Colorado and Wyoming have reciprocity as to Bar membership, with only the requirements of five years of active practice and in good standing in the present Bar. The process of admission, however, seemed to take a tedious amount of time.

A small side note: In 1945, I graduated number one in my law school class at the University of Colorado School of Law. I lived in Boulder, Colorado, where the school is located, while attending law school and my husband was away serving in World War II. So, I met the Colorado requirements for Bar admission of graduation from an accredited law school and, I thought, of residency. But I had not then been eligible to take the Colorado Bar examination, despite my graduation from the Colorado law school. Why not? Because I did not meet the residency requirement, although I had actually lived in Colorado the required time. This was all a long time ago, and the Colorado Bar authorities told me that the domicile of the husband was the domicile of the wife. My husband had been domiciled in Wyoming and had entered the armed services from that state and, therefore, my domicile was also Wyoming. Hence, I did not meet the residency requirement to take the Colorado Bar examination.

WYOMING SUPREME COURT REFERENCE LETTERS

HERE IS another digression. Hopefully, the Reader will forgive me for disclosing that, as I later learned, I was the first woman who "really practiced law" in Wyoming, the state's first woman trial lawyer, and the first lawyer whom the Wyoming Supreme Court had ever appointed to represent an indigent defendant whose conviction had aroused public support of the need for an appeal. So I was proud and deeply touched by the four Wyoming Supreme Court justices' generous judicial offer to recommend me for admission to the Colorado Bar.

Now frankly immodest: I received a telephone call from the then chief justice of the Wyoming Supreme Court stating that the court had heard of my imminent move to Denver, and each of the three justices wanted to write a letter of recommendation for me. When I filed my application for my admission to the Colorado Bar, I attached these letters to my application; I was pleased that my admission soon followed. I made copies of these letters on the then-primitive copy machine and saved them for over forty years.

October 11, 1968

Board of Law Examiners
State of Colorado
Denver, Colorado

Re: Brooke Wunnicke

Gentlemen:

        I am informed that Mrs. Wunnicke has filed an application
with your board for admission to the Bar of the State of
Colorado and in support of such application is in need of a
certificate from a member or members of this court furnishing
to your board certain information.

        I hereby certify that I have been personally acquainted
with Mrs. Wunnicke for several years. She was admitted to the
unified Wyoming State Bar on May 7, 1946, and is presently a
member in good standing. On several occasions she has appeared
and competently presented and argued important cases in this
court and also before the several trial courts of this state.
I have no hesitancy in recommending her admission to your Bar.
I regard Mrs. Wunnicke as an able, experienced, industrious,
and honorable lawyer; of high morals and good character; and
her enthusiasm, support, and personal participation in Bar
activities and in community affairs have been of no small bene-
fit in improving the "public image" of the Bar.

        Dated at Cheyenne, Wyoming, this 11th day of October, 1968.

                                    Norman B. Gray, Justice
                                    Wyoming Supreme Court

Figure 2.25. 1968 letters of recommendation offered to Brooke by the four justices of the Wyoming Supreme Court for Brooke's application to the Bar of the State of Colorado, and the January 1969 letter by Judge Ewing T. Kerr, United States District Court Judge for the District of Wyoming.

The Supreme Court of Wyoming
Cheyenne

HARRY S. HARNSBERGER, Chief Justice
NORMAN B. GRAY
JOHN J. McINTYRE } Justices
GLENN PARKER

ANN OELAND, Clerk
RITA M. WHITE, Deputy Clerk

November 7, 1968

Board of Law Examiners
Denver
Colorado

Gentlemen:

Understanding that Brooke Wunnicke is making application for admission to the Bar of the State of Colorado, I am pleased to inform you that, having observed Mrs. Wunnicke for more than fifteen years in her practice before the court of which I am presently Chief Justice, she is a most accomplished lawyer and possessed of an impressive talent for oral presentation and argument. Her ability to succinctly, concisely, and convincingly brief her cases and then advocate her contentions is of superior quality.

Mrs. Wunnicke excels in bonding, finance, and negligence, as well as in criminal matters.

I am sure she will be a worth-while addition to the Colorado Bar and will quickly gain the regard and respect of your bench and bar.

Respectfully,

Harry S. Harnsberger
Harry S. Harnsberger
Chief Justice

Mrs. Wunnicke is held in high esteem by members of the Wyoming State Bar and is a past president of the Laramie County Bar Association. Although I have not had occasion to observe her trial work, I can say she does exceptionally fine appellate work.

DATED at Cheyenne, Wyoming, this 11th day of October, 1968.

John J. McIntyre
JOHN J. McINTYRE
Justice, Wyoming Supreme Court

October 10, 1968

Board of Law Examiners
State of Colorado
Denver, Colorado

Gentlemen:

Re: Mrs. Brooke Wunnicke

This will certify that I have been well acquainted with
Mrs. Brooke Wunnicke during her professional career--some twenty
years of practice in Wyoming courts--and especially during my
tenure as trial judge in the Second Judicial District from 1949
to 1955 and since that time while I have been a member of the
Supreme Court.

Mrs. Wunnicke is a brilliant student of fine personality
and a most effective advocate. I consider her to be one of the
outstanding lawyers in the State. I understand that she has
arranged to move to Denver and is applying for admission to the
Bar of Colorado. I can recommend her most highly as a proficient
and experienced lawyer whose ethics and standing are above
question. I am sure she will be a credit to any bar of which
she may be a member.

Glenn Parker, Justice
Wyoming Supreme Court

UNITED STATES DISTRICT COURT
DISTRICT OF WYOMING
P.O. BOX 888
CHEYENNE, WYOMING 82001

January 20, 1969

Mr. C. R. Locke, Director
National Conference of Bar Examiners
1155 East 60th Street
Chicago, Illinois 60637

Dear Mr. Locke:

This will acknowledge receipt of your letter
of January 17, 1969, with reference to the character of Brooke von Falkenstein Wunnicke. I am
pleased to make a report thereon.

I have known Mrs. Wunnicke since she was
admitted to the Bar of this state in 1947. She
has appeared in this court on numerous occasions
and always acquitted herself creditably, both as
a trial lawyer and in the research of the law.
I have made it a practice to appoint her to defend indigent women charged with the commission
of federal crimes. She has been conscientious
in all of her duties.

I commend her as an excellent student of the
law, having earned a Phi Beta Kappa key and other
singular honors while a student.

I have little or no doubt that all Justices
of the Supreme Court will be pleased to give her
an equally good recommendation.

Her integrity, legal ability and fitness to
practice law will justify her admission to the
Colorado Bar.

Sincerely yours,

EWING T. KERR

U. S. District Judge.

OF COUNSEL: MAJOR OIL AND GAS LEGAL PROJECT AND COMMERCIAL REAL PROPERTY LAW

AFTER MY admission to the Colorado Bar, I was busy with our move from our home of the past twenty-three years in Cheyenne, Wyoming, to Denver. My husband soon left for an African safari that had been planned for several months. I knew few people in Denver and much missed my friends and colleagues in Wyoming. After only several weeks of feeling forlorn, the telephone rang—a welcome sound—it was my first professional call on our Denver telephone. The man calling introduced himself as a Denver lawyer. He said that he had heard about my moving to Denver and badly needed an experienced oil and gas lawyer to work on a major project. Could he interest me and if so, how soon would I be available? I felt like a hungry trout must when it thinks it sees tempting bait with a hidden hook. I replied, "Yes. How about one o'clock this afternoon?" I heard sort of a short gasp at the other end of the line and then the caller said, "Well, I had not expected that soon, but that would be excellent." So I donned a business suit and duly presented myself at the appointed time. Between the telephone call and my appointment, I had called one of the two Denver lawyers whom I knew professionally from my handling litigation for his firm in Wyoming and inquired about the lawyer who had called me. He informed me that the man had a fine reputation both as a person and as a lawyer but cautioned me that he was known as a "nitpicker for accuracy." I responded, "Good. So am I." And so it proved. I accepted his offer to be Of Counsel (meaning that you are past the bloom of youth and will "counsel" with the firm's lawyers, but not primarily with the firm's clients). When we two nitpickers worked together on a project, it was always a mutual pleasure.

When I had finished the major oil and gas project—which was unique and fascinating—I then engaged in other areas of practice with the firm, including commercial property. I enjoyed the varied legal work that I was doing, which usually needed a senior lawyer and almost always seemed to be unusual and challenging work. For example, I did all the legal work for one of the first shopping malls in metropolitan Denver.

MAJOR BANKRUPTCY—COURT-APPOINTED
LAWYER FOR THE TRUSTEE

ONE DAY, the lead partner who had engaged me asked if I had ever done bankruptcies. I responded that I had but that I did not like that legal area, either business or personal bankruptcies. He then asked me to undertake a very interesting statewide bankruptcy that I could not resist. I would be a successor lawyer serving the Trustee of the estate of the bankrupt debtor, a chain of statewide weekly newspapers. The predecessor lawyer had apparently failed in his performance, and the court wanted to appoint a replacement. The bankruptcy judge later became the Chief Judge of the United States District Court of Colorado and eventually served as a Senior Judge, always as an outstanding judge.

SECURITIES LAW

I ALSO started practicing securities law, which I found to be plainly prescribed by statute and regulations. During this era, I was convinced that our local branch of the Securities and Exchange Commission (SEC) was a role model for a federal agency. The regional director was the excellent Dan Stocking; when he retired, we of the local Securities Bar campaigned for his deputy, Robert Davenport, to be his successor. Political neophytes that we were, we were fortunate to be successful. As a result: more years of an excellent SEC for our region. I prepared a few S-1 forms, the full registration statement for a new issue of securities. A fond memory is one deal when the underwriter's New York counsel was insisting that our client's securities counsel confer with him in New York. His office was in Buffalo, New York, where I had never been. I liked the lawyer when I met him in Buffalo, even when he said that he liked to work on a project all night and would I mind? I was intrigued and replied that I would be glad to do so. We did indeed work all night, resolved amicably all questions, and he bought me a delicious breakfast. He had arranged for me to get some sleep at a local hotel, then he and his wife would pick me up for a late lunch, and I could get a late afternoon plane trip back to Denver. His wife was as nice as her husband—a charming and interesting couple. Lunch was memorable. It was on the top floor of a building where my hosts had reserved a table with a wonderful view of Niagara Falls, which I had never before seen. The lunch was delicious, my company delightful, and I can still see in memory the magnificence of the falls. When I took the late afternoon plane from Buffalo, the pilot announced that he was going to take a detour over Niagara Falls so we could see them as the sun was starting to set—and we saw unforgettable glorious beauty.

My new-found Buffalo friend was a prominent New York corporate counsel, and we kept in touch with personal correspondence—long before convenient e-mail—about needed reforms in corporate law until his decease.

THE COLORADO BAR; NUDES WITH LUNCH

I WAS active in the Denver and Colorado Bar Associations. I have always believed that lawyers serve the public interest by being active in a good Bar association that is dedicated to protecting the public by means of its services.

When I attended my first Denver Bar Association monthly lunch, I was impressed that it was held in one of Denver's main downtown hotels. I divulge the name because the hotel was imploded years ago—the Hotel Albany. When lunch was served, I was shocked. The plate was covered with a thin layer of canned beans and at the side of the plate was one-half—yes, one-half!—of a hot dog cut lengthwise and cooked until it was curled as if in pain. I thought that the prisoners at a state penitentiary would have rioted if served such a meal.

I was soon appointed to chair the Topical Luncheon Committee. I was determined to schedule it at a place with good food. I first arranged for an interesting and timely program, and then sought a good place to eat. A restaurant across from Denver's historic Brown Palace Hotel and convenient to downtown law offices had recently been re-opened under new owners and was reputed to have very good food. Its predecessor had been excellent and the small building, historically known as The Navarre, was rumored to have had a rather lurid history. The second floor was a facility for group dining, and so I scheduled lunch to be held there—but did not go to see the room. The new owners were pleasant to work with and promised a fine menu at the usual lunch price for the Bar. When the day of the meeting arrived, and I went upstairs to the meeting room, I was horrified. The table arrangement was perfect, with snowy white linen and good silver service. But the walls! They were covered with huge pictures in heavy gilt frames—oil paintings in living color of voluptuous nude women, all in provocative poses! The lunch was delicious, and the program well-worth hearing.

At the end of the meeting, one of the lawyers stood up and, looking admiringly at the walls of the room, said: "Let's give three cheers for the little lawyer from Wyoming for a fine program, good lunch, and unusual but fun ambience!" And my new colleagues at the Bar gave me three rousing cheers. I looked about the room and could not help but laugh, and then we all laughed together. I thanked them for their cheers and felt at home in the Colorado Bar.

IMPORTANCE OF BAR COMMITTEES

IT WAS very comforting to feel again accepted in the Bar where I practiced. I continued to be active in the local Securities Bar, even lecturing several times at our luncheon meetings. I enjoyed these meetings because I found the Securities Bar as congenial for me as my Oil and Gas Bar colleagues. I became active on the Ethics Committee of the Colorado Bar Association, which for some years met on the entire Saturday morning once a month. I have always had a deep, abiding concern about the ethics of the legal profession, especially since I have seen its focus shift to billable hours and the bottom line. For many years, I also served on the Awards Committee for both the Denver and Colorado Bar Associations. I believe that recognition is due to those members of our profession who serve to foster its high standards of competence and dedication to integrity.

As I continued my activities in the Bar, I was elected to the statewide five-member Mineral Law Council, to the Board of Trustees of the Denver Bar Association, and to the Board of Governors of the Colorado Bar Association. In time, I was selected for their highest honor, the Award of Merit, by each of the Colorado and Denver Bar Associations.

Colorado Bar Association

101st Annual Convention

Saturday, September 25, 1999

Vail Marriott Mountain Resort

Luncheon Program

[*COMPILER'S NOTE:* From Brooke's file, an excerpt from the presentation remarks: "If I had a martini, I'd lift it to Brooke Wunnicke, an amazing combination of brilliance, talent, tenacity, and charm. . . . Today, we add to her 'collection' (of awards and honors) with the best one we have. Thank you, Brooke, for leading the way."]

PROGRAM

Welcoming Remarks...H. Barton Mendenhall

Award Presentations:

  Award of Merit Recipient ....Brooke Wunnicke

  Outstanding Young Lawyer Award Recipient.....................Brandon P. Hull

  Jacob V. Schaetzel Award Recipient ....James R. Leh
                                            Maggie Atkinson
                          13th Judicial District Bar Association

  Donald W. Hoagland Award Recipient...............................Doris Truhlar

  Pro Bono Coordinator of the Year Award Recipient ....Barbara Chamberlain

Annual Business Meeting ....H. Barton Mendenhall

Introduction of Speaker..H. Barton Mendenhall

Address ....Tim Gill

"Steamrollered by Technology: Looking into the 21st Century"

Figure 2.26. Colorado Bar Association 1999 Award of Merit awarded to Brooke, first two pages from the September 25, 1999, program.

*The Museum will
be open for DBA
guests to enjoy
until 9 p.m.!*

*6 p.m. Welcome by DBA President Joe Dischinger,
presentation of awards and passing of gavel to incoming
DBA President Mary Jo Gross*

2004 Awards

Award of Merit . . . . Brooke Wunnicke

Volunteer Lawyer of the Year . . . . Stacy Carpenter

Young Lawyer of the Year . . . . Megan Brynhildsen

Judicial Excellence . . . . Judge Herbert Galchinsky

OUR 50-YEAR HONOREES WERE RECOGNIZED
ON MAY 19, 2004

George W. Bermant	James A. May
Theodore A. Borrillo	Gordon H. Mayberry
Willis V. Carpenter	George McMahill
James J. Cronin	Peter H. Merlin
Carl F. Eiberger, Jr.	Joseph M. Montano
Jack A. Engles	Leonard A. Mues
Bruce L. Evans	William G. Odell
Samuel R. Freeman	John "Jack" Pfeiffer
Richard P. Hall	George Pulver
Ralph D. Johnson	Robert J. Ring
Thomas J. Kerwin	William F. Schenkein
Dolores B. Kopel	Richard L. Schrepferman
Joseph R. Lincoln	John L. Terborg
Robert Lipton	Martin Zerobnick
Jay E. Lutz	

Figure 2.27. Denver Bar Association 2004 Award of Merit awarded to Brooke, page from the evening's program. Brooke's comments at the occasion quoted from famous Judge Learned Hand: "What has brought us up from savagery is a loyalty to truth—and trust cannot emerge unless it is subject to utmost scrutiny." And, "Not in the books that law can live. But in the conscience of society as a whole."

YEARNING FOR APPEALS

I SERVED for three and a half years as Of Counsel, from mid-1969 to 1973, to the law firm practicing in the areas I have written about here. My yearning for appeals, however, continued unabated. I missed reading the many volumes of trial records, the legal research, the analysis of the evidence in the record in light of applicable law, followed by crafting the legal briefs for filing in the appellate court, and the oral arguments before that court. My yearning became acute when the firm's appellate lawyer lost an appeal that turned on a single issue and lost again the following year representing the opposite side of the same issue! And I still harbored my years-long dream of serving on a state supreme court and writing correctly written and carefully reasoned opinions.

Meantime, I was grateful for my pleasant and interesting law firm affiliation and my heartwarming acceptance by my new colleagues in the Colorado Bar.

Public Service in Criminal Cases and Mentoring "Brooke's Children" (1973–1986)

CHIEF APPELLATE DEPUTY DISTRICT ATTORNEY

On a Sunday afternoon in late 1972 the telephone rang, and Denver's newly elected District Attorney Dale Tooley asked if he could come to my home in the next hour and talk to me. I did not know him, but he said that he lived near me and would not take long so I said "yes." When he came, my husband and I both visited with him, found him to be a very personable, and—as he soon proved—a persuasive person. He said that he had heard of me as a very successful Wyoming appellate lawyer, about my move to Denver, and very much wanted me to be his Chief Appellate Deputy District Attorney. After thanking him, I told him that although not active politically I had long been registered in the party other than his party. He replied that he had known that before he came to see me. He said what we later applied to acquisitions of lawyers for the District Attorney's Office, "I want the best legal talent that I can get with the taxpayers' money." Then my husband joined the district attorney to say that he thought it would be a great idea for me to return to the appellate work I had so long liked. I agreed to obtain a year's leave of absence from the firm where I was and enter the world of criminal prosecution.

ABOUT A week after my acceptance of heading the appellate division, the district attorney called me to apologize. When he offered me the position, he had not yet learned that the Chief Appellate Deputy also headed the law student Intern Program, but he could change that if I preferred not to do it. I replied that I had never mentored but would be pleased to undertake doing so. And so I fortunately brought into my life—and a permanent place in my heart—many talented young law students whose later careers have filled me with pride.

MENTORING: "BROOKE'S CHILDREN"

MY "MENTEES" are known as "Brooke's Children," and they generously refer publicly to themselves by that designation. First, I tell you that I did not return to the private sector of law practice for over twelve years, and a major impetus for that decision was my "children." I am very proud to record here that my more than sixty-five "children" at law now include one governor, six district court judges, five elected district attorneys, five recipients of Distinguished Alumni Awards from their respective Colorado law schools, two past presidents of the Denver Bar Association, one of whom also is a past president of the Colorado Bar Association, and senior trial and appellate lawyers and administrators in public offices and with prestigious law firms. And they are all as loyal and loving to me as they are talented contributors to the legal profession.

I had never formally mentored but hoped that I could spare these young soon-to-be-lawyers some of the wounds and scars that I had sustained as a young lawyer. When I started to practice "solo," because no one then wanted to practice with a woman lawyer, law schools did not offer "practicum" courses that included lower court experience under a supervising lawyer. Continuing Legal Education was years in the future, and not even any "how-to" law books were yet available for the young lawyer.

To schedule a first meeting for a chat with interns already in the District Attorney's Office, I arranged an evening meeting so as not to conflict with their law class schedules. All five of them were attending the University of Colorado School of Law in Boulder, thirty miles from Denver. (I also later had interns from the University of Denver College of Law.) The night of the meeting the weather was bad, snowing heavily, but they all came. They later told me how disappointed they were when they met me, even remembering how I looked. I was wearing a fur coat and matching fur hat that my husband had given me. He was over six feet tall and, dear man, never seemed to realize that I was sadly only five foot one inch. So my (then in fashion) fur coat that night was black with a large white fur collar and cuffs and the matching hat was a monstrously large fur tam, with a big white furry button on its top. I always felt like the short stem of a large mushroom in that outfit, but my husband liked it on me. Understandably, I was not a reassuring professional sight to those young law school interns.

After starting at the District Attorney's Office, where I had a scruffy little office in the very old building where it was housed, I began mentoring. I decided that one-on-one working together was the best way to mentor, and I still believe that to be true.

DIGRESSION: A WARNING ABOUT YOUNG LAWYERS

FAIR WARNING: this is going to be a long digression, but it will caution you about young lawyers. I begin with physicians. Newly graduating physicians are required to enter into a residency program, working for from three to seven years under the supervision of a senior physician. Additional residency is required to become board-certified in a specialized area of medicine. Now, for comparison, consider the young lawyer. After law school graduation and passing the required two-day Bar examination, the young lawyer is eligible to practice law, free of any supervision. A certain amount of annual continuing legal education is now required in most states, but this is being a member of an audience attending a lecture. Do law firms provide mentoring? Some do; most do not. Based only on my personal observation in one city, I believe that mentoring programs decreased with the advent of the now prevalent system of lawyers billing by the hour. At the end of the law firm's fiscal year, when the profit "melon" is cut for the respective shares of its members, the number of billable hours is determinative of the member's share of the melon. Hence, the senior lawyer who mentors the new young associates will find this a costly personal undertaking. Some firms claim to have a mentoring program in which the firm has some of its more senior lawyers "spread their feathers" to show what they can do in court or to relate their transactional successes or their other skills. Believe me, such "show and tell" programs, as other lawyers have told me, and I agree, are worthless for teaching young lawyers. If I am wrong in my assessment of lawyer mentoring currently, and proof is provided to me that I am wrong, I shall be pleased.

MENTORING INTERNS

BACK TO my interns, whom I tried to help by working with each one individually. I would have the intern sit right next to my left elbow, and we would go over the intern's written product word by word, addressing both style and content. Effective communication, both oral and written, is essential for an able lawyer. And, of course, that includes being able to write well. I wish you could hear several of my "children" when they do a public imitation of my correcting some of their memorable errors. One now very prominent lawyer likes to tell about the trial court brief he authored for a heroin case. Throughout the brief, he spelled the drug "heroine"! Years later, he still laughed at my repeating, "no 'e' at the end, dear," as I crossed out each one. Another intern tells of his draft of a brief having so much of my editorial pen's red ink on it that it "looked like it was bleeding to death"—as indeed it should have. A Phi Beta Kappa intern produced such a pitiful project that I buried it in a bottom drawer of my desk, and then I quickly wrote another one for court filing. He later became a proficient intern and excellent lawyer. I still believe that young talent should never be harshly judged or made to feel frustrated or to become discouraged. So, I always tried to encourage them as they were learning how to use the tools of practicing law.

WHAT DID INTERNS DO?

WHAT DID the interns do? They were the legal support for the almost fifty deputy district attorneys. We wrote all the trial court briefs, and several of the trial judges were so pleased with the availability of having their legal questions briefed that our volume of trial court briefs soon increased. Indeed, we had one judge who always wanted two briefs on a single question, and we used to say that he would want a brief on "Who is Buried in Grant's Tomb?" We also provided an "emergency legal service" on questions of law and evidence that suddenly erupted during trial. The deputy district attorney would ask the judge for a short recess, call our direct telephone number, and the interns and I would scurry to find and relay the answer.

This emergency legal service got badly out of hand on one occasion, and I was to blame. This is the first time that I have ever told about it, and in writing no less, but enough years have elapsed that no harm can ensue. A young deputy district attorney and former intern called me from County Court (Colorado's lowest trial court) to ask a question about evidence, telling me that the judge had allowed a short recess for him to make the call. After I had answered his question, he asked if I would mind answering a question for the public defender, his opposing counsel. Our deputy said that the "PD is really nice," and as young an attorney as our young deputy, but that public defender had no one to call in the public defender's office for answers to a question. So I agreed and answered the young public defender's question. Then our deputy said that the judge, who was quite new to the bench, had asked if I would answer a question for him also, which I did. After I hung up the telephone, I chided myself severely. Talk about avoiding conflicts of interest? I had represented both parties and the judge!

THE APPELLATE DIVISION

BACK TO our Appellate Division: in addition to our trial court services, we did indeed handle appeals to Colorado's appellate courts, the Colorado Court of Appeals and the Colorado Supreme Court. Our appeals fell into two categories. First, we filed appeals on questions of law. Winning these appeals could not result in the retrial of a defendant because of our constitutional prohibition against placing a defendant in "double jeopardy" for the same crime. Nonetheless, these appeals, that were notably successful, provided useful precedent for future prosecutions by helping trial judges to make correct decisions in a case as to the law and evidence, as well as served to curb grave judicial abuses. For example, I reversed one district court judge sixteen times out of seventeen appeals. Another, I reversed fourteen times out of fifteen appeals. I avoided appeals on violations of mere technicalities but tried always to select questions of law when a needed reversal of error would serve the public interest. And I always enjoyed my return to reading the record (comprised of transcripts of trial testimony and evidentiary exhibits), preparing briefs, and making appellate arguments.

Our second area of appeals was interlocutory appeals, based on the court's allegedly wrongful pretrial granting of defendant's motion to suppress evidence. Sadly, several of the then district court judges seemed to believe that they were less likely to be reversed by the appellate court if they suppressed the defendant's confession or evidence seized in a search and seizure wrongfully claimed to have been illegal. The factual circumstances in some of these cases do not bear repeating, but one was the main headline on the local Sunday newspaper! The interlocutory appeals, often successful, fostered fair trials with the jury hearing evidence properly admitted—and thereby serving the public interest.

Another function, rarely necessary to perform, was the filing of "original proceedings." These are special emergency proceedings, based on the common law, quickly to remedy serious judicial errors. Some state supreme courts, depending on who the judges are, seldom if ever grant an "original writ." Fortunately, when I did my stint of public service in the District Attorney's Office, our then state supreme court would grant relief when justified. Let me give you an example. A Colorado statute at the time prescribed the procedure for release of a person convicted of a felony but found to be insane and sent to the state mental hospital instead of the penitentiary. The procedure included specific provisions protective of the public safety. In the case I have chosen for an example, the deputy district attorney objected to the release because the felon seeking his release from the mental hospital, and his lawyer had obviously failed to comply with the plain language of the statute. The judge approved the release, stating "I don't care what the statute says, I am ordering this man's release." Within the hour, the deputy was in my office, very upset: "Brooke, I talked to the mental hospital and the doctor says the man is dangerous!" In my opinion, the court had carried judicial "activism" much too far, and within two hours I was at the state supreme court with my newly filed Original Proceeding and urgently seeking to stop the release. The then Chief Justice said, "Brooke, that is what the appellate courts do. They take care of these matters on appeal—the trial judge has a right to be wrong and then we correct it." I was too indignant at the trial judge's cavalier ignoring of the statute's plain wording to be tactful and snapped: "No judge has a right to be this wrong." And bless the Chief Justice's heart, my request for relief from the release was granted. I later learned that further tests had disclosed the man was indeed very dangerous and had to be kept confined for both his and the public's safety.

In addition to over 200 state court appeals handled by the Appellate Division, I filed two petitions for *writ of certiorari* with the United States Supreme Court. A petition for *certiorari* is a request that the Supreme Court order a lower court to send to it the record of the case for review. Only minute fractions of such petitions are granted. I prepared the first petition for *writ of certiorari* in *Colorado v. Quintero*, 464 U.S. 1014 (1983), concerning an order suppressing evidence. The Supreme Court granted *writ of certiorari*, but the petition was later dismissed because Respondent Fidel Quintero died. I also prepared the petition for *writ of certiorari* granted by the United States Supreme Court in *Colorado v. Connelly*, 479 U.S. 157 (1986). The case involved a confession by a man who simply walked up to a policeman on a downtown Denver street and volunteered that four months earlier he had murdered a fourteen-year-old girl. His detailed information proved correct, and the murder charge was filed against him. The trial court ruled the confession was involuntary, and the case would have been dismissed but for the successful *certiorari* and reversal by the Supreme Court. I give fair credit to the local newspapers, whose reporting of the case I attached to the petition.

THE "APPELLATE PANTRY"

THE DISTRICT attorney was very proud and supportive of the Appellate Division, which he called the "Appellate Pantry," with ample justification. I assure you that young law students are always hungry, and I am not referring to hunger for knowledge. I was empathetic having always, despite my small size, had a big appetite. So when they arrived from law school to work all afternoon in the Appellate Division, I would send an intern to a little shop about a block from our building to bring back a sack of good doughnuts, which would instantly disappear. On Fridays, when their schedules would allow them to arrive at lunch time, all of us—our interns, my two assistant deputy DAs, legal assistants, and secretaries—would go out to lunch together. We had several favorite places, where the delicious food servings were large and the prices small. On warm, sunny Fridays, we went to a Mexican restaurant, now expanded into a large attractive building, but then in a small, private home. We would eat at a large table in the back garden under a big tree, and I would buy the pitcher(s) of beer for everyone to have a modest amount to drink. We also had several other places where we could sit in a private area, eat plenty of good food, and I unapologetically would buy the pitcher(s) of beer for limited consumption. The camaraderie was warm, and we would all return to work refreshed and eager to delve into the law. We even had a Thanksgiving dinner on Thanksgiving Eve in our office's law library, complete with turkey, dressing, mashed potatoes, gravy, and all the trimmings, prepared by the interns! Our district attorney was understandably astounded!

Figure 2.28. Thanksgiving dinner arranged in the "Appellate Pantry" and law library of the Denver District Attorney's Office, in about 1981. O. Otto Moore is at one end of the table and Brooke is at the other.

We were always a happy division of workers, including our secretaries, two of whom became distinguished lawyers—and who had been trained in using our law library and writing trial court briefs while in the Appellate Division. We had a third secretary who became a senior legal assistant, skilled in legal research and brief writing. I am pleased to report that our little group, which changed every two years as the interns graduated and became lawyers, always was very productive and excellent. As a result, we acquired national recognition from several national professional organizations.

Then early one summer, the district attorney told me that he had invited a young lawyer from the East to be a "summer intern" and hoped that would not be a problem for me. I assured the district attorney that it would not because we could always use more help. When the new young lawyer arrived, he was nice and quite normal but was unused to our more open, Western ways. We tried to make him feel welcome and took him with us on our Friday lunches. As time went on, he also seemed to enjoy the food that was almost always present on the big table in our law library. Office staff would bring in leftover-but-still-fresh birthday cakes, muffins, cookies, and other assorted goodies—and they could retrieve their empty plates within a very short time. Then the Friday came when, driving back to the office, we saw a truck parked that was selling whole watermelons. As we neared, the truck driver sliced open one, and we could see how deliciously red it was. So we stopped, and I treated the Appellate Pantry to a watermelon. When we reached our building, the young Easterner said that he would carry the watermelon up the steps and to our law library. As we reached the front door, it opened, and there stood the district attorney, a man with a great sense of humor. He looked at his young import from the East holding the big green watermelon and blurted: "I don't believe it!"

That afternoon the district attorney revealed the horrid truth. Our young Easterner was a "mole," a representative of some national research organization that did some kind of investigation and peering into public agencies. The organization had heard of our Appellate Division's excellence and, with the district attorney's connivance, had sent this person to check us out. By now the Easterner had become a bona fide participant in the gustatory activities of the Appellate Pantry, and a capable member of the legal team. We were sorry to see him leave, and he said that he would never forget his time with us, which I am sure proved to be true.

MESSAGE TO MY BELOVED "CHILDREN"

DECADES LATER, many of my "children" and staff still keep in contact with me. As I was writing this, my telephone rang from one of my "children" who had been the second Black attorney appointed as the City Attorney for the City and County of Denver. He called from the Seattle airport, where he had a long wait before the plane that would take him and his wife to the port to leave on an Alaskan cruise. He said, "Brooke, I was thinking about you and how grateful I am for all that you taught me." Then he went on to say that he was always confident that he was doing "the right thing in court" from his first court appearance, all the little things such as where to stand and how to

Figure 2.29. Denver District Attorney's Office attorneys, interns, and staff at front of the former historic West Side Court Building at 924 W. Colfax, in about 1981.

First row (left to right): LaDonne Bush, Donna Skinner Reed, Gertrude Grant, Dale Tooley, Norm Early, Brooke Wunnicke, Richard Spriggs. *Second row*: Guy Till, Brenda Taylor, Michael Cohen, O. Otto Moore, Mike Little, Chuck Lepley, Tom Casey, Jeff Bayless. *Third row*: Rich Caschette,Bill Buckley, Ann Frick, Mark Fogg, Dave Thomas, Dan Fischer, Lee Anderson, Espinoza Gilberto. *Fourth row*: Larry Gagnon, Dan Lynch, Suzanne Lynch, Pete Ramirez, Yvette Kane, Christopher Cross, Ken Keene, Dave Stark, Bill Lucero, Neal Richardson. *Fifth row*: Chris Munch, Velveta Golightly-Howell, Bonnie Wright Benedetti, Diane Balkin, Jim Weissman, Sheila Rappaport, Castelar Garcia, Paul Wolf, John Coughlin. *Sixth row*: Dave Olivas, David Purdy, Robin Whitley, Jim Hurd, Karen Steinhauser, Charles Murray, Gary Jackson, Steve Munsinger. *Seventh row*: Paul Markson, Scott Shockley, John Olsen, Keith Johnson, Dave Connor, Stan Garnett, Bill Ritter, Craig Silverman, Rich Keenan, Dave Heckenbach, Steve Marsters, Jack Rotole, unknown; Carl Eklund, Dave Costello, Peter Bornstein, Lamar Sims, James Allison.

address the court. I was so proud and happy with his call—to hear again that I had spared a talented young lawyer some of my early embarrassments. He calls me "My Mother in the Law."

When my "children" visit me, many happily recall our Friday afternoon special lunches, the plenitude of available food, and the camaraderie that made their work pleasurable. Several have called their tenure as interns as

Figure 2.30. In the District Attorney's Office "Appellate Pantry" with a cake for the occasion of celebrating their total of one hundred years at the Bar in May 1984 are Brooke for thirty-eight years and O. Otto Moore for sixty-two years.

"Camelot" and the best time of their career. I too shall never forget my time as Denver's Chief Appellate Deputy District Attorney. I shall never forget the pleasurable success of my many appeals involving the criminal law. I shall never forget the interns whom I mentored—my beloved "children."

I close here with a short message to each of my beloved "children" at law: when you visit me and hug me as you leave, saying softly, "I love you," joy surges within me together with my pride in your fine contributions to the legal profession and the law that I love.

> [*COMPILER'S NOTE: Honorable O. Otto Moore (1896–1990) was Chief Justice of the Colorado Supreme Court while serving as a justice from 1948 to 1969. He was a judicial crusader for civil rights and, after retiring from the bench, rewrote the Colorado Criminal Code and served as a Denver assistant district attorney.*

On January 14, 1986, to honor Brooke, as she returned to practice civil law instead of criminal law, the District Attorney's Office honored her twelve years with a large dinner party with a program, including rhymes and chorus of familiar melodies with new lyrics.

For the occasion, also well known for his rhymes, Judge Moore wrote the following:

Brooke Wunnicke will always be
the one most high in memory
when thoughts are turned to things well done
because of which a case was won.
   It saddens us to know that now
we'll have to get along some how
without her never erring voice
in helping us to make a choice
by pointing up the things to do
to prove the point we urged was true.
   As Brooke moves on to this new life
of law applied to civil strife,
we know that she will find success
which leads to fulfilled happiness;
and knowing this we'll dry our tears
remembering the happy years
in which we labored hand in hand
to lessen crime throughout the land.
We love you Brooke—there'll never be
   another like Brooke Wunnicke

Not to be outdone by the Judge, the following rhyme was anonymously written by some attorneys in the District Attorney's Office for the same occasion, and Brooke archived it with other happy memorabilia.

Thanks for the Memories
   Thanks for the memories,
   The early days with Dale,
   You kept us out of jail.
   The briefs you wrote, we loved to quote,
   You never let us fail.
   Oh, thank you so much.
   Thanks for the memories.
   With you and Moore,
   The judges knew the score,

The P.D.'s shook, as did the crooks,
We slammed the jailhouse door,
Oh, thank you so much.

Thanks for the memories,
You were at our beck and call,
You always knew it all,
The troops you led,
Were all well fed,
And always on the ball,
Oh, thank you so much.

Thanks for the memories,
Your charm and your kind grace,
Have always warmed our place,
The smiles you wore,
Your open door,
Will never be replaced,
Oh, thank you so much.

Thanks for the memories,
A Mom to everyone,
It's sure been lots of fun,
Although you leave,
We all believe,
That we remain as one,
Oh, Thank you so much . . .

Of Counsel (1986–2011)

I n 1986, I decided to return to the private sector of law practice, having had my fill of criminal law and appeals only for criminal cases, as Chief Appellate Deputy District Attorney for Denver from 1973 to 1986. (See this in Part Two's "The Colorado Lawyer," about Public Service in Criminal Cases and Mentoring "Brooke's Children" [1973–1986].) I affiliated Of Counsel with Hall & Evans, LLC, a fine litigation firm in downtown Denver that promised me the opportunity to provide counsel for the firm's trial and appellate practices. Because of my age, I told the firm that I no longer did trial work, but even after over 200 appeals in two states and federal court, I still loved that area of the law. The firm also enabled me to arrange my time for lectures, writing, and teaching.

[COMPILER'S NOTE: The rest of this subsection was written by the Compiler (in italics), after Brooke's death, and it also includes some postmortem text from the law firm and quotes Brooke's 2005 thank you note to the firm.]

Brooke became good friends with Richard D. (Dick) Hall, retired partner and then Of Counsel (and eponym) for Hall & Evans. Their Monday lunches during football season included detailed analyses of the games, plus the law. Dick's 1997 obituary included that "Brooke Wunnicke, a lawyer serving as Of Counsel to Hall & Evans, was one of Mr. Hall's greatest friends and admirers. She comments, 'Dick touched many lives. He was a scholar, a gentleman, a fine lawyer, and a truly good person.'"

Figure 2.31. Brooke, in the library of Hall & Evans, 1995.

Brooke always enjoyed a party, and colleagues and friends always enjoyed a party with and for her. Hall & Evans regularly arranged celebrations of her birthday with flowers for her office and, in its large conference room, a generous birthday party for all attorneys and staff. The following is one of Brooke's email thank you notes:

Figure 2.32. Brooke at the January 28, 2006, formal reception hosted by Hall & Evans to honor her sixty years (1946–2006) at the Bars of Wyoming and Colorado. To her left is the billboard of her professional biography and to her right, on the wall, is the firm's portrait of her friend Richard D. Hall.

To all at Hall & Evans—I thank each and every one of you for my splendid birthday party on May 9 [2005]. The food was delicious, and the bouquet is still spectacular. I am truly grateful that you make my days at the firm so pleasurable. . . . Your friendly greetings and daily kindness to me are a cherished part of my life. I still love the law and lawyering, and you have done much to ensure that this love has not lost its luster. I am grateful to all of you for my memorably fine birthday party and for my happy life here at Hall & Evans. Fondly, Brooke

Celebrating her two sixtieth anniversaries—her 1945 graduation from the University of Colorado School of Law and her admission to the Wyoming Bar—in 2006, the firm hosted a widely attended, elaborate, formal reception for Brooke's many colleagues in the Colorado Bar. In its memorial tribute to her in 2014, the law firm wrote about Brooke's twenty-five-year affiliation, until her retirement in 2011.

Brooke joined us at Hall & Evans in 1986, after leaving the Denver District Attorney's Office. She remained a vital cornerstone of the firm until 2011. While at Hall & Evans she contributed on many levels, including work on appellate matters, and a remarkably wide breadth of legal issues. It seemed that no matter was too complex for her legal acumen, and she had a knack for distilling complex issues into simple terms. The trial lawyers of the firm learned from her how to mix strong advocacy with charm, how to maintain a professional approach in the heat of battle, how to approach the practice of law with great respect for its institutions and constituents, and how to treat all persons, regardless of stature or position, with respect and dignity. No one could hold the stage and tell a story better than Brooke. She was a sought-after public speaker, and would engage her audiences with substance, humor, always concluding with an important and relevant lesson.

After withdrawing from the active practice of law, Brooke remained at Hall & Evans and continued her work as a prolific author, expert witness, public speaker, and contributor to the firm. . . . Professional ethics was among Brooke's areas of expertise, and she was a tremendous resource to the firm in that regard. Brooke was an active participant of the firm's conflicts committee, and always provided careful and useful guidance. The standing instruction in the firm on all questions of professional responsibility was to ask Brooke.

Monday mornings were often filled with her always perceptive analysis of the latest Broncos victory or defeat. Brooke took personal interest in every person in our organization from the most senior attorney to the recently hired hourly staff. We have missed her in the office since she decided to continue her work at home. Hall & Evans will always be grateful for our association with our colleague and friend.

On behalf of Brooke, Diane Wunnicke adds a personal note of special gratitude to Ken Lyman, Bruce Menk, and Kevin O'Brien who, as executives for the firm, led Hall & Evans to provide twenty-five years of comforts and pleasures for Brooke; to list but a few: nice sunny offices, very convenient parking, transportation if needed, birthday and special parties, flowers for every important and personal occasion, a conference room in her name including some of her honorary memorabilia, social occasions for her 2011 retirement, for many years funding in her name an annual scholarship at the University of Colorado Law School and, in her memory, generous funding for the law school's permanent Brooke Wunnicke Endowed Scholarship.]

Give a Helping Hand

When active in Wyoming, I really liked many of my "fellow" (I was then the only woman) lawyers in the Cheyenne Bar and appreciated what had become their kind acceptance of me. As my "thank you" for their camaraderie, I was always glad to give a helping hand, if my schedule permitted.

Over the many years while in Colorado, when asked and before I retired, I still tried to mentor, counsel, or help other lawyers.

Usually forgettably routine, some incidents of helping are still memorable for me. So, I thought that maybe you would be interested or amused.

"Don't Let Them Cross-Examine Me"

I RECALL when one of the younger lawyers in Cheyenne called to say that he had a free trip to Las Vegas that weekend, and he very much wanted to go. Las Vegas was just starting to bloom as was that lawyer's practice. Problem: the lawyer had a small trial to the judge, without jury, on Friday that would prevent his trip. Could I do the trial for him? My calendar was free that Friday, so I said, "Yes." When his client showed up, he had the shiftiest pair of eyes that I have seen on a person, either before or since. I thought, "If the judge notices his eyes, this fellow will have zero credibility."

As we walked the one block from my office to the courthouse on that Friday, the client said: "Don't let the other side's lawyer cross-examine me."

I explained that the opposing counsel had a right to cross-examine him and that I could not prevent this. Whereupon the fellow said: "Well, I have a bad heart. If during cross-examination I get upset and have a heart attack, I have nitroglycerin pills in my coat pocket. Reach in quickly to get a pill and give it to me." He survived the trial and so obviously, but grimly, did I.

"Bury This Bill," New Level Grave Markers

ANOTHER MEMORABLE incident of "helping out" during my years as a Cheyenne lawyer also arose out of Las Vegas as an emerging holiday destination. A lawyer friend called to tell me that he had two friends going to Las Vegas for a fun long weekend, returning Monday evening, and they had invited him to join them. Unfortunately, he had a hearing scheduled that Monday afternoon to fight a bill before a committee of the Wyoming State Legislature, then in session. His clients were flying in from their home office in a midwestern state to appear before the committee with my lawyer friend to represent them in objecting to a bill.

The lawyer appealingly asked, "Would you?" I said, "Yes, I'll represent your clients at the hearing. What is the bill about?" Apparently, his clients had been very successful in buying land for cemeteries and developing them with grave markers limited to being level with the ground. Funeral directors throughout the state had joined to support a bill that would ban this type of cemetery. The lawyer did not have time to stay and explain the grounds for the funeral directors' objection to these cemeteries and scampered off happily to Las Vegas.

On Monday afternoon, I duly appeared with the clients for the legislative committee hearing. The clients were two youngish men the size of pro football defensive ends, and I could tell that they were disappointed in their substitute counsel. I looked out at the opposition and was uneasy when I saw so many funeral directors, all dressed in dark blue or black suits with dark ties—and their able lawyer. Frankly, I felt forlorn.

Then the committee entered the room. I was acquainted with the chairman (as was then the term, now a "chair"), who was an upstate lawyer. He was of Irish descent with twinkling eyes and a known sense of humor. When he saw me, he looked surprised and, without warning, started the meeting by calling on me. He asked me to identify the persons who I was representing and to state our position. Our position? I was ignorant of the legal aspects of cemeteries. What could or should I say? I responded by simply stating in eight words all I knew about our position: "We ask the committee to bury this bill." The chairman, obviously choking back laughter, promptly adjourned the meeting for a short recess. The bill was buried, the frolicking lawyer and his clients were happy, and I was not proud of my professional contribution to the hearing.

He Was Too Frightened to Try the Case

THEN IN Colorado, where we moved to Denver in 1969 after my husband's retirement from business in Wyoming, I decided to cut back on my arduous life as a trial lawyer. I affiliated as Of Counsel with a Denver law firm, retiring from physically strenuous trial work—and expected to no longer be a "helping hand" to my new colleagues "at the Bar." I enjoyed being solely a "transaction" lawyer, doing some interesting oil and gas, securities and real estate projects, areas in which I had practiced in Wyoming. But soon, another lawyer needed a "helping hand."

Although an excellent small firm, in 1969 it did not encourage associates to seek help and seemed to look down on those who did. Despite the firm's disfavor, a young and distressed associate at the firm came to see me one day. I had thought him very intelligent and hardworking but was surprised when I learned that he wanted to be a trial lawyer and had been assigned to work with the several trial lawyers at the firm. The associate was reserved, soft-spoken, and rather shy. Why would he desire to be a trial lawyer? I thought of some of my trials and how this nice young fellow would have been "mince-meat" long before the trial was over; trials are not a gentle exercise.

Back to the associate's visit to me: "How can I help you?" I asked. He told me that he had his first trial "alone" the next day, and he was scared about how to do it. He had only "carried the briefcases" for one of the experienced trial lawyers in several previous cases. I asked him to tell me about his first solo case. It was a simple short one, to be tried to the judge without a jury, and should take less than a day. Then he disclosed the horrifying truth: "I am too frightened to try the case. I don't know what to do." Me, all caution gone: "Would you like me to try it for you?" I asked. "Would you?" he pled. "Of course. The trial is in another county though, and I don't drive that far. Give me your file, pick me up at home tomorrow morning, drive me to court. I'll try the case, then drive me home, and no one at the firm need know." So, I told my secretary that I would not be coming in the following day.

The trial was held on a beautiful day filled with Colorado sunshine. We had a nice drive to the rather distant courthouse; I tried the case, we won, and the associate drove me home. The firm never knew about the lawyer switch and was pleased with the victory but disappointed that the associate announced his departure because he had decided that he did not want to be a trial lawyer. I was pleased by his wise career decision.

The Judge: "Where Have You Been All My Life?!"

ANOTHER INCIDENT—AND I shall never forget it—involved my giving minor help. Among other trial and appellate matters, I did municipal bond test litigation. Shortly after I moved to Colorado, I was tracked to my Of Counsel firm and asked to do another test of the validity of a municipal bond issue. I have heard, but never bothered to check, that some of the eastern states have a procedure where such municipal bond test suits can be filed directly in the state's highest court—a sensible route. In Colorado and Wyoming, the test suit has to be filed in the state's highest trial court, called the "district court" in both states, and a staged hearing is held. Bond counsel lists every point that trial counsel must bring up so as to include it in the record for the necessary appeal. The trial court hearing is "staged," with bond counsel writing the scenario. The lawyer attacking the validity of the proposed bonds raises all grounds for the attack, and the "winning" lawyer raises all the persuasive reasons for the bonds' validity. The objective of the litigation is to try to ensure that the highest appellate court upholds the validity of the bonds and that the court's opinion covers every issue that bond counsel has included in the scenario for the hearing.

For the staged hearing that consisted of stipulated facts and opposing legal arguments, I would be one of the lawyers and we needed to select another "opposing" lawyer. As bond counsel and I considered a choice, I said to him, "Why don't you do it?" He was an experienced, able, highly regarded municipal bond lawyer and a very nice person. He laughed at my question, but I pursued the suggestion. Finally, he said, "My children don't think that I am a real lawyer because I have never been in a court, and they watch Perry Mason on TV. I'll do it." And I replied, "Great! And don't worry because I'll be there and make sure that nothing bad happens to you."

When the great day for our hearing came, my "opposing" counsel picked me up at home because the hearing was in a county north of Denver and beyond my driving range. At that time the county had a very new courthouse that was round—yes, you read it correctly, round! When we entered, we asked where our courtroom was, and the receptionist replied, "Turn to your right—well, that won't work will it? And it won't work if I tell you to turn left, will it?" I replied, "Don't worry. We'll just walk until we find it." And so we did, and like Alice, entered into a wonderland, walking the circle until we found the courtroom and judge.

I had heard of the judge, who was known for his volatility rather than his wisdom. He was quite short of stature and seemed somewhat excitable. I was the lawyer who spoke first and had told bond counsel just to do as I did. I warned him to watch closely when I introduced a documentary exhibit into evidence because the required steps for introduction are as inflexible as the steps in a minuet. Then came bond counsel on his maiden voyage in court, and he did very well indeed.

After my closing argument and without warning, the little judge leaped down from the bench, rushed up to me, threw his arms around me, and, hugging me, shouted: "Where have you been all my life?" I wish that you could have seen the poor bond counsel's face! Very large eyes, mouth slightly ajar, and visibly shocked! As bond counsel drove me the long drive home, I repeatedly emphasized the truth to him: I had never seen any judge do anything like that to me or to any other lawyer or even heard of such an occurrence. Sadly, I could feel that the bond counsel did not believe me—but I'm sure that he never forgot his first day in court.

Another Starting Trial Lawyer, "Just Can't Do It!"

I MISSED appellate work more than I had anticipated and left private practice in 1973 for a dozen years of public service as Chief Appellate Deputy District Attorney in the Denver District Attorney's Office. Here, I just relate briefly my foolishly giving a helping hand when in the District Attorney's Office. I did not do trial work—just my first love in the law, appellate work. The young deputies all knew, however, that I was an experienced trial lawyer, as I mentored them.

About four o'clock on a Thursday afternoon, a young deputy district attorney who already had a reputation for being inept in court came to my office, claiming to be desperate for help. He had a hearing the next morning in federal court that involved only legal argument on a motion opposing counsel had filed. The hearing, however, was before a federal judge who instilled dread in some lawyers—in my opinion, justifiably so—if they were ill-prepared or did not know what they were doing. The young lawyer assured me that all he asked was for me to come and sit beside him at counsel table to give him needed courage. So I made the big mistake of feeling sorry for the young lawyer and could not say "no" to his humble request to just come sit by him.

The hearing was set for 8:30 a.m. I arrived in court at 8:20 a.m. to find the lawyer-by-whom-I-would-sit already in a funk. "You are late! I was so afraid that you were not coming!" The hearing began at the appointed time of 8:30 a.m., and the movant, the hapless lawyer who had filed the motion, began his argument that seemed interminable. I did not listen to his droning voice that could have brought slumber to the most afflicted insomniac. I managed to keep my eyes open and marveled at the judge's patience as the lawyer kept on droning. Finally, the lawyer sat down, and the judge nodded to our counsel table. The young lawyer leaned to me and said: "I can't do it!" Me: "What do you mean you can't do it? I have never even seen the file in this case!" He: "I just can't."

The judge barked at us to begin, the young lawyer seemed literally rooted in his chair, and I rose and went to the podium. I shall not shock you with what I was thinking about that young excuse-for-a-lawyer—but only momentarily. More immediately, what could I say? "Your Honor, what is this case about?" That obviously would not do. So, remembering the lengthy droner who had preceded me, I simply said: "Your Honor, (stated my name) representing the defendants (I did not know their names). Our position is that the movant's brief and argument here this morning establish that the motion lacks credible grounds in fact and in law. Does the court want further argument?" Ah, His Honor took the bait of not having to listen to another lawyer argue and ruled: "No further argument. Motion denied." I still think this an unusual victory.

What Fun! Same Day, a Defective Complaint for an Easy Win

THAT DAY in federal court was not yet ended. As I left the courtroom, a young man from our office was waiting for me. The district attorney was scheduled to argue a motion to dismiss a civil suit alleging various claims against the District Attorney's Office. Because a major emergency had just erupted, he could not leave the office. The district attorney found out that I was at the federal courthouse appearing before the same judge as would be hearing his motion and sent a messenger scurrying to ask me to "Please, please," take care of the matter for him. I had fifteen minutes before the hearing and decided to skim the plaintiff's complaint and our Motion to Dismiss, and the brief supporting the motion if I had time. Ho-ho! No need to read the motion or the brief—the complaint had a fatal flaw. What fun!

When the hearing began, I spoke first as the movant for dismissal. When I reached the podium, before I could even address the court, the judge said to me: "Counsel, tell him." So I turned to opposing counsel, and in an easily audible voice, said: "You do not have a jurisdictional paragraph in your complaint." The judge nodded with an approving smile and declared: "Case dismissed." Lest you think this harshly unfair, plaintiff could refile the suit, doing so correctly. As you probably know, "jurisdiction" is the power of a court to hear and decide cases. A federal district court does not have "plenary jurisdiction," and so it is elementary for the lawyer to state the source of jurisdiction in filing the complaint to start the lawsuit. I hope that the lawyer did not bill his client for the second corrected suit filing.

Hearing My Obituary as a Trial Lawyer

IN 1986, I had been at Hall & Evans only a few weeks when—you guessed—a lawyer at the firm, whom I liked and had known before becoming Of Counsel, called me to lend a helping hand. Although acknowledging that he knew I had stipulated "no more trial court," he had an essential appearance to make out of town for important clients at the same time that he was scheduled to argue a motion before the Chief Judge of our federal district court. Would I? Yes, because I thought that I had a moral obligation to do so, and one more trial court appearance would not hurt me.

When I got to the courtroom, I sat down at the customary counsel table for the defense. When plaintiff's counsel arrived, he was a big, tall young man, who snapped at me: "You are sitting at the wrong table." I thought, "Things have really changed since I last came to a trial court." So I meekly changed counsel tables. Then the court bailiff entered the courtroom, looked at us, and said: "Counsel are sitting at the wrong tables." Ah, this small appearance was not off to a promising start. Next came the judge, who I have always admired for judicial skill and legal scholarship. The judge looked at plaintiff's lawyer, who had filed the motion that was to be argued, and said: "I have read the file in this case, including your motion and brief, and have made up my mind with respect to your motion. Do you still want to argue?" "Yes." And argue he did, not omitting it seemed a single, pearly word of his lengthy, unpersuasive argument. I thought, "Why doesn't the lawyer look at the judge's expression?" But it was not to be—he finally finished. The judge then nodded to me.

When I reached the podium, after the initial formal address I always made to the court, I asked: "Does the court wish further argument?" "No. Motion denied." I returned to my counsel table, but the judge did not immediately end the proceeding. Instead, he asked the court reporter to include what he was going to read into the court's transcript. I then had the rare and exquisite pleasure of hearing my own trial lawyer obituary, presented by a fine judge. What a wonderful way to end my trial lawyer career!

When I left the courtroom and got to the elevator, opposing counsel was waiting for me. He leaned down and snarled, "I don't think that it is fair that they sent you!" I thought it safer not to respond, and we rode down in silence—but I was still basking that the judge read his recognition of me into the court's permanent record.

Expert Witness Takes Over the Settlement

MY YEARS as a lawyer continued at Hall & Evans with me as staid Of Counsel, giving occasional lectures to lawyers and serving as an arbitrator. My liveliest activity was serving as an expert witness, and one incident belongs here about giving a "helping hand." I had been retained to serve as an expert witness with respect to a letter of credit issue, being coauthor of a book titled *Standby and Commercial Letters of Credit*.

I had accepted to serve because the trial was to be in Florida, and I thought that the locale would be enjoyable. The law firm that retained me was prestigious, the young Cuban American lawyer who talked to me about the case was likable and explained that a senior lawyer was in the background. I arrived the day before trial was to begin, and it had been arranged for me to testify the first day. Nothing went according to plan. The corporate parties to the lawsuit were headquartered in South America in a country that had just acquired a new dictator. The activities involved in the lawsuit were sufficient to permit jurisdiction of the dispute to be in the United States. Anyway, on the day that I arrived, the dictator had taken over one of the corporate parties because it had the misfortune to have a lot of cash on hand, and the dictator wanted and took it. A foreign subsidiary of the now cash-poor parent corporation remained as a party to the lawsuit. And all the parties decided that it was in their mutual self-interest to settle this lawsuit and do so quickly.

The young lawyer with whom I had been working was aghast when he told me about the parties' decision for a prompt settlement. He was a junior partner, had prepared very hard for this, his first solo trial, and a junior partner apparently had a sort of probationary period before being elevated to the top roster of partner. Now, no trial! And his voice shook when he told me the news and said: "I have never settled a case or drafted a settlement agreement. And (naming the senior partner on the case) left the country this morning for some depositions overseas." He looked so forlorn and was such a nice, young lawyer. I heard my voice say, "Would you like me to handle the settlement for you?" "Yes, yes. Would you?" "Yes." So the next day, the now-vacated trial day, I negotiated a very favorable settlement for "our side," drafted the settlement agreement, had it properly executed, and handed it to my young lawyer. Both he and his client were very happy, and I was pleased for them. The young lawyer, to celebrate, took me to what he said was the finest Cuban restaurant in town. He selected from the menu and the wine for us. Although some of the dishes and even the wine I did not recognize, everything was memorably delicious—including the joy of my young host, who had known when *and been willing* to ask for a helping hand.

Hospitalized, Still Ready to Help My Nurse

MORE YEARS passed; no more trial court appearances; no more appellate arguments, which I still missed. Then in 2007 I was in the hospital for a week. One of the attending specialist physicians had left written word with staff on the floor and a bold, large-print sign on the door where I was placed that I "Must Not Have An IV." About 2:00 a.m., a doctor came through to look at the patients on that floor. Never coming closer to me than twenty feet, and despite the sign, the doctor barked at the young nurse taking care of me, "Put an IV on her. Everyone on this floor must have an IV at all times." Then the doctor sailed on like a galleon under full sail.

My quiet, brave, young nurse looked kindly at me and said firmly: "I am not going there." As I lay there in the hospital bed, flat as a water lily pad, I heard my reply: "Good for you!" And, confident that somehow I could and would, "Don't worry. If you have a problem, I'm a lawyer and I will defend you," and then I contentedly went to sleep.

Adjunct Professor of Law (1977–1997)

S everal years after my moving to Denver, the University of Denver College of Law fully accredited Evening Division contacted me about joining the faculty. I was flattered, because I had learned that distinguished lawyers and respected judges were the evening faculty. I declined, however, because I wanted to spend my evenings with my husband.

TEACHING "PROBLEMS IN LEGAL PRACTICE" AND ABOUT BASICS OF WRITING

WHEN MY husband died a few years later in 1977, leaving me desolate with grief, I thought that practicing law all day would tire me enough to sleep at night. Wrong! I have never taken a sleeping pill, so instead I called the University of Denver College of Law (DU Law) to ask if I was still wanted as a teacher in the evening division. "Yes" was the welcome answer. I was asked to teach a course called Problems in Legal Practice. I gratefully accepted, then found out no textbook was available, and I was to design the course.

Thus, I began twenty years of serving as an Adjunct Professor of Law, teaching for two hours in the evening twice a week. The old downtown law school building had attractive architecture with pleasant appearing amenities. In winter, however, the heat was unreliable, and the air conditioning worked fine until the weather was hot—then it vanished. I found all this out the hard way. I froze teaching in winter quarter and panted through summer quarter.

I soon became very fond of my students. They worked full-time at assorted jobs and then came to law school for four to five nights per week for four hours of classes. "Dinner" was maybe a hamburger on the way to school or a very late supper after classes.

In my class Problems of Legal Practice, they were to acquire some knowledge about the real world of practicing law. They learned what they would be expected to do when starting as an associate in a law firm, as well as how to draft a few simple legal instruments, a trial court brief for a law firm partner, a short witness examination in a deposition, and a short oral legal argument. My literally hungry students lapped up all these realities. I taught them how to draft a simple will and was surprised (and a bit worried) when the students later told me that they were now preparing wills for their relatives. As the class and I worked together, we became like a close-knit little community. A nice memory is when one of our best students, who had obviously worked diligently to prepare her oral argument, had to stop after only about two minutes because she apparently could not speak in public. So she sat down, fighting tears, while we continued with other members of the class. Then I said to her, "Would you like to try again?" She nodded her head and rose to address the class, doing a good job all the way to the end. I was proud of her and of the class, which broke into enthusiastic applause when she finished.

One last word on this, my first law school class. I learned, to my dismay, that these talented young people had not been taught the basics of writing in the English language. So, for their next trial court brief assignment, I tabbed the worst errors. At class, I left the papers in my briefcase while I told the students about the evils of not writing correctly and how important it was for lawyers to learn to write well and unambiguously. Then, I said, "Let me read you some examples."

I fished out of my briefcase a blank folder in which I had placed some of the worst examples. When I read them to the class, they broke into laughter at many and looked puzzled by others. Then I revealed the startling truth: "Everything I read to you was from your papers." Finally, I told the class about a very small, inexpensive book that would set them on the proper course to improve quickly how they wrote: *The Elements of Style*. And I am still a devoted fan of William Strunk and E. B. White.

"OILS WELL THAT ENDS WELL, IT HAS BEEN A GAS"—OIL AND GAS LAW

THE NEXT event in my nighttime career as an Adjunct Professor of Law occurred when the prior fine oil and gas adjunct professor and equally fine man decided to retire from teaching. He told the law school to try and get me to teach the course. I had really enjoyed the practice of oil and gas law, both in Wyoming and during my first four years in Denver. So, I started teaching Oil and Gas Law and continued to do so for twenty years. I was deeply honored and very pleased when the Rocky Mountain Mineral Law Foundation (RMMLF) gave me a special award for my teaching of Oil and Gas Law. The RMMLF, as it is unhandily known, is an internationally prestigious organization dedicated to educational seminars and publishing outstanding papers in the RMMLF legal areas. I wish that I could express how much this recognition meant to me, but, as I told some of the members, I hope that I taught them correctly because they are now working in the oil and gas business throughout the area.

CASEBOOK SYSTEM COMPLAINT

THIS IS as good a place as any to make a complaint and to record a confession. I presume law schools are still using the "casebook system." The casebook will contain nothing but cases in the particular area of law, for example, constitutional law, contracts, etc. At the end of the case, or usually excerpts from it, are questions for discussion (usually a handbook with the answers is available to teachers). From these cases, I suppose the student is supposed to learn the rules of law applicable to the particular area—and to learn them by inductive reasoning? Maybe I am wrong about this, but I never could perceive how the hapless student was supposed to learn this way. Well, I did not do this for my Oil and Gas Law class. My predecessor had told me that he used a "Hornbook" on oil and gas law, which is truly excellent. For years, every oil and gas lawyer I knew had a copy of Hemingway's *The Law of Oil and Gas* in the lawyer's office. The book gave the students a firm foundation in the basics of oil and gas law. Sometimes when a prospective employer would call me to ask about a graduate, I could say: "He (or she) has studied the 505 pages of Hemingway," and the caller would always be pleased to get a new graduate who knew the "basics."

WE WERE ALL ALWAYS HUNGRY;
A STUDY IN MEANNESS

MY STUDENTS were always a delight. They sacrificed heavily to attend law school and were truly grateful to have the law that I was teaching laid out "cold" for them. I learned more about my students when chatting during our first hour's fifteen-minute break. Every classroom had a sign prohibiting any food or drink. I never enforced the rule, because the floor was just cement that had become stained and spotted, and my class was hungry. And to be honest, I was also hungry. I never objected, but one year was very difficult for me, because a student in the front row seated almost directly in front of me always came with a really delicious looking hamburger that he happily munched as I lectured.

I also learned new lessons in meanness. As I was leaving the classroom one evening, I walked past one student still there with his head down on the desk. I wondered if he were sick or asleep, so I stopped to make sure that he was all right. He lifted a tear-stained, weary face. When I asked what was wrong, the sad tale poured out. He was a law clerk to a state district court judge, and his classes were on Tuesday and Thursday evening. Every Tuesday and Thursday only, the judge would keep him for unpaid overtime, so that he would miss the first half-hour or more of class, which was my class. I told him not to worry, that I could give him notes for what he missed. I also gave him my home telephone number and told him to be sure and call me for anything he didn't understand. A painting of his face could have been titled "Gratitude."

For many years, the law school was downtown and then moved from its downtown building to east Denver. On the way to either location, I drove past supermarkets with excellent delicatessens. For the last day of class, which was a review session, I would stop at the market to pick up my previously ordered sandwich plate—a very large plastic platter heaped with different kinds of sandwiches guaranteed to feed the number that I needed. Next, I would get cans of mixed nuts (no peanuts), paper plates and cups, and the store would put all this in the trunk of my car. Then I would stop at a nearby liquor store to get some acceptable bulk wine. The feast was always greeted with much appetite and appreciation. Not a crumb or a nut or a drop of wine would be left and, oh, the joy when at the outset I gave several of the men the keys to my car and sent them to get the food.

Just one more memory of my Oil and Gas classes. Well, really two of them. One class presented me with a gift draped in a white cloth. When I whisked

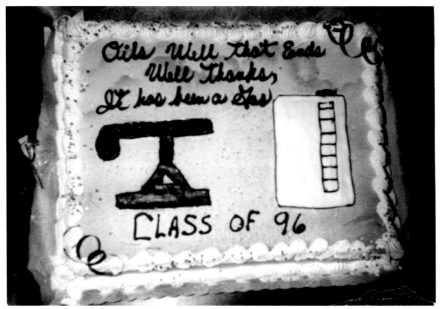

Figure 2.33. Cake inscribed for Brooke from her DU Law Oil & Gas Law class of 1996.

it off, I had a sixteen-inch-high replica of an old oil drilling rig. One student's father was an old-time oil man in Oklahoma, who had informed his son that I would enjoy this gift. Indeed, I do, and it lives near me in my now home office. The other memory is another last night of review and feasting. I digress to tell you that I could not teach without some quotation from Shakespeare, who was so often relevant. On this particular occasion for Last Night of Class, when I came to the classroom, it was guarded by two of my students. Then the door opened, and a student's head popped out saying, admittedly rudely, "She can't come in yet." The door shut. A minute or two later, the door opened and "She can come in now." On the table next to the podium was a very large sheet cake so that everyone in the class could have a piece. On the cake, between icing images of an oil well pumper and a storage tank with ladder, the icing inscribed the following lines:

> Oils Well that Ends Well
> Thanks,
> It has been a Gas.
> Class of '96

CONSTITUTIONAL LAW

BEFORE THE law school moved to east Denver, and was still in its downtown building, I was asked to teach Constitutional Law as an "emergency." The law school had a scheduling problem for the course, and yet the Bar examination then always had a constitutional law essay question. I had become known for my appellate work in both civil and criminal appeals, had received very favorable evaluations for my prior teaching, and so I seemed an acceptable choice.

When I first met my Constitutional Law class, I was appalled. They were a hostile group, who had all petitioned the school to make Constitutional Law available before they graduated—and they all were entering their senior year. They called themselves the "Trailer Class." So here we all were, cold and hungry, the students with a substitute professor in answer to their petitions, and me, their only choice for the substitute professor.

All turned out well, however. I had long had a passion for constitutional law and had truly enjoyed the appeals I had handled that involved constitutional law questions. So teaching it was a pleasure for me. The students, after working all day, missed having dinner. To appease their hunger, some bought a burrito out of a machine in the building. In that hot building, they would munch the poor small, cold, greenish burritos, which I found an appetite depressant. To this day, I cannot comfortably face a burrito.

The summer quarter proved to be exceptionally hot, and I told the class that they need not wear all their work clothes to class. First to go were the neckties, and it seemed to me that they all wore less and less until finally I warned: "No more clothes come off!" They were a good class, eager to learn, coupled with ability. I made sure that we studied the United States Supreme Court cases, which I thought were important and so did the Bar examiners that year.

The last session of my Constitutional Law class is memorable, even after many years. The class had made arrangements for a singing telegram and written poems for the singer's lyrics. The singer was an attractive young woman, about six feet tall, dressed as a bumble bee. Tears came to my eyes while I smiled from one ear to the other as the bumble bee put her arm around my shoulder and sang the poems that the students had written in my honor.

I will detour here to tell you a result of my teaching a class in constitutional law at the Denver police training academy—an experiment of the police chief and district attorney. One Saturday morning, driving an empty but major boulevard, I made a U-turn for a parking spot. A young motorcycle officer, siren blaring, stopped me. When he came to my car window, he recognized me and repeatedly said, "You taught me constitutional law. But you made a U-turn!" The fifth time he said it, I again apologized and then said, "There is nothing unconstitutional about a U-Turn." Whereupon, he smiled, said "Oh," refused to give me a ticket, and left.

FOND MEMORIES

BEFORE THE law school left downtown Denver, I sometimes took the bus home after teaching because my vision was not the best for night driving. When my class found out, a student who did not have a second class that night would walk me past the city park, with its dubious habitués, to the bus stop and wait to put me on it. One night as the bus stopped on its way down Broadway, a waitress still in uniform got on. She was apparently a regular rider as were some of the rather rough looking passengers on the bus, who greeted her. Soon she stood up, faced them, and said, "Fellows, you gotta go to that art museum [which was then about a block away from us]. They got a special show with the purtiest pitchers [*sic*] you ever seen. They are so purty! And it costs only a dollar to get in and see the show." She was talking about the beautiful Baron von Thyssen special exhibit that people had been coming by busload from southern Wyoming and western Nebraska to see—and yes, the waitress was right. And as I listened to her praise and saw her tired face light up, I felt a surge of appreciation for how great art enhances our lives.

The law school moved to its new building in 1984. I was delighted, because the school was less than a fifteen minutes' drive from my home, and I would have a warm winter quarter of teaching. Wrong! The drive was fine, but I wanted to meet whoever signed the completion certificate for that new building. The heating system did not work, and I taught my first class in there wearing a fur coat over my wool office suit. The building's problems did not, however, interfere with a wonderful class of students; and as always, I enjoyed teaching Oil and Gas Law, which is a blend of contract law and real property law together with a common law developed during years of petroleum industry operations.

I shall spare the Reader recounting more fond memories. Instead, I shall go to a new venture in my teaching career.

FUTURE INTERESTS FOR TWELVE YEARS:
REPUTED AS A MOST DIFFICULT COURSE

THE ASSISTANT dean, James Wallace, had always been helpful and consider-
ate to me. When he asked me to teach a second course, which meant I would
be teaching two semesters (no more quarters) a year, from September to May,
I could not say "No." The problem was that the school had no one to teach
Future Interests the next semester. Would I teach it for a year? Hah! It was
twelve—yes, twelve—years before another teacher was found.

Future Interests, which is a combination of advanced trust law and real
property law, had long had the dubious reputation of being one of the two
most difficult courses in law school, the other being Conflict of Laws. I had
always really liked this area of law, undoubtedly because of my law school
professor. Professor Simes was the author of the definitive book about Future
Interests, a large, grim-looking, black-bound volume. He was teaching only
for the summer when I had him as a professor: old, white-haired, and fragile in appearance. At the outset of the class, a small one because the course
was a dreaded elective, he said, "I believe that by the end of this course, all of
you will have come to really care about Future Interests." I'm sure that we all
mentally sniffed at that prospect, but he was right as far as I was concerned.
He had the gift of making all the rules and principles so lucid that you never
realized how complex it all was. Anyway, I agreed to teach Future Interests,
and although an additional burden on my time and energy, I found it a worth-
while project.

My Future Interests students and I got along fine. To begin with, I used two
paperback books for texts, saving the students the ever-increasing high costs of
the large casebooks. One book, which we used first, was like an 8.5-by-11-inch
notebook, with illustrative diagrams which I called our "picture book." This
enabled me to teach my class basic real property law, which had not been adequately taught to them in that course, and to introduce the students to what
was to come. The other was a combination text and casebook, which had
endeared itself to me by having a pertinent cartoon from the *New Yorker* magazine for its frontispiece. Also helpful was my adjunct professor experience in
teaching fractions, which I had learned in the fourth grade, to my Oil and Gas
Law class—all of whom had a four-year undergraduate degree plus two years of
law school—and to whom fractions were a strange new world.

[COMPILER'S NOTE: My brief informal explanation of the term "future interests" for the non-lawyer Reader: a future interest is the right to possess property in the future; topics involve estates, wills, trusts; entire or fractional future interests for ownerships of properties versus present interests for ownerships.]

Rule against Perpetuities and the Fertile Octogenarian Rule

ONE LAST paragraph about Future Interests. This is the source of the famous or infamous, depending on your point of view, Rule against Perpetuities. Here is the venerable Rule against Perpetuities: "No interest is good unless it must vest, if at all, within twenty-one years after the death of a life in being at the time of the creation of the interest." Correct application of this rule is essential for the competent estate planning counsel, commercial real estate lawyer, and personal bankruptcy lawyer, to name a few areas. Another venerable rule is known as the Fertile Octogenarian Rule, which declares there is a conclusive presumption that a man is always able to father children, no matter how old he is. The class never had trouble with this rule, and no student ever missed it in answering an examination question, no matter how subtly I thought it concealed. And a final memory of teaching Future Interests is when the class proudly presented me with a scarlet T-shirt that had emblazoned on its back in large black letters "Fertile Octogenarians." Imagine the puzzlement of my neighbors when I worked in my front garden wearing that garment!

Figure 2.34. The cartooned T-shirt inscribed "Fertile Octogenarians," a unique gift to Brooke from one of her DU Law classes in Future Interests.

TEACHING EMERGENCY CLASSES FOR THE LAW SCHOOL

DURING MY twenty years of teaching law in the evenings, I taught several summer seminars on the law of western coal, which is different from that of eastern coal law in many respects. I had talented students in these seminars, including several with substantial experience working for coal companies.

Real Property: Their Professor's Social Life Was Too Busy!

THE LAW school asked me to teach one-half of the first-year law school students the basic first-year Real Property Law course. I had taught the Bar Refresher course in real property law, so this was no chore, and I enjoyed the first-year students. For the other one-half of the students, the school had found someone who proved to be a poor choice. She was a young lawyer, with apparently an active social life, who would greet the students with a sign on the classroom door such as "No class tonight. Had a dinner party." So the "other one-half" started coming to my class, and the then dean complained to me, wanting me to take roll and tell the "Abandoned Students" to leave! Here, nicely put, is the substance of my response: "Forget it." And so we finished one large class, and for years I kept in the top drawer of my office desk the card that had accompanied the beautiful bouquet the first-year real property law class sent me, which read: "To the best ever Real Property Law teacher."

Flowers and Chivas Regal for Pinch-Hitting on Real Property Law

I TAUGHT one more time in an emergency. The assistant dean called me to say, "Brooke, we need your help. And we will really pay you well!" I didn't believe the promise about remuneration. All the adjuncts, including me, taught for the love of the law and of teaching eager young students. This time, however, I was astounded by the promised compensation. The school had assigned a regular faculty member who had never practiced or taught real property law to teach this required first-year course. The result was that two groups of the class, which together was 100 percent of them, had petitioned the dean for a special review class, complaining that they had learned nothing about the subject. I responded that I thought the law school had always had graduate students do these review sessions. "Not this one. We have a very serious problem. Please help us—even four Saturday morning sessions will do." I had the annual supplement due soon to the publisher of one of my law books, then in its second edition (and now in its third). So I replied that I could squeeze only three sessions into my schedule, and we settled for that.

When I arrived for the first session, I was shocked. The two groups had met to mark the items in the table of contents to their casebook where they needed help, and they had concluded that they needed help on "everything." Portable PCs had now arrived, and extension cords were draped all over the steps that I had to walk down to reach the teaching podium.

The students were correct—they seemed to have learned virtually nothing. So, for three consecutive Saturday mornings from 9:00 a.m. until noon (no breaks), the classroom was a model of diligence. I lectured, and they feverishly took notes.

When I arrived on the last Saturday morning, a gift of flowers was on the table in front of the podium. The flowers were in a very large arrangement and looked to be in the shape of a casket piece. As I walked down the steps, treading carefully over cords, the class kept calling, "Look on the other side of the podium." So when I came to the podium, at its back was an extremely large bottle. I did not know that Chivas Regal came in a bottle so large that it had a handle. I was overwhelmed by the gifts of flowers and scotch. Then a spokesman for the class said that they had talked to my Oil and Gas Law class and learned that when I got home about 8:30 p.m. from teaching, and after practicing law all day, I enjoyed one scotch-and-soda before my supper, which my dear daughter would have prepared for me. It took three of the young men to carry the flowers and the scotch to my car after our class.

ABOUT TEACHING LAW

THE TIME came when, because of my age, I knew that I should no longer teach. I told the law school of my intent and that I would wait until I received my evaluations for the class that I was then teaching. When I received the evaluations and discussed my resignation with the dean, he said that my evaluations were always enthusiastically favorable. I replied that for this I was grateful, because then I could retire with peace of mind.

I conclude with a few comments about teaching law.

First and foremost, I love the law and enjoyed sharing basic knowledge of the law with the fine young people I had as students. I always added some ethics into my lecture, trying to instill a firm commitment to the honorable pursuit of our profession.

Second, I never taught that also I did not learn. I updated my information before each lecture to make sure that I was teaching the current law. I had heard tales of yellowed lecture notes and had professors like that when I was in school. Not mine—my information was up to date.

Third, the young students brought much joy to my life. I still miss them and always shall.

For years, when walking down the street on my way to or from lunch, someone would put their arms around my neck from behind and say: "Professor, I

UNIVERSITY of DENVER

College of Law
Office of the Dean

September 5, 1997

Brooke Wunnicke
Hall & Evans, LLC
1200 Seventeenth Street Suite 1700
Denver, Colorado 80202-5800

Dear Professor Wunnicke:

It is with great pleasure that I inform you of your designation as the 1997 Frank H. Ricketson, Jr. Adjunct Professor of Law (fall semester). This honor has been created to recognize the valuable contributions made by the adjunct faculty at the University of Denver College of Law, and carries with it a $500 honorarium. You have been chosen as the first recipient of this award in recognition of not just your many, many years of teaching, but also the love and respect your students have expressed for you, consistently and perennially.

Please be our guest of honor for the presentation of this award at a faculty luncheon on October 8, 1997, at 12:00 noon in the Hart Faculty Forum.

Feel free to call me or my assistant, Susan Murphy-Jacobs, if we can be of assistance to you in any way. I am delighted to be able to participate in honoring you in this way.

Very truly yours,

Sheila K. Hyatt

Sheila K. Hyatt
Associate Dean for
    Academic Affairs
(303) 871-6105
(303) 871-6378 fax

cc: Dean Robert Yegge

Figure 2.35. University of Denver College of Law letter dated September 5, 1997, to Brooke informing her that she is the first recipient of the Frank H. Ricketson Jr. Adjunct Professor of Law, "in recognition of . . . the love and respect your students have expressed for you."

was in your (naming the class) and shall always be grateful to you." And then delight would overcome my regret at no longer being physically frisky enough to teach.

My student evaluations always warmed my ego . . . the one I always liked best said "Get rid of the dean but keep this professor!" The dean at that time was one about whom I agreed with the student—get rid of him.

POSITIVE AND NEGATIVE COMMENTS ABOUT THE PROFESSOR:

Professor W. is always prepared and interested in the course material. What's more, she's A REAL ATTORNEY. Imagine that? There is hope for D.U. after all, if they're smart enough to hire someone who is in the practice. Good course.

One of the most professional proffesors I ever had in 3 yrs —
   knowledgable, gives both practical and acedemic information
      thoroughly enjoyed the class —

- SHARP AS A TACK
- VERY NICE
- MADE A DULL SUBJECT VERY INTERESTING

One of the nicest ladies I've ever met.

Figure 2.36. Brooke was an awarded Adjunct Professor of Law from 1977 to 1997 at the University of Denver College of Law. In the 1990s, the law school sent her some evaluations from students in her classes about oil and gas law and the law of future interests.

Books

INVITED TO WRITE

This is a short discussion but is about a vital part of my professional life. By the early 1980s in both Colorado and elsewhere, I had become rather widely known in legal circles for my ethics lectures. I tell you more about the importance of ethics and my lectures in the following discussions.

"SHE! SHE! I DIDN'T KNOW BROOKE WUNNICKE WAS A WOMAN!"

ONE DAY at my office my secretary came to me and said, "Brooke, I have a call you need to make, and I'm so afraid I might have done something to hurt your opportunity." I said, "What happened, who called?" She told me: "This man asked for you, and I asked, 'May I say who's calling?' He gave his name and said I'm with the publishing company John Wiley & Sons. I said, 'I'm sorry, sir, she's on the other telephone. If you give me your number, she will call you. Brooke, he said, 'She! She! I didn't know Brooke Wunnicke was *a woman*!' I didn't know what to answer but anyway, here's his number."

So, I telephoned, and in a very chilly voice he made a date to have lunch with me in Denver. We met, and he said, "We have had several lawyers contact us saying that we should get you to write a book for us on legal ethics. We did not know that you were a woman, and we have never published a woman author." I was then quite ignorant of law book publishers and said, "How long

175

has your publishing company been in business?" He replied, "Our company published the first American edition of James Fenimore Cooper's *The Last of the Mohicans*." Me: "Oh." So, I agreed to do a book for them and frankly was so flattered that I would have agreed to write one on pornography.

LEARNING TO TYPE, AND MY FIRST PC

NOW I must digress. I had never learned to type, and a personal computer was to me some weird invention that had no part in my life. When the publisher sent me the Author's Questionnaire, one of the questions was, "Will you be writing this book on a computer?" I whooped with laughter as I read it to my daughter, and she replied firmly, "Write yes." That made all the difference in my life as a lawyer. It added decades to how long I was able to practice law and enabled me to write lectures, articles, and books even as I grew old. But learning to type was not easy. So, one day at home I started, while my daughter trimmed a hedge and fielded questions outside the window where I was teaching myself to type and to use a PC. All I remember of this period was that I was a slow learner and recall saying to her that I would buy her a new "delete" key for her PC.

ETHICS COMPLIANCE FOR BUSINESS LAWYERS, 1987

FINALLY, MY first book was completed: *Ethics Compliance for Business Lawyers*, published by John Wiley & Sons, Wiley Law, in 1987. Five years later, the Wyoming Supreme Court stated in *Bowen v. Smith*, 838 P.2d 186, 195 (Wyo. 1992): "Likely the most practical and definitive resource regarding ethical requirements of business lawyers is provided by Brooke Wunnicke, *Ethics Compliance for Business Lawyers* (1987)."

STANDBY AND COMMERCIAL LETTERS OF CREDIT, 1989 TO 2013

A YEAR went by and again Wiley Law called me. They told me my book was so well written and well received, would I like to write another book for them. About that time, my daughter had involved me, because of her corporate finance work, in issues of the then burgeoning use of standby letters of credit. I had been trying to be helpful for about two years, and I learned more and more about standby letters of credit. So, I recall these circumstances plainly. My daughter told me about a call she had received from a large Canadian bank about her help on letters of credit and calls from other prestigious banks because her name was becoming known in the area of standby letters of credit. Then, the day came when she told me about a small European bank that had called her for assistance on that topic and, something snapped in me. I said, "We should be getting paid for all this advice we're giving about law and business practice with respect to standby letters of credit." Thus was born in 1989 the first edition of our joint book about letters of credit, which eventually grew into its third edition of 1,400 loose-leaf pages. We annually supplemented this tome for twenty-three years, then looked at each other and said, "Enough is enough."

LEGAL OPINION LETTERS FORMBOOK, 1994–2011

OUR LETTERS of credit book was doing very well when Wiley Law asked me to be the editor and to write a book on the rapidly developing separate area of legal opinion practice. Again, I was easily flattered but said that I didn't think I was the right person. I thought this book needed to have one of the eastern business lawyers write it because they were the ones who were giving most of these opinions. Wiley Law said, "But you are so well known, Brooke." I said, "Yes, here in Colorado and Wyoming where we'd be lucky to sell a dozen copies of the book." Then they asked if I would consider doing it with an eastern lawyer, and that was irresistible. Thereby hangs a happy tale.

I searched a big legal directory and found the list of names I would consider, three of them; but my first choice was a man named A. Sidney Holderness Jr. I notified Wiley Law of my choice and said I do not know him, but his experience and credentials were splendid for the tasks for this book. And the publisher said it would send a representative to meet him and ask him to join me. The publisher reported that the meeting went well and that Sidney would call me. One, two, three, four weeks went by without a call. With his Ivy League background I thought he would have the courtesy of calling me eventually, which he did. In the conversation the reason for his delay became obvious. He was a senior partner in a major Wall Street firm where he had practiced for thirty years. He said that he had never worked with a woman lawyer. I responded that his friends need not know, because my first name was ambivalent. So, on this basis, began a devoted professional and personal friendship that survived until his untimely death in 2010.

I had business that took me to New York City and made arrangements to meet Sidney for the first time one evening while I was there on my short trip. When he came in the restaurant, I was a bit surprised, because he was so very tall. He was six foot five inches, and I only five foot one inch. Although I, a westerner, and he, a New Yorker, we were sympatico from the first meeting. He took me to meet his lady friend at her apartment, and Sidney and I visited until two o'clock in the morning. Our book *Legal Opinion Letters Formbook* went into three editions; the title was purchased by Wolters Kluwer Law and Business for its second and third editions. And, again, I was confronted with annual supplements.

Pleasurable for you, I hope, is from a dear friend of Sidney's who, on an airplane, started to review the third edition of our book, found it fun, and some of his comments here follow. Enjoying my Chapter 2's "Basics of Writing," he comments on some quotations' sources, being from books in our family library that I used for my writings, lectures, and remarks.

> Now let me turn to the fun side of the book. The book opens with a
> French phrase. From there, to make its points, it draws on Confucius,
> Oliver Wendell Holmes, Little Johnny Possum, James Madison,
> Lord Chesterfield, Blackstone, Sir Francis Bacon, Quintus Horatius
> Flaccus [aka Horace] and Justice Cardozo, most of them in the first
> twenty pages! I began to read this book on an airplane. By page 26 I
> was chuckling to myself (well, not quite to myself!)—pages 26 and 27
> dealing with Words and Phrases to Avoid. The man next to me asked
> what I found so funny in this rather hefty tome. When he saw it was
> a book on legal opinions I was laughing about, he edged a bit further
> away in his seat. But the grace of this book is that the authors have
> approached a subject often written about in rather pedantic tones, in a
> light-hearted manner.

The "Basics of Writing" includes my "A,B,C's, Accuracy, Brevity, and Clarity." In comments about writing correctly, hoping a bit of humor might attract readers, included is a list of the "Substitutes: The 'Chain Gang' and Other Abominable Phrases." I enjoyed writing the books. There is something

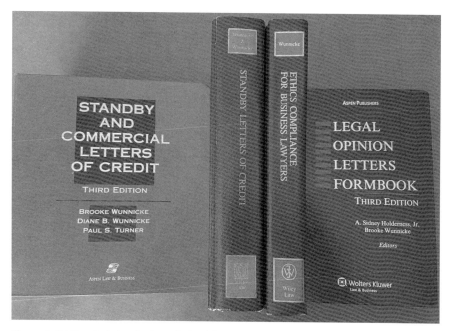

Figure 2.37. Brooke's books, heavily hard-bound by the publishers, to be permanent.

about sharing knowledge about certain areas of learning that is gratifying, because you feel useful.

Then, I decided to write this book, because I have so much to share about the inside workings of the legal system. Also, I wanted to share a few short essays about the rule of law and ethics, that are in Part Three of this book.

Legal Ethics
NATIONAL LECTURER

HOW DID IT START?

A s AN introductory note, I became a national lecturer on legal ethics. How did it all start? I was busy as a practicing lawyer when in 1978 I received a telephone call from a prominent patent lawyer, whom I did not know personally. He asked me if I would be willing to be a lecturer on legal ethics for his organization, The International Practicum Institute (IPI). I had never thought about speaking on this topic and was curious why he called me. He replied that his IPI partner was assistant dean of the University of Denver College of Law where I taught as an adjunct professor in its evening division. The assistant dean had suggested contacting me because he had been impressed by my student evaluations, which always warmed my ego. (Examples: "Professor Wunnicke is both inspirational and delightful" and "Brooke rocks!") I checked: the patent lawyer was nationally rated very highly, and the assistant dean was a retired general in the Air Force who had been on the faculty of the Air Force Academy when he retired. So, I said yes, I would be pleased to do an ethics lecture. When they gave me the details, I was very surprised, because the lecture was scheduled to be two hours long. The Reader should know that the lecture had to be accredited by the Colorado state judicial department for the mandatory Continuing Legal Education (CLE) requirements. That's how thirty years of these lectures all began.

My first lecture went well. It was a topic, more than a topic, in which I had always been interested and about which I deeply cared. I still do. Today, I have seen the legal profession complete a total change from what it was when I started to practice, and now it is driven by the "bottom line." I know lawyers, who are financially successful, who never violated an ethics rule but practiced with their toes on the borderline of ethical practice. Fortunately, I know the majority who practice in obedience to both our rules and the spirit of those rules.

RULES, RULES, RULES

WHAT ARE the rules of ethics that lawyers are supposed to obey? The history of formal rules for lawyers nationwide begins in 1908 when the American Bar Association adopted the Canons of Professional Ethics. Please note that "Canons" is spelled in the middle with one "n," not two. The Canons were few in number but were deemed adequate for sixty-one years. They were the rules in effect when I began the practice of law and always governed me because I think they embodied the spirit of true ethical practice. In 1969, the American Bar Association responded to requests from many at the Bar to adopt more "modern" rules of ethics. The result was the Code of Professional Responsibility, much longer and more detailed than the previous Canons. Each rule had a "DR," Disciplinary Rule, or several DRs, which mandated certain conduct. In addition, each rule had an "EC," Ethical Consideration. These Ethical Considerations were not mandatory but were deemed "inspirational." The Code did not last as long as the Canons. Instead, only fourteen years later in 1983, the American Bar Association adopted our current *Model Rules of Professional Conduct* that govern ethics by lawyers, which have been continually amended but not yet replaced in total. These American Bar Association rules of ethics—Canons, Codes, and Rules—have been adopted by all the states, some with substantial differences such as California.

WHY THE LECTURES WERE POPULAR

ANY LECTURE on legal ethics would be, in my opinion, doomed to failure if it tried to cover all the rules. Instead, I recommend doing what I did: speaking about those that are surprising, difficult, or most frequently encountered. I always began with Rule 1.1 and its first sentence: "A lawyer shall provide competent representation to a client." I always included in my classes as an adjunct professor, whether Oil and Gas Law or Future Interests, this sentence as the very first rule. *I never failed having several students say, "I didn't not know that competence had anything to do with ethics."* I believe that there are also lawyers out there that do not know competence is an integral part of legal ethics.

The next rule on which I would elaborate is the rule governing confidentiality, Rule 1.6, governing communications between lawyer and client. There are a number of subsections to this rule and a number of situations in which determining whether confidentiality would be violated or compromised unethically. Resolution of these problems is not easy.

The next Rule, 1.7, addresses the most pervasive of all ethical problems that a lawyer and a law firm confront: the prohibition against representing conflicting interests. Will this proposed defense violate the Rule against conflicting interests? Will a major witness be ineligible to use because it would engender conflict? And if opposing counsel decides to call that witness, will the conflicted lawyer have to withdraw as counsel? Some law firms have senior members who serve the firm also as experts on determining whether a forbidden conflict would occur if the firm were to accept a representation. This was a major problem that I addressed during my lecture. I tried to be as helpful as possible in helping the lawyers in attendance to deal with the "conflicts" problem.

SNAKE SKINS

SO MANY years, so many *conflict of interest* problems! I could recount many instances and situations where a conflict of interest occurred. I should stress here that determining whether an impermissible conflict would occur in a representation is often not an easy decision. So rather than burdening the Reader with a series of examples, I shall close this portion with just one example that occurred late in my years of practice. I was now Of Counsel in a law firm and in that capacity already a step into retirement, when one of the law firm's senior and able lawyers came to my office. He asked if I would be willing to do a trial court brief for him and his co-counsel, who was another fine, able senior lawyer in the firm. The lawyer said to me that opposing counsel had such a shocking conflict of interest that they just could not trust themselves to respond to it. Here were the facts. A lawsuit was filed by a company, naming three other companies as defendants. It was a bad case to defend, and our two lawyers represented only one of the three defendants, whom I shall here call "C." The other two defendants, "A" and "B," were defended by a New York City law firm. While the suit was ongoing, plaintiff's lawyer merged with the New York City law firm that was defending A and B. Plaintiff had an excellent claim which could produce a large fee for plaintiff's lawyer. The New York City firm decided it would rather represent plaintiff than A and B. That firm had represented A for almost twenty years in all its corporate affairs requiring legal services. That firm was also then representing B in another ongoing lawsuit. The New York City firm was not deterred by these facts. It wrote to A stating that it terminated its lawyer-client relationship. It wrote to B stating that it was withdrawing as its lawyer in the other lawsuit and that B would have to find other counsel. The conflict was obvious because it gave plaintiff direct access to all the inner workings of A and B. So, I wrote a short trial brief, and I stated in that brief: "In Colorado, lawyers do not shed their clients like snakes do their skins."

The trial judge liked that, apparently, and quoted that several times in his ruling that the New York City law firm needed to withdraw as plaintiff's counsel because of conflict of interest. Our counsel reported to me that the plaintiff's lawyers were furious. I was proud of the court for its firm and appropriate stance.

ETHICS LECTURES HITHER AND YON

I WAS gratified that my ethics lectures were always well attended. In Colorado for many years (1979–2002), I gave two two-hour lectures every autumn as lawyers realized that year-end was approaching, and they had to meet their annual Continuing Legal Education (CLE) ethics requirement. I was surprised when I learned that I was being dubbed "the conscience of the Bar." My surprise was changed to pride that I had been able to fulfill my purpose. I thought it important, and still do, not only to know the rules of ethics that govern us but also to be aware and take care to practice in accord with the highest principles of serving as a lawyer. This involves more than honesty but complete integrity in the service and, sometimes, requires not being able to give first place to the "bottom line." I was very pleased when I was invited to speak to lawyers on ethics in several other places. These included Chicago, Boston, Mississippi (several times), New Orleans, West Virginia, Iowa, Oregon, New Mexico, Arizona, Utah, San Francisco, and Coronado, California. I enjoyed everywhere I went and every group of lawyers to whom I had the pleasure of speaking.

Of course, when you go different places, the sleeping accommodations were always excellent, but this was not always true of the speaking accommodations! Scares for me were temporary platforms that shook and wobbled under my feet; I had several memorable incidents. And I could write an essay on sick and unreliable microphones. Those early microphones would sometimes whistle at you or echo you, blare at the audience, or turn themselves off. I believe those microphones of the early years had independent lives filled with devilish mischief. Often, I would just turn off the microphone and speak with enough volume for the audience to hear easily. This was also handy when arguing motions or trying cases in a state that had no microphones and poor acoustics in the courtrooms. I am reminded of my early case in Rawlins, Wyoming, with trucks changing gears on the hill near the courthouse when a juror commented that I was the only speaker they had heard throughout the trial.

I should confess that one of my faults is a lifelong dislike of getting up early. I was scheduled to be the ethics speaker on the second day in a conference in the East, and I had rashly said that any time would be acceptable. When I got there, the printed program listed my speech as starting the day at eight o'clock in the morning. And I can remember like yesterday greeting the audience at the same moment realizing that it was 6:00 a.m. in my home.

"THERE'S A MAN'S HAND GROPING MY FOOT"

TO GET an audience's undivided attention, here's an amusing incident I would share. I stood up to address on ethics 350-plus lawyers in a nice resort and realized that I only knew one lawyer there. As I began to speak, I felt something crawling as it seemed on my left foot. It became more irritating, and I never before had foot trouble. So, I was frank and said to the audience, "Something's going on with my foot and I'm going to bend down and check it out." When I bent down, as was usual there had been a curtain put around the bottom of the speaker's stand and crouched under there was a young man with a huge hand groping my foot. I stood up and said to the audience, "There's a man's large hand groping my foot. I'm going to bend down again to check it out." I bent down and met the anguished face of a young man who said, "I was trying to keep you from tripping on the wires." I stood up and would you believe that I had the undivided attention of everyone in that audience? I bent down and said to the young man, "I'm fine. Come out, and I'll help you leave." Out he crawled, all six-foot-plus of him, and I said to the audience, "He was trying to keep me safe, so let's give him a hand." So I clapped, and they clapped; and, of course his closest exit was locked. The poor young fellow had to walk the full length of the auditorium to the back, and we applauded him the whole way. The day I left, I ran into him. He said, "Goodbye. I'll never forget you." I never have known what he meant—plus or minus?

ALWAYS PACK A DRESSING GOWN OR ROBE

A MEMORABLE lecture trip was to speak at a lawyers' conference in Phoenix, Arizona, inexplicably scheduled for July, when very hot. I gave my all in the lecture where I spoke loudly enough to drown the noise of the air conditioning, and all went well. My hosts had booked me into a fine new garden motel where the rooms were on the second floor surrounding a courtyard filled with flowers and a beautiful fountain splashing in the middle. When I went to bed, I thought I'll never sleep over that loud noise from the air conditioning—this was all a long time ago. I had neglected to pack a dressing gown, but I thought no one knows me, I'll just slip out and lean over the railing above that beautiful fountain and be cool. So, out I traipsed in my nightgown, and it was lovely to see the fountain, leaning over the railing and being content, when a man's voice said, "Aren't you our speaker today?" I thought, "On no, this cannot be!" I looked to my right and there is a man, and he doesn't look too great either. He's wearing a pair of boxer shorts. We looked at each other and then both laughed and had a bit of chat and then retired to the humdrum racket of our respective air conditioners.

SIR FRANCES BACON AND SHAKESPEARE

I SHOULD also confess that I tried in my every lecture on ethics to awaken or renew a spirit of respect for ethics and its largest sense in each lawyer who was present. I ended my lectures with quoting the words of Sir Francis Bacon, as first published in 1630. I only alter the words to include women lawyers:

> I hold every lawyer a debtor to the lawyer's profession, from the which, as lawyers of course do seek to receive . . . profit, so ought they of duty to endeavor themselves by way of amends to be a help and ornament thereunto; this is performed in some degree, by the honest and liberal practice of a profession, when lawyers shall carry a respect not to

descend unto any court that is corrupt, and unworthy thereof, and preserve themselves free from the abuses wherewith the same profession is noted to be infected; but much more is this performed, if a lawyer be able to visit and strengthen the roots and foundation of the science itself, thereby not only gracing it in reputation and dignity, but also amplifying it in perfection and substance.

My legal ethics lectures always included my following personal testament, which because of its importance to me, I will deliberately elsewhere repeat in this book.

If what I have been saying seems to be a preachment, I apologize. The feeling that fills my heart is that somehow I can re-kindle in each of our hearts an inextinguishable fire to be always dedicated lawyers: lawyers who serve your clients with skill and integrity; lawyers who promote and protect a sound legal system and the rule of law so that law cannot end nor tyranny begin in the United States of America.

And then my very last words to them were my wedding present from my parents when I eloped at the ending phase of the Great Depression, with priceless words paraphrased from William Shakespeare, *Hamlet*, Act 1, Sc. 3: "Do what thou hast to do and to thine own self be true."

I Am Not
"Goody Two Shoes"

AN ATTORNEY CONFRONTED BY CHILD ABUSE

Who was Goody Two Shoes? She was the heroine of a 1765 nursery tale who was cloyingly virtuous in a sentimental way. The following is relevant to the fact that for many years, after I moved to Colorado, I was a lecturer to lawyers on professional ethics, speaking about ethics at national, state, and local seminars throughout the country. I've told you about this in my previous discussion, Legal Ethics: National Lecturer. This preface paragraph is necessary because I am going to share with you two events from earlier in my Wyoming legal career: one when I acted illegally, and the other when I deliberately gave clients illegal advice. As I look back over these events of very long ago, I ask whether I would behave the same today and unrepentant, I answer "Yes."

This all happened in a small Wyoming community of then about 30,000 at a time when almost all the local lawyers engaged in a general practice. And we were sought out for problems far removed from the sophisticated practices of most lawyers in large cities. Both events triggered my illegal conduct because I have a strong adverse reaction to child abuse.

One day when I had been practicing law for only several years, my secretary notified me that a woman had come in to see me and would not disclose any reason for her visit. When I invited the shabbily dressed woman into my office, she was very nervous, and she opened with: "Are you going to charge me for speaking to you?" I said "No, unless I take care of a particular legal problem you have." She said "No. That's not why I wanted to see you. I have something very bad to tell you about and thought that you, being the woman lawyer, would know what to do for the child." When I heard the word "child," my interest quickened. I then asked her to tell me about the problem with the child. She told me a memorably horrid tale. She lived on the south side of town, the then poor part of town, in an area with shack-like houses, where neighbors were very close together. In the house next to her lived a family of four: father and son, one young daughter, and the mother, an alcoholic. The father and twenty-two-year-old son frequently raped the little girl. I can recall the woman's nasal but earnest voice saying, "Mrs. Lawyer, it *'fare tares'* ['fair tears'] my heart when I hear the girl screaming and then hear her loud sobbing for a long time. My husband would be real mad if he knew I came to see you to tell about our neighbor, but I just had to." I assured her she owed me no money, and I would do something to protect the child, and her husband need never know that she came to see me.

When the woman left, I dutifully called the state welfare office (we had no local one) to report the matter and give the address. The welfare person was nice, thanked me for my interest in reporting the matter, and said that the department currently had a very busy case load. She said that the department would investigate the matter in a few weeks and report the findings to me. I thanked her, hung up, and called the chief of police.

Now, I knowingly digress briefly. Formerly, when I was still handling Police Court cases, the chief of police had been hostile to me as a woman attorney. Then one day, I received a ticket for parking too far away from the curb, and outraged, I called him directly to complain that if I had parked any closer to the curb, my car would have been badly stuck in the snow. I dared him to come park legally where I had been, and he would find out. He was fair because he called me later to say that he had taken the dare, been badly stuck, and told me to tear up that ticket. Since then, we had developed a mutual trust and respect. So I told the chief of police about the child, her abuse, and the welfare person's response of "weeks" until an "investigation" was undertaken. I said: "I thought that you would do something more quickly to protect her." He replied that he would go there right away and get the child, and I told him that I would defend him without charge if any trouble came from his taking the girl.

Good to his word, the chief of police called me later that day to report that the child was with his wife at their home, that they had no children, and she was very happy to love and take care of the girl. Then he told me that what he had walked into was not fit for me to hear and that the child would never be returned. Later, I terminated parental rights, under a statute that I had earlier drafted and lobbied for its passage. The little girl now had loving parents, later was a graduate of the University of Wyoming, married a good man, and lived in northern Wyoming. Yes, I knew then, as is still true today, that the chief of police acted illegally in bursting into the house without a warrant and taking the child. Yes, I would have defended him and insisted that he acted on legal advice. Yes, I knew then and know now that I acted both unethically and illegally—but know that if I had it to do over again, I would do the same.

The second event that my conscience causes me to disclose in writing is my expressly giving illegal advice. A young couple had called for an appointment with me about "an urgent legal matter." When they arrived, I thought them a very nice appearing young couple and waited to hear their legal problem. The young wife told me that it was her grave concern for her younger sister, and then told me a lurid tale of incest. She came from a small town in Wisconsin, and from the time that she had been thirteen years old, her father had been raping her. She said that her mother had never intervened and told me of her sufferings until she ran away at age seventeen. Her husband was aware of this incestuous background, had always been very understanding, and shared her concern for her young sister, who was now being subjected to the same incestuous abuse. Remembering the incident of some years ago, I suggested that she write her little sister to call the chief of police in her town. The young wife replied, "But our father is the Chief of Police." Oh, then write her to contact the judge in your town. Her eyes filled with tears, and she replied: "The judge is my uncle, my father's brother, and they are close." "How old is your little sister?" The reply was, "She just turned fifteen, and our father started raping her at thirteen, just like he did with me."

Then I deliberately gave illegal advice about protecting this young minor girl. I told her older sister that she could forward money for a bus ticket to Minneapolis which was not very distant from the small town where the younger sister lived, "Enclose money for the ticket and tell her to take a taxi from the bus depot to the Minneapolis airport." My client could buy an airline ticket for her younger sister to pick up and take a plane that then had a direct flight to Cheyenne, where she and her husband could meet her at the airport. Also, I asked if either of them had a friend or relative in a large city in the East, and the young husband said that he had a close friend in New York City. I then told them to have the little sister write a letter saying that she was fine, living with nice people, and no longer abused; enclose that letter to your friend in New York City, and ask him to post it from the main post office.

They left happy with a solution provided by a lawyer. This time, my lawyer's conscience hurt. By now, our district court had two judges, and the new one was a good man, who had been an excellent trial lawyer for many years, before his election. I called this judge (yes, in those days, one could call a judge directly) and asked if I could see him for a few minutes. As I walked to the courthouse, I mused that the judge and his wife had no children and wondered how he would react. He listened without comment as I told him about my advising unauthorized removal of a minor from her home and hiding her whereabouts. Then he said, "Brooke, I would have done the same thing that you did. If you have a problem come up, come see me and I'll back you up." I wish that he could know these many years later how I still remember and am grateful for his reassurance that I had given right, although illegal, advice to protect a defenseless young teen from cruel abuse.

A happy postscript: The young couple took the wife's younger sister into their home, sent her later to the University of Wyoming, and sent me a clipping of her picture and news story when she was named the university's Homecoming Queen.

I do not write a moral to this short discussion because I do not know what I could write. Maybe that is because there is no moral. Judge me as you will; I am grateful that I could protect those children.

[COMPILER'S NOTE: *In Brooke's files, further to the children in abusive situations, here is an excerpt of her February 19, 2004, email upon inquiry from a Wyoming State archivist about the 1950s and her being Executive Secretary of the Wyoming Youth Council:*]

When the Wyoming Youth Council was created, Wyoming was about the only state with no juvenile court system, which was then in the prime of its acceptance. The Council worked diligently on preparing a legislative draft which was enacted as Wyoming's first juvenile court law. Also, Wyoming had a practically non-existent procedure for terminating parental rights—a sad handicap when a child was in a very abusive situation. The Council drafted a proposed termination bill which was enacted.]

Wyoming Youth Council

April 1, 1960

Mrs. Brooke Wunnicke
Outgoing Executive Secretary
Wyoming Youth Council
Cheyenne, Wyoming

Dear Mrs. Wunnicke:

The members of the Wyoming Youth Council, as a group, and each of us individually, wish to extend to you at the time of your resignation from the
position of Executive Secretary, our sincere appreciation for your outstanding
service and devotion to Wyoming and its youth.

It is with deep personal regret that we accept your resignation. We feel your
hard work, sincerity, and everlasting optimism have done much both to improve
the position of the youth of Wyoming and to enable the Youth Council to continue on its road stronger and more secure in its statutory purpose.

It is the unanimous wish of the Wyoming Youth Council that a copy of this
letter be filed in the official archives of the State of Wyoming to memorialize your work in organizing, molding and perpetuating the Wyoming Youth
Council.

In testimony whereof, we, the members of the Wyoming Youth Council, have here-
unto subscribed our names.

WYOMING YOUTH COUNCIL

[signatures]

Figure 2.38. The April 1, 1960, letter of appreciation to Brooke signed by each of the Wyoming Youth Council's members, in part stating: "It is the unanimous wish of the Wyoming Youth Council that a copy of this letter be filed in the official archives of the State of Wyoming to memorialize your work in organizing, molding, and perpetuating the Wyoming Youth Council."

Ethics

ATTRIBUTES OF A GOOD LAWYER AND A GOOD CITIZEN

INTRODUCTION FROM THIS "LEGAL LEGEND"

D EAR READER: I hope that you will enjoy and consider what I still believe are the attributes of a good lawyer and helpful guidance to be a good citizen.

In 1981, I was invited to be the first woman speaker at the graduation ceremony of my law school alma mater, the University of Colorado School of Law. I include here a part of my remarks, what I consider the attributes of a good lawyer. Decades later, I make no change. I ask myself, "Have I learned nothing in the ensuing years or have these attributes remained the same?" Here, I boldly and unequivocally state that I still believe based upon my many years as a practicing lawyer, that my following summary sets forth the essential attributes of the good lawyer. And, my opinion is confirmed by the many years I have been asked to present these attributes as the core of my national and local lectures on ethics.

In 2011, by invitation from the Colorado Bar Association as its first "Legal Legend, A Fireside Chat," I presented my well-known lecture to a large audience and was widely seen statewide via the internet. Although at age ninety-three it was my last lecture, I still was gratified by another standing ovation for my presentation of these eight attributes and my personal testament and credos.

I still remember how I started the task of preparing my 1981 remarks, customarily written out by speakers for the law school's graduation ceremony. My goal was to be able to inspire the graduates to serve the legal profession with competence, integrity, and zeal for service to the law. I sat at my desk in the library at home and pondered: what had I learned over the years that made a good lawyer? I had known almost every conceivable type of lawyer, and now, based on substantial experience, what did I think made a good lawyer? So that is what I wrote about for my keynote address. When I was writing this book, I fished out of my files that 1981 graduation speech and reread it after all these years to find out whether it was quaint. Instead, what a pleasant surprise! My speech still reflects my fervent beliefs about the attributes of a good lawyer. Nonlawyers have commented that most of these attributes apply to all people who are "good."

This speech had become the core of my lectures locally and nationally, leading to many recognitions and awards, and being referred to a national publisher to write my first book, *Ethics Compliance for Business Lawyers*, published by Wiley Law in 1987. Reprinted here are my 1981 remarks, except the then statistics about legal malpractice that are now obsolete, although they continue to be woeful.

SPEECH: EIGHT ATTRIBUTES OF A GOOD LAWYER WITH PERSONAL TESTAMENT AND CREDOS

SPEECH TO UNIVERSITY OF COLORADO LAW SCHOOL 1981 GRADUATES

From: Brooke Wunnicke

Friends and Colleagues:

The honor and pleasant duty are mine to welcome these graduates to the legal profession. Congratulations to each of you who today received your juris doctor.[1] I confirm to your families and friends that yours is a hard-won achievement: beginning with the almost fatal LSAT and followed by years of intensive study, punctuated grimly with "final exams." Can you even estimate how many hundreds of cases and thousands of pages that you have read during your law school studies? Today marks the culmination of your years of labor. Today you have achieved the honored status of graduate lawyers.

What a signal and heartwarming honor to be asked by my alma mater to be the keynote speaker at law school graduation! Mine was the law class of 1945 which, to save you subtracting, was 36 years ago. With this honor, however, came worry, and my remarks to you have been difficult to prepare. What message could I give that would be worthy for you to hear on this great day in your lives?

I have never held political office and I have never been a judge. Rather, I am proud to address you as an active practitioner at the Bar for 36 years (now writing this, it's sixty-six years!). My message is intended to convey more than that survival is possible. I sorted my memories: the hot pit of the trial court, the austere chamber of appellate court, and the law office with its long and demanding hours. Then I decided that instead of preparing a formal address, I wanted to share with you some reflections on being a lawyer. My hope is to strengthen your dedication to the lawyer's duty and to the legal profession.

The attributes of a good lawyer are many and difficult to acquire, *ad astra per aspera*—to the stars by the hard ways. I urge you to travel those hard ways. Do not become discouraged, because as the great American lawyer, Joseph H. Choate, said: "Common sense and common honesty combined with uncommon industry will make a successful lawyer, and give [a lawyer] an honorable place in any generation at the bar."[2]

I believe that every good lawyer should have eight attributes, and it is about these attributes that I talk to you today. To paraphrase after the first two lines from *Jerusalem* by the English poet, William Blake:

> I give you the end of a golden string,
> Only wind it into a ball,[3]
> It will lead you to profit and honor
> And to serve justice above all.

1. Humility

I have never known a competent lawyer or able judge who did not have humility in the law. The law is too vast and complex to know it all or even a major part. No lawyer should ever hesitate to admit "I don't know"—and then proceed to find out. On your graduation day, I must reluctantly tell you that you will be studying the law all your lives.

2. Long and patient labor

The practice of law is hard work. The lawyer's obligation is to put forth all the work appropriate to serve well and truly the client's cause. The wage of glibness and an ability to "wing it" is malpractice.

3. Wise and resourceful counsel

Hasty judgments are the antithesis of sound counsel. Consideration of all facets of a problem and deliberation are prerequisite to proper legal advice. Do not become too easily content with general principles of law, because your concern should be with the solution of a particular case.

In finding the solution, be resourceful. Were every lawyer constrained to do only that which has been done before, law would become static and thereby no longer responsive to the changing legal needs of society. As Justice Holmes said:

> The life of the law has not been logic:
> it has been experience.[4]

In my years at the Bar, I have seen developed the law of products liability, new business torts, whole new areas of securities law, as well as new application of the doctrine of *res ipsa loquitur*[5]—to list but a few. Recent developments in the law are examples of lawyer resourcefulness in solving problems. Justice Holmes truly spoke, almost a hundred years ago, that "the law is made by the Bar, even more than by the Bench."

4. Broad cultural interests

. . . which words I use for want of a better phrase. This attribute is not to be mistaken for recommending that a lawyer should be a pedant or a snob. Rather, a true correlation exists between a lawyer's excellence and a lawyer's general knowledge. Remember the unkind caution of Edmund Burke:

> Law sharpens the mind by narrowing it.[6]

I suggest that history, the arts, music, drama, poetry, philosophy and all the now called liberal arts provide breadth and depth to the lawyer's ability and character. Surely we should all have some acquaintance with Plato, Aristotle, Homer, Shakespeare, Bacon, Milton, Dante,

Montaigne, and Montesquieu. Surely we all know as friends the great writers on jurisprudence: Lord Coke, Blackstone, Pollock, Maitland, Cardozo, and Holmes, to name but a few from an illustrious roster.

Justice Holmes rightly deplored that the practical-minded undervalued the importance of jurisprudence. Jurisprudence is the philosophy and science of law. Jurisprudence is the root of the law that we practice. A lawyer who is ignorant of or pays no heed to jurisprudence only ploddingly plies a trade. A knowledge of jurisprudence enables a lawyer to apply resourcefully and credibly broad rules to particular cases.

5. Courtesy

A hallmark of a great lawyer is courtesy: to court, litigants, and other lawyers. A lawyer demeans the profession by indulging in the now too frequent bitter personal colloquy with opposing counsel. Even Shakespeare, who was no admirer of lawyers, had Tranio say in the *Taming of the Shrew*:

> And do as adversaries do in law,
> Strive mightily, but eat and drink as friends.[7]

Some months ago, I heard of an incident in Denver where a lawyer addressed a young minority lawyer with an opprobrious racial epithet. Such appalling conduct is not typical. Subtler, but as pernicious and more common, is lack of courtesy to and merited respect for African American, Latino, and women lawyers. Lawyers are all colleagues at the Bar, and I submit that sincere courtesy between and among lawyers in their dealings with each other is an essential attribute of professional excellence. (Courtesy, now termed "civility," or rather the lack thereof, is a grave concern of lawyers and judges, in this first decade of the twenty-first century.)

6. Faithful performance of the lawyer's duty to client

The lawyer's obligation to the client has remained constant for almost 600 years. In *Blackstone's Commentaries*, we read:

> So early as the statute 4 Hen. IV. C. 18 it was enacted, that attorneys should be examined by the judges, and none admitted but such as were virtuous, learned and sworn to do their duty.[8]

No more stringent fiduciary duty exists than that between lawyer and client. Yet, in the most recent calendar years for which figures are available, grievances filed and malpractice claims against lawyers in our country are an evil list (the original now stale statistics omitted; the Reader can insert the current figures obtainable on the internet). The lawyer's duty to the client is simply stated: to serve the client with integrity, fidelity, and competence. Whether fulfillment of that duty be easy or burdensome, the duty remains the same.

7. Service to the Organized Bar

We would be inexcusably naïve not to recognize that public respect for law, lawyers, and judges is now at dangerously low ebb. (Still true.) I grant you that this is not a new phenomenon. As long ago as in the Bible's New Testament, the Gospel of Luke declares,

> Woe unto you also, ye lawyers!
> for ye lade men with
> burdens grievous to be borne . . .[9]

We all recall the famous lines in Shakespeare's *Henry VI*:

> The first thing we do, let's kill all the lawyers.[10]

The task of rehabilitating the legal profession to its former status of the most honored profession is a heavy but necessary one. Public respect for law, public confidence in the judicial system by which law is administered and public faith in lawyers is essential to fulfillment of the American ideals of liberty and justice.

I have not the time nor the wisdom to say how all this is to be accomplished. But I subscribe to the belief of the great jurist Learned Hand:

> It is not in books that the law can live but in the consciousness of the profession as a whole.[11]

I urge you, therefore, to give unstinting service to the organized Bar; local and state Bar associations, as well as to the American Bar Association. I commend this course to you because the conjoined efforts of all able and honest lawyers can more effectively, than by separate effort, purify the wellsprings of our profession.

I trust that each of you will exert the strength and enthusiasm of your youth to restore a learned, fearless, independent, and esteemed Bar.

8. *Ethical Conduct*

Although mentioned last, I submit that the primary attribute of a lawyer should be ethical conduct, in every circumstance and always. "Ethics" is a word derived from the Greek word which pertains to character, so when I speak of ethics for a lawyer, I speak of a lawyer's character. But I do not propose to inflict a textbook discourse on legal ethics. You have all taken a required course in Legal Ethics while in Law School.

Rather, let me express some personal observations. The cliché to obey not only the letter but also the spirit of the law is not a cliché in the context of legal ethics. To know the contents of the Code of Professional Responsibility (now the Rules of Professional Conduct) and to keep apprised of newly issued advisory ethics opinions are basic obligations—but they do not suffice. To be an ethical lawyer demands a commitment of spirit and a respect for what is right. Let me state some specific observations. I have come to believe that an incompetent lawyer cannot be an ethical lawyer. When the client pays a fee to the lawyer, the client justifiably expects and is entitled to skilled legal service. For the young lawyer, this is not an insuperable task: Learn how to do it before you do it, although for the first few years of practice the law library (now legal research is usually done "online") may seem your only habitat. The world of the legal practitioner demands practical and effective legal work.

Competence alone, of course, does not equate with legal ethics. A lawyer should repudiate the doctrine that the end justifies the means. The legal profession should not tolerate the lawyer who believes and practices that the "name of the game" is winning, no matter how the victory be won.

If these views seem harsh, I remind you of the high purposes of the legal profession: To nurture an orderly society by aiding to solve the numerous and diverse questions—legal, constitutional—to which the daily affairs and business of our society give rise; to foster and protect the rights of all persons, and to promote justice. These purposes provide a noble and continuing challenge, which only a legal profession with a high ethical standard can meet.

The new lawyer properly asks: how do I know whether in a particular matter my conduct would be ethical? No simple answer could be adequate, but I can give you several guides. I remember the first time when I heard a lawyer rebuked for his conduct. A distinguished jurist in open court said to my opposing counsel: "Counsel, I caution you. A lawyer should be like Caesar's wife, above reproach." What a memorable way to express the ethical canon that "a lawyer should avoid even the appearance of professional impropriety." To this canon I add "in both the lawyer's legal and social pursuits." I would add this because from the instant when you will be sworn in as a member of the Bar, you have the status of lawyer, with the lawyer's obligations, every second of your life. These obligations include behavior that will restore to our profession the dignity that its practice should deserve.

My personal guidelines to ethical behavior are quite homely. One is that being ethical is like being pregnant. Either you are or you are not. Similarly, a lawyer cannot be somewhat ethical in handling a legal matter. My other guideline is this: if you ask yourself whether you may ethically do something, don't do it. The fact that the question arose in your mind is itself sufficient warning not to take the proposed action. Borderline ethical conduct may conform to the letter, but is contrary to the spirit, of the ethical standards of our profession.

I urge you not to be tolerant of those lawyers who demean the profession that they have been privileged to join, and paraphrase the great text of John Donne:

> No lawyer is an island, entire of itself . . . any lawyer's betrayal of the lawyer's trust diminishes me as a lawyer.[12]

If you are thinking that my views are inconsistent with earning good profits from your chosen means of livelihood, I give you my personal assurance, based upon experience, that this is not so. Indeed I caution you that to survive the realities of law practice, you should promptly discard any illusions about our profession. But never discard your ideals.

Personal Testament and Credos

In concluding, I share with you Sir Francis Bacon's words, which I have altered only so as to include women lawyers. In 1630, as first published, he wrote:

I hold every lawyer a debtor to the lawyer's profession, from the which, as lawyers of course do seek to receive . . . profit, so ought they of duty to endeavor themselves by way of amends to be a help and ornament thereunto; this is performed in some degree, by the honest and liberal practice of a profession, when lawyers shall carry a respect not to descend into any court that is corrupt, and unworthy thereof, and preserve themselves free from the abuses wherewith the same profession is noted to be infected; but much more is this performed, if a lawyer be able to visit and strengthen the roots and foundation of the science itself, thereby not only gracing it in reputation and dignity, but also amplifying it in perfection and substance.[13]

Since 1946, this has been my personal testament as a lawyer. I recommend it to the Law Class of 1981 for your covenant—it will serve you well. (Brooke's comment for this book: My legal ethics lectures every year until 2011 also always included this quotation, a testament I deliberately repeat here.)

Finally, I share with you two personal credos. If all else that I have said today shall pass quickly from your memories, recall the words:

To thine own self be true, and do what thou hast to do.[14]

Second, a quotation from Marcus Aurelius served as my credo for all my sixty-five years as a lawyer—they too will serve you well:

Never esteem aught (anything) of advantage which will oblige you to break your faith, or to desert your honor.[15]

If what I have been saying seems to be a preachment, I apologize. The feeling that fills my heart is that somehow I can re-kindle in each of our hearts an inextinguishable fire to be always dedicated lawyers: lawyers who serve your clients with skill and integrity; lawyers who promote and protect a sound legal system and the rule of law so that law cannot end nor tyranny begin in the United States of America.

[COMPILER'S NOTE: Below, for your convenient use, are some explanations, comments, and references, as numbered for you in Brooke's speech. Some editions are from collectible books in Brooke's library. These older books are now subsequently reprinted, and many are probably available in part or whole on the internet, but the page numbers will differ. Among other sources, Wikipedia is a good place for further information and interesting comments, too. The Reader may enjoy browsing these writings, and they are good sources for other quotations, too.]

1. Juris Doctor (JD) is the degree earned by completing law school. "Juris" usually refers to "of law."

2. Joseph Hodges Choate (1832–1917), address at the Nineteenth Annual Commencement of the Columbia Law School, New York, May 16, 1878, and titled "The Young Lawyer" and included in *American Addresses* (New York: Century Co., 1911), 94. So text applies to both men and women lawyers: "a *man* an honorable place" changed to "a *lawyer*."

3. William Blake (1757–1827), a famous poet, painter, and printmaker; *Jerusalem: The Emanation of the Gian Albian* (London: Trianon Press, 1951 [facsimile]; original completed in 1820), plate 77, "To The Christians"; see also many collections of the poetical works of William Blake.

4. Oliver Wendell Holmes Jr. (1841–1936), *The Common Law*, 1st ed. (London: Macmillan, 1882), 1.

5. *Res ipsa liquitur* means the "thing speaks for itself." Put simply, the presumption that the defendant was negligent if the accident was one that ordinarily does not happen, in the absence of negligence.

6. Attributed to Edmund Burke (1729–1797), a famous and often cited British statesman and philosopher, for one of many examples, by Oliver Wendell Holmes Jr., *Collected Legal Papers* (New York: Harcourt, Brace and Co., 1921), 164–65; see also Edmund Burke, *The Works of the Right Honorable Edmund Burke* (George Bell and Sons, 1887).

7. William Shakespeare (1564–1616), *Taming of the Shrew*, Act 1, Sc. 2.

8. William Blackstone (1723–1780), an English judge and author of the influential treatise *Commentaries on the Laws of England*, 1st ed. (Oxford: Clarendon Press, 1765–1769), Book The Third (1768), Of Private Wrongs, Ch. 3 Of Courts in General, 26.

9. *The Bible*, King James Version, New Testament, Gospel of Luke, 11:46.

10. William Shakespeare (1564–1616), *King Henry VI*, Part 2, Act 4, Sc. 2.

11. Learned Hand (1872–1961); attribution by Brooke Wunnicke in her writings and speeches since 1981. Learned Hand was a judge on the United States District Court for the Southern District of New York (1909–1924) and later the United States Court of Appeals for the Second Circuit (1924–1961) and prolific scholarly writer of quotable comments.

12. John Donne (1572–1631), an English poet and scholar; *Devotions upon Emergent Occasions*, Meditation 17, 1624; many printings. Here paraphrased.

13. Sir Francis Bacon (1561–1626), an English philosopher and statesman who served Attorney General and as Lord Chancellor of England; *The Elements of the Common Lawes of England*, printed by the Assignes of I. More Esq., (London, 1630), Preface. Many subsequent printings and editions.

14. Parents of Brooke von Falkenstein Wunnicke, their guidance to her soon after her marriage, early 1940. Paraphrased from William Shakespeare, *Hamlet*, Act 1, Sc. 3, 7.

15. Marcus Aurelius (AD 121–180), Roman Emperor (AD 161–180) and Stoic philosopher; *Meditations*, Third Book, 7; here 1902 rendered by George W. Chrystal based on Foulis translation of 1742.

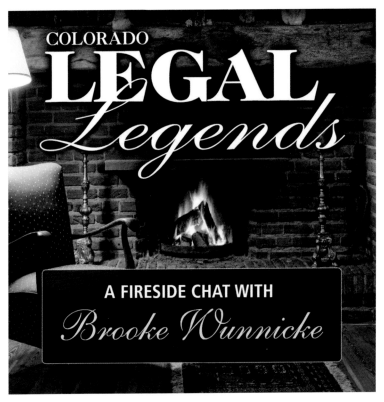

Figure 3.1. To introduce Brooke's live program and statewide website of December 14, 2010, this was the image for the brochure for a "fireside chat" with one of Colorado's "legal legends."

Part Three

The Law

Where-ever [*sic*] law ends, tyranny begins.
  John Locke, Two Treatises of Government, *Chap. XVIII "Of Tyranny," Sec.*
  202 (1689)

ACQUIRE OR RENEW YOUR FAITH IN THE LAW

PART THREE is why I wrote this book. I love the law. The practice of law has not been fun. I have known cruel discrimination. I have suffered wrenching disappointment. I have known years of hard work with many hours of laborious study. Yet I still love the law and my intent is that my book will cause you, the Reader, to love the law.

Parts One and Two were to introduce me to you and to share with you memories of some of my trials, appeals, and travails as well as rewards of general practice. Now, I hope that you will continue to enjoy my insider's look at the law as practiced by most lawyers in private—that is, non-governmental—practice. Most lawyers in the United States engaged in private practice do so in small towns and mid-size cities as I have done for many years. I am not qualified, because of no experience, to write about practice in large cities, such as New York or Los Angeles. But you have had a look at what legal practice is really like for most American lawyers.

Also, Part Three has brief essays about—most importantly for you—your rights under the law together with my insider's look at the perils to those rights.

A parting word before you begin reading Part Three: I hope that, having read my background in Part One and my memories as a lawyer in Part Two, you feel that you know and trust me. I believe that the law is our guarantee of the right to freedom in a fair society. now please come with me to acquire or renew your faith in the law.

What the Law Means for Us

But that to come shall all be done by the rule.
William Shakespeare, Antony and Cleopatra, *Act 2, Sc. 3*

It's a poor rule that won't work both ways.
O. Henry, The Whirligig of Life, *paraphrased*

I N SEPTEMBER 2000, my daughter was returning to our Denver home when she had to change airplanes in Chicago. As she walked past a newsstand with newspapers from different parts of the United States, imagine her shock when she saw hanging up in front of the newsstand her mother's picture filling the Spotlight cover page of the *Rocky Mountain News*! She was quickly reassured when she saw that I was smiling and pointing at the camera, with the title "Loooong Arm of the Law: Lawyer's Professional Passion Burns Bright after 54 Years." (See figure 2.1 at beginning of Part Two.)

I do indeed love the law, warts and all.

When I tell you that, you understandably ask what I mean by "the law." My answer is that I love the rules that human beings have developed for many centuries in an effort to promote ethics, morality, and justice among free persons individually and collectively. These goals may never be reached. What is meant by "ethics" has been debated since Aristotle, and Bar associations and legislatures keep changing their codes of ethics. What constitutes "morality" varies widely among people and their respective cultures, both past and present. The late great Supreme Court Justice Oliver Wendell Holmes Jr. put it wisely and well: "The law is the witness and external deposit of our moral life. Its history is the history of the moral development of the race." And "justice" is still the subject of disputed definition. Even accepting that these goals of the law are still elusive in both their meaning and achievement, we can each serve to help attain those goals.

Most important of all, to me and I hope you agree, are my short essays in Part Three about our rights as Americans under the law. What do these rights really mean? How important to us are our rights embedded in our 1787 Constitution?

The answers to these questions begin with our legal system. The law for different peoples in different countries depends on the applicable legal system. The history of legal systems is fascinating because it reflects the efforts of people to have rules that try to enforce ethics, morality, and justice. The concepts for the earliest legal system, of which we know, seem to have started in ancient Egypt as early as 4000 BCE. The ancient Egyptians even had a word meaning "true" and hence "just." The ancient Egyptian kings sometimes added to their title, "Sun of Maat" or "Justice." Records of ancient Egyptian legal systems include rules and judicial rulings and reflect the efforts of most human beings to live fairly together.

The next great legal system in antiquity began to develop in the Mesopotamian area about 2100 BCE. This system is of special interest for its rules governing commercial transactions—business law had its inception! The greatest of the three codes of law adopted in the Mesopotamian region is the Hammurabi Code of about 1760 BCE, which reflects that ancient Babylonia had a well-developed banking system and commercial activities. That code included, for example, provisions relating to agency, brokerage, and partnerships. Its English translation is well worth reading. The Chinese, in the Yellow River Region, also started to develop legal systems in ancient times, about 3500 BCE.

I mention just two more ancient legal systems. In Roman times, the Theodosian Code that compiled the laws since 312 BCE, was published in 438 CE. Then, the famed Justinian Code, issued between 529 and 534 CE, is the basis of the *Corpus Juris Civilis*, or in English, the "Body of Civil Law" (not the laws about crimes), for legal systems in force today throughout Western Europe and influencing modern public international law. I would very much like to share with you more history of the law, but I accept that I should quit here recounting ancient history. I add, in self-defense, that these early legal systems are the roots of our laws today.

I conclude here with two quotations. The first is from William Blackstone, whose four-volume *Commentaries on the Laws of England*, published in 1755, is an essential part of Anglo-American jurisprudence:

"The first and primary end of human laws is to maintain and regulate these absolute rights of individuals."

The second famous quotation is one with which I often ended my lectures to lawyers. The author is the noted Englishman John Locke in the chapter "Of Tyranny" in his *Two Treatises of Government* (1689); his writings undergird the Constitution of our United States of America:

"Where-ever law ceases, tyranny begins."

AND IN JOHN LOCKE'S PRECEPT, I FERVENTLY BELIEVE.

THE MAGNA CARTA—WHAT'S IT TO YOU?

AMONG OTHER important protections, the Magna Carta in the year 1215 established that no one—not even the king—is above the law.

Do any of our American middle schools or high schools teach the students about the Magna Carta? Students many years ago used to be taught about it, and we were required to learn its date. Perhaps my early teachings about the Magna Carta are why it has been important to me all my adult life.

Over forty years ago, on my first holiday trip to England, I took a bus tour that was routed to drive by the meadow at Runnymede where, on June 15, 1215, King John affixed his great seal to the Magna Carta. When the bus slowed for the tour guide to tell our busload of American tourists about the great event that happened at Runnymede over 700 years ago, I can still feel my excitement. The plain-looking landscape seemed to become crowded with the barons, archbishops, and abbots in their medieval dress demanding certain human rights that eventually became integral to our American Constitution. The tour guide could see my excitement and asked the cause. When I told him, he asked me to share with my fellow-travelers what the Magna Carta had given to all of us, which I did. I was glad to see that they also became enthralled by what happened centuries ago at the very place at which we stared. The tour guide asked my name, to which I replied that he would find my last name difficult to remember so just remember "Brooke, the woman lawyer from Wyoming," where I then lived and practiced law. For years afterward, I had people returning from a visit to England telling me that their tour guide had asked if they knew me!

In preparing to write this, I wanted to make certain that all I wrote about that great document was still accurate. So being now well-used to online research, I checked and found that the Magna Carta is currently known to have been reissued several times, has had some textual changes, and may (scholars disagree) have been signed elsewhere than Runnymede meadow. The Great Charter's affirmation of human rights, however, has remained unchanged.

Here are three of its important provisions (the numbers refer to the charter's paragraphs).

39. "No free man will be taken or imprisoned or disseised [deprived of possession of a freehold estate] or outlawed or exiled or in any way ruined, nor shall we go or send against him, save [except] by the lawful judgment of his peers [jury] or by the law of the land."

    My comment: this is the equivalent of our guarantee of due process granted by the Fifth and Fourteenth Amendments to the United States Constitution.

40. "To no one shall we sell, to no one shall we deny or delay right or justice."

    My comment: I quote this provision of the Magna Carta at the beginning of every lecture that I give to lawyers. I believe it is an eloquent and enduring ideal for the American system of justice.

45. "We shall not make justices, constables, sheriffs, or bailiffs who do not know the law of the land and wish to observe it well." My comment: we are still striving to this end. In the United States, election of judges is now in disfavor because of scandals in campaign financing. The favored American Bar Association (ABA) method of appointment, in practice, assures only that the appointed judge has excellent political credentials. the appointee may be qualified, but that is not assured by the appointment process.

The Magna Carta is indeed the Great Charter. The British Museum has one of its original copies and looking at it in its glass case is an unforgettable experience. The Magna Carta's provisions seeking to ensure freedom and justice are at the core of our United States Constitution and are still our fervent desire as Americans.

[COMPILER'S NOTE: Sadly, deceased in September 2014, Brooke missed the Magna Carta's 800th birthday celebrations. The Magna Carta and its 800th birthday celebration on June 15, 2015, are explained at a wonderful website, http://magnacarta800th.com. As a present for her ninety-sixth birthday, I arranged for Brooke Wunnicke to be a Sponsor of the American Bar Association's ABA Edition of a fine book of history over the many centuries, Magna Carta: The Foundation of Freedom 1215–2015 and the Rule of Law.]

BEDROCK OF JUSTICE—THE COMMON LAW

THIS DISCUSSION shares with the Reader how wonderfully and richly the common law has contributed to America's efforts for justice to prevail in our courts.

I begin many years ago when I was in law school and a required course was one year of Common Law. When I looked at our textbook, it consisted of English cases starting in the thirteenth century, and some of the decisions were written in very old English that was difficult to understand. Not much time elapsed before I realized how exciting and important the common law was—and continues to be. I have remained firm in my belief that a knowledge of and respect for the common law is essential for the legal profession to fulfill its role of fostering justice—and for citizens to understand why the common law can protect them.

What is common law? Prepare for a long answer. I ask you to come with me to 1200 in England, when Westminster Hall started as a central court to hear and decide civil cases—in which the Crown was not involved—as well as the trial and punishment of crimes. And what a courtroom it was: 290 feet long (a football field, between the goal lines, is 300 feet long), 70 feet wide and 90 feet high—and probably gloomy. I have seen a portrait of how the judge looked as he sat on his high bench. He was an imposing figure: clad in a scarlet velvet robe with white fur cuffs to the elbow, a large white fur collar, and a very large white wig. An impressive surrounding indeed for a judge and jury seeking to reach a just result in resolving the civil disputes that inevitably arise between people. Here is a partial list of the myriad of problems for which the common law developed rules as hundreds upon hundreds of cases were tried and decided over centuries: negligence, trespass, fraud, bailments, ownership of property, contracts, and succession of property at death when deceased died without a will.

I can guess that your next question would be: "Why is this old common law of any interest today?" For an answer, I start with the Bill of Rights to the

Constitution of the United States, in which the Seventh Amendment grants us our right to a jury trial and reads:

> In Suits at *common law*, where the value in controversy shall exceed twenty dollars, the right of trial by jury shall be preserved, and no fact tried by a jury, shall be otherwise re-examined in any court of the United States than according to the rules of the *common law*. (My emphasis added.)

Although now replaced in large part by state constitutions, statutes, and judicial decisions in forty-nine of our fifty states, the common law remains as the roots of those laws, and still applies when needed. One state, Louisiana, does not have its legal roots in the English common law but instead in the Napoleonic Code, based on the excellent Roman Justinian Code. The reason: in 1803, the then young United States bought the Louisiana Territory from France, and French law governed in its New World colony, where it is still pervasive in the state of Louisiana.

With that brief historical digression, I turn attention to common law in the United States in modern times. When I started to practice law in Wyoming, its statutes then all fit in a single thick, black-bound volume with the poorest index that I have ever encountered. To digress again, I had bought a used copy of the statute book and its index opened automatically to a page headed with "parsnip"—but major subjects were omitted. Anyway, I started reading the statute book and was startled to read this verbose statute (enacted by the Council and House of Representatives of the Territory of Wyoming), which I strongly recommend that the Reader only skim:

> Section 1. The common law of England as modified by judicial decisions, so far as the same is of a general nature and not inapplicable, and all declaratory or remedial acts or statutes made in aid of, or to supply defects of the common law prior to the fourth year of James the First (excepting the second section of the sixth chapter of forty-third Elizabeth, the eighth chapter of thirteenth Elizabeth, and ninth chapter of thirty-seventh Henry Eighth) and which are of a general nature, and not local to England, shall be the rule of decision in this Territory when not inconsistent with the laws thereof, and shall be considered as of full force, until repealed by legislative authority.

Sec. 2. This act shall take effect and be in full force from and after its passage.

Approved, December 2^d, 1869.

The statute has remained unchanged, except for changing "Territory" to "State" when Wyoming became a state in 1890. When my husband retired from business and we moved to Denver where I have practiced law for many years, I had to familiarize myself, of course, with Colorado law. My curiosity caused me soon to check whether Colorado also had a statute adopting the common law of England. And indeed it did. Section 2-4-211 of the Colorado Revised Statutes, in language similar to that of the Wyoming statute, declares that the common law of England remains in effect unless repealed by the Colorado General Assembly. So if the Reader is also curious about your state, you will need only seconds to find out on your personal computer. You can go to Google and type in your state + statutes + common law and presto! You will have your answer.

I thought that you might be interested in several examples of the common law of England, still law today. I have selected examples involving the law of negligence, because suits for personal injury probably receive more publicity than other areas of civil law. An essential element of the tort of negligence is a "duty owed" to plaintiff. When did this legal requirement to prove a defendant's negligence have its start? In the fourteenth century, so long ago that the online legal research services do not have the case available. So I checked my worn copy of Justice Holmes's classic text *Common Law* (my 1923 reprint is its forty-fifth printing!), and he wrote a summary of the case as I had remembered it. He did not include the name of the case, but I recalled it as the "Horse Doctor's Case." The facts are simple: the defendant undertook to cure the plaintiff's sick horse, but the defendant doctor was negligent in his treatment and the horse died. The court held in favor of plaintiff, stating the now familiar rule of negligence law· having undertaken the duty for plaintiff, defendant undertook to perform it well. This case laid down the precedent that was followed in 1375 after the Great Plague, in suits against physicians—and is an underlying rule of law still applicable in medical malpractice suits.

I now jump six centuries to 1863, the English case of *Byrne v. Boadle*, and the rule of *res ipsa loquitur*, literally "the thing speaks for itself," applied in a negligence case. The facts can be briefly stated: plaintiff was walking down a London street, when a barrel of flour fell out of a second story window, hitting and seriously injuring plaintiff. Plaintiff sued the owner of the flour shop and his employees, but plaintiff did not know whose negligence had caused the barrel to fall out of the window. Nonetheless, plaintiff won because the three requirements for the rule of *res ipsa loquitur* to apply had all been met:

1. The accident was of a type that ordinarily would not happen in the absence of someone's negligence.
2. Plaintiff's injuries were not contributed to by plaintiff or by any third party.
3. The instrumentality, condition, or thing causing the injury must have been in the exclusive control of the defendant(s).

If the court determines that the rule of *res ipsa loquitur* applies, the plaintiff suing to recover for injuries caused by defendant's alleged negligence must also still prove that defendant's exclusive control of the source of plaintiff's injury and that the alleged source was the proximate cause of the injury.

For the last example, also involving the law of negligence, I move from England and *Byrne v. Boadle* in 1863 to the United States, where in 1944 we find the famous California case of *Ybarra v. Spangard*, 25 Cal. 2d 486 (1944), that made legal history. The doctrine of *res ipsa loquitur* was applied to these facts: plaintiff was hospitalized for an appendectomy. When he recovered consciousness after his surgery removing his appendix, his shoulder and arm had been injured resulting in paralysis. One does not have to be an expert in either anatomy or appendix surgery to realize that this result is not normal in the absence of someone's negligence. Plaintiff sued all the surgical team and the hospital owner. Plaintiff had, of course, been unconscious for his surgery, and hence obviously could not know whose conduct had caused his injury. After two appeals to the California Court of Appeals, the California Supreme Court affirmed the judgment in favor of plaintiff. The appellate courts all held that the rule of *res ipsa loquitur* had been fairly applied to the multiple defendants. This case laid a firm foundation for numerous subsequent lawsuits, with *res ipsa loquitur* being applied not only in medical malpractice suits, but other factual situations that ingenious lawyers perceive meet the three-fold requirement for the rule to apply.

Regretfully I now write "good-bye" to writing about the common law because I acknowledge having written probably more than enough about the topic for this book. I am proud of the company that I have in my admiration for the common law, about which it has been said over a century ago that "It is the gathered wisdom of a thousand years."

Great American jurists have extolled the virtues of the common law and its contribution to our American system of justice. We should remember that the common law is not the product of one judge or a group of judges, but as the late great Justice Joseph Story described the common law, it is "the wisdom, counsel, experience, and observation of many ages of wise and observing persons."

I hope that you have found this chapter intriguing and that it has aroused in you a lasting affection for the common law and for what it can give to our system of justice.

THE JUDICIARY—WHAT IT MEANS FOR YOU

WHEN I was very young, my family made me aware of how important were current historic events. I remember being informed that when Benito Mussolini came to power as Italy's dictator, his first official act was to shut down the courts. I remember reading in the newspapers about a man named Adolf Hitler becoming dictator of Germany, who soon closed down the judicial system. I remember when Fidel Castro, Cuba's dictator for decades, early in assuming power got rid of the independent judiciary. Thus, I have long realized that an independent, competent, and fearless judiciary was necessary for people to remain free from tyranny.

Separation of Powers, Your Constitution

OUR FOUNDING fathers granted the people of the United States the enduring governmental structure of a government with three independent parts, the basis for our "separation of powers" doctrine that undergirds our government. Articles I, II, and III of the United States Constitution provide for these three parts, each with its own powers: legislative, executive, and judicial, the pillars of our federal government.

Our founders emphasized that ours was to be *a government by laws*, not by persons.

This essay is divided into two sections: the federal judiciary, and a general overview of the states' judiciary. I hope and trust that you will find it both interesting and important.

Obviously, a very large subject matter, our country's judiciary is more deserving of a candid book than of a brief essay in a book. But at least, I can give the Reader an insider's look as a lawyer into our country's judiciary.

The Federal Judiciary

ARTICLE III, Section 1 of the United States Constitution provides that "[t]he judicial power of the United States, shall be vested in one supreme Court, and in such inferior Courts as the Congress may from time to time ordain and establish. The Judges, both of the supreme court and in inferior Courts, shall hold their Offices during good Behaviour."

No larger or juicier plum hangs on the political tree than appointment as a federal judge under Article III. No federal judge ever stands for an election. The president of the United States nominates the lawyer or judge to be named as a federal judge, and the nomination is subject to confirmation by the United States Senate. Article III federal judges are appointed for an indefinite term, expressed as "during good Behaviour." The reality is that federal judges are appointed for life: "shall hold their offices during good Behaviour." They receive comfortable base salaries plus generous benefits, "perks," and pensions. The judges have law clerks who do the judges' research and help draft their opinions.

You can be assured that every appointee as a federal judge has impeccable political credentials. When we are fortunate, the appointee is worthy in experience, competence, integrity, and dedicated to justice. Sometimes we are not so fortunate.

So, here is a short description of each of the major federal courts. Not included are specialized courts such as bankruptcy courts, United States Tax Court, Court of Appeals for Armed Forces, Court of Appeals for Veterans Claims. To introduce them, below is a simple diagram.

Supreme Court of the United States

THE SUPREME Court of the United States is the only court for which the Constitution of the United States makes specific provision. Article II Section 2 of our Constitution provides for the president of the United States to appoint the justices "by and with the advice and consent of the Senate" of the United States. The name of the presidential nominee is sent to the Senate Judiciary Committee for hearings and, when contentious, media reporting occurs. If the Judiciary Committee approves, the nomination goes to the Senate for a full vote, a majority being required. The Constitution does not state the number of justices to serve on the Supreme Court. The court started with six but for a very long time has had nine justices.

"PACKING THE COURT"

THE CONSTITUTION'S omission of a prescribed number of justices allowed then President Franklin Delano Roosevelt to seek to "Pack the Court," as the news media quickly dubbed his efforts to increase the number of justices. His motivation was the Supreme Court's then composition of very conservative justices who were striking down as unconstitutional his New Deal legislation.

I have a vivid, pleasant memory of the "Pack the Court" drama. I was then a college undergraduate, and despite a full scholarship, was—as were many of my school colleagues—lean and hungry for money, any money. We had been enduring years of the Great Depression. When the college posted a notice announcing an extemporaneous speaking contest on whether "Packing the Supreme Court" was a good or bad idea, many of us rushed to enter the contest. The first prize was $75—an excitingly large amount back then. I was among the majority who were committed to "packing the court." We believed in the New Deal and desperately wanted a change.

On the day of the contest, I thought that I had an eloquent plea for the need to increase the number of Supreme Court Justices. When my turn came and I saw the contest judges up close, my reaction was "oh-oh"—they looked tougher than Attila the Hun and were obviously miffed by what they had been hearing. I immediately forgot my mentally prepared "eloquent plea" and instead gave an "extemporaneous extempore" presentation on the evils of "packing the court" and the merits of a nine-justice court. Yes, I won the contest and the $75. Yes, my conscience troubled me. But I welcomed the money with which I bought a pair of needed new shoes and proudly gave the rest to my family.

JUDICIAL GIANTS IN FIRST HALF OF TWENTIETH CENTURY

IN THE first half of the twentieth century, we had several judicial giants, not equaled since: Justices Oliver Wendell Holmes Jr., Nathan Cardozo, and Louis D. Brandeis. A fourth judicial giant was Judge Learned Hand, Judge of the United States Circuit Court of Appeals for the Second Circuit, which includes New York. Judge Hand was a brilliant, rational jurist, whose opinions are still quoted by many courts including the Supreme Court, although he was never appointed to that Court. I recommend for an inspiring read his small book *The Spirit of Liberty*, a compilation of his lectures and essays.

JUDICIAL "ACTIVISM" IN SECOND HALF OF TWENTIETH CENTURY

IN THE second half of the twentieth century, judicial activism proliferated. I confess that I am vigorously and unalterably opposed to activist judges at any level of the judiciary. I define an activist judge as one who substitutes his or her opinion of what the result should be in the case before the court—though the evidence and sound legal precedent directs a contrary result. I submit to the Reader that judicial activism violates our vaunted system of representative government by laws, not by persons.

Judicial activism flourished with Supreme Court Chief Justice Earl Warren (1953–69), formerly governor of California. I consider Earl Warren to have been the first high-ranking justice to be an "overtly" activist justice.

Article I, Section 9 of the United States Constitution includes this ban:

No *ex post facto* law shall be passed.

What is an *ex post facto* law? A law that imposes a criminal penalty on a person for an act lawful when done but is later made a crime by a law passed after the act was done. I am sure that you agree an ex post facto law is inherently unfair. So, imagine my surprise when many years ago on a grey, dismal Saturday afternoon I was doing some legal research in our Wyoming state law library. My husband was golfing, and our daughter was at a birthday party. I thought it a perfect time to do some research on an interesting appeal that had been forwarded to me. Then my attention was riveted by reading a then recent United States Supreme Court opinion, authored by Chief Justice Warren as I recall, that the ex post facto clause did not apply to income tax laws intended to raise revenue and that imposed a criminal penalty. The judicial determination was that the ban—"No . . . ex post facto laws shall be passed"—should not apply to a law intended to get more tax money. Hmm.

Before I leave this Supreme Court discussion, some important facts: the Court has both original jurisdiction and appellate jurisdiction* to review decisions of lower courts, if it grants a lawyer's petition for a *writ of certiorari*. A lawyer petitions for a *writ of certiorari*. "Certiorari" has a slushy pronunciation: sur-shee-rair-ee. A *writ of certiorari*, briefly pronounced "cert," refers to a writ issued by a superior court to an inferior court ordering an examination of the records of the inferior court to determine whether the lower court acted correctly or incorrectly in a specific case. Thousands of "petitions for cert" as lawyers commonly refer to them, are filed annually with the Supreme Court. The justices then decide which cases they would like to hear and decide.

---

* EDITOR'S NOTE: Original jurisdiction involves disputes between the states or disputes arising among ambassadors and other high-ranking officials. In other circumstances, the court is required to take (1) an interlocutory appeal from a decision of three federal district court judges, (2) an appeal rendering a federal statute to be unconstitutional, and (3) any other appeal where required by law.

United States Courts of Appeals

APPEALS MAY be taken from adverse judgments in the federal trial court of general jurisdiction, called the United States District Court, to the federal Circuit Courts of Appeals. At the present time, there are eleven numbered Circuit Courts, the First through Eleventh Circuit, each with its own member states. For example, the Tenth Circuit hears appeals from the states of Colorado, Kansas, New Mexico, Oklahoma, Utah, and Wyoming. In addition, there are the Circuit Court of Appeals for the District of Columbia Circuit, and the Court of Appeals for the Federal Circuit, which has nationwide jurisdiction to hear certain types of cases. A reminder: I am omitting several other appellate courts with only special jurisdictions.

The appellate court's task is to determine whether the law was applied correctly in the trial court. Appeals courts consist of three judges, or more, and do not use a jury.

Judges for the Circuit Courts of Appeals are nominated by the president of the United States and appointed by and with the consent and advice of the Senate. Each vacancy is filled by a person from the same state in the circuit as the departed judge. Always and appropriately the objective is to have each state in a circuit have a judge on its Circuit Court of Appeals. Where does the president get the names of the nominees? The political leaders of the pertinent state notify the state's United States senator(s), if of the same political party, of the name to be submitted to the president for appointment. The appointment is made without notice to constituents and usually without prior publicity.

The judges are appointed to serve "during good behaviour," which in reality is for life. The salaries are always in the six figures, with good benefits, "perks," and handsome pensions. You can find out quickly on the internet in which circuit you reside. You will find on line maps that show the circuits, and the number of states—which varies by circuit. The federal Circuit Courts of Appeals have varying reputations in the legal community, ranging from a "strong" court to a "weak" court. Here, my promised insider's look at our legal system is shut down. Prudence dictates that I do not write which are the "weak" Courts of Appeals, but lawyers know and are careful not to cite their opinions in briefs because they have almost no weight. For decades, the Second Circuit, which includes New York, has always had enough excellent judges to qualify it as a "strong" court, especially in the area of business law, and the same is true for the Seventh Circuit, which includes Illinois. The Fifth Circuit, which includes some of our biggest oil-producing states, has long dominated the area of oil and gas law. Some legal scholars and lawyers consider the Circuit Courts of Appeals to be the most powerful courts in our legal system. Maybe they are right, but I hope not, because they vary so much in merit.

Federal District Courts

THE NINETY-FOUR federal United States District Courts are the "work-horses" of the federal judiciary. They are the trial courts with jurisdiction over all cases involving federal law, both civil and criminal. Again, of course, I have omitted special jurisdictional law such as military law. Some states, for example California, have more than one district, for example, the United States District Court for the Central District of California. Other states, such as Colorado and Wyoming, have only one district, for example, the United States District Court for the District of Colorado. Each district includes a United States Bankruptcy Court.

Again, appointment as a federal district court judge is a political appointment. Again, the base salaries, benefits, "perks," and pensions assure the appointee of financial comfort for tenure "during good behaviour," which, with rare exceptions, is for life.

As is true for the Courts of Appeals, so it is with the District Courts: some are outstanding, some are adequate—and others are not. Despite a reputation for impurity of its politics, somehow New York City has always managed to get some fine judges on the United States District Court for the Southern District of New York, which includes New York City. This district court, thanks to an omnipresent cadre of fine jurists, has earned the reputation of making the business law of our country—and doing a good job of it. In some cases, the plaintiff may have a choice of district courts in which states to bring its lawsuit. Some states have federal district courts that are notoriously poor, and legal counsel may try to avoid filing a suit in such a court.

The States' Judiciary

OBVIOUSLY, I can do no more than generalize about the state judiciary in our fifty states. All the states have a system of lower courts that hear misdemeanor criminal cases and civil suits up to a maximum amount of dollars that varies from state-to-state. All states have trial courts of general jurisdiction that hear criminal felony cases and civil suits with no maximum dollar amount limitation. Many, but not all, of the states have intermediate courts of appeal. Every state has a state supreme court. Confusing names: in New York, the highest appellate court is not called a "supreme court" but is the "Court of Appeals;" and the state trial courts are called "Supreme Court."

How do the states get the judges for the state courts? The two major ways are by election and by the so-called "merit selection" of judges. The American Bar Association and probably a majority of state Bar associations strongly urge rejection of an elected judiciary, on the ground that this method is tainted by corruption attributable to corporate campaign contributions. These Bar associations and their leaders tirelessly advocate adoption of the so-called merit selection of judges.

How does the merit selection of judges operate? Although undoubtedly differences are found in the details of this method, the basic system is uniform in the states that have adopted it. Usually the governor appoints a commission, with its membership comprised of lawyers and nonlawyers. The commission reviews the applications of those applying for the judgeship and screens, through interviews with the commission, those applicants that it deems judicially qualified or politically designated. Following the interviews, selected applicants are certified to the governor for appointment.

At this juncture, fairness requires me to disclose that colleagues alleged that I was a victim of a covert political strategy resulting in my not being appointed as a judge to a state supreme court. Their opinion, as relayed to me, was that my thirty-plus-years of well-known appellate record, in all of civil and constitutional and criminal matters, had caused me to be recognized for appointment. A commission, at that time, chose a small list (three or four) for possible appointment and that list then was certified to the governor; but in 1979 in Colorado, the names were not released to the public. The commission may have had at least one more member of the governor's political party; a governor could more readily dictate which names were on that short list for selecting his appointee. Thus, a governor could appoint a Supreme Court justice to fulfill a political commitment or a strategy. A committee of the state legislature investigated, and procedures were changed for future disclosure of possible appointees. I shall let the Reader decide whether such a system removes judicial selection from political taint or merely changes from overt to covert politics as the determinative factor in the selection of a state's judiciary.

Tenure under the "merit system" of judicial appointment? After a governor's appointment and a period of time on the bench, the judge must run for office; but no other candidates are allowed. Instead the appointed judge runs "on the judge's record." Now, Reader, be honest—how many of you, lawyers and nonlawyers alike—are familiar with any trial or appellate judge's "record"? So the Judicial Commission, at least in Colorado, publishes its evaluation and recommendations before each election.

The Judicial Commission in my area has seemed automatically to state its recommendation, "Be Retained." Thus, let's look at an example of an election that included voting whether to retain a judge for the highest court in the state. The Judicial Commission's report of evaluations by lawyers and nonlawyer resulted in a score of "70" (out of "100"). The report included evaluations of the judge's failure for opinions to be well-reasoned coupled with failure to follow sound legal precedent, but at least the judge was always gracious and courteous. The Judicial Commission's recommendation: "Be Retained." And the same recommendation of retention was stated for a senior judge in our state's lower trial court, whose evaluation was only a mere "65" (out of "100").

GRAVE WARNING

I END this book's discussion of the judiciary with a grave warning:

> *DANGER! We cannot afford as a free people to be apathetic about the persons chosen to serve as federal and state court judges. We must be vigilant in decrying poor choices and vocally urging appointment of lawyers qualified by experience, intelligence, and integrity to serve us as our judges.*

Inside a Civil Jury Trial

It is not sufficient to know what one ought to say,
but one must also know how to say it.
Aristotle, Rhetoric, *Book III*

D EAR READER, if you read this introductory essay, you will find the next few explanatory essays more pleasurable. This essay is divided into two parts: Part A, pretrial process, uses and abuses; Part B, parts of a civil jury trial. The pretrial process and the parts of a typical civil jury trial in both state and federal courts are the same, as well as the sequence and content of the trial's parts. Criminal trials differ mainly in burden of proof and applicable rules of evidence, but this part of my book is primarily about civil trials, the majority of my trial practice.

PRETRIAL PROCESS: USES AND ABUSES

I BEGIN before actual trial, because certain pretrial activities are an integral part of the trial process.

Discovery

WHEN MANY years ago I started to practice law in Wyoming, the then new (only three years old) Federal Rules of Civil Procedure of course applied in our federal court, but in state courts we had code pleading, which did not provide for any discovery. I can remember during trial looking at the witnesses for the other side and wondering to what matters their testimony would relate. I also remember when Alfred P. Murrah, then Chief Judge of the United States Court of Appeals for the Tenth Circuit, came to Cheyenne to speak to our Bar association to urge adoption in our state courts of the Federal Rules of Civil Procedure. (Judge Murrah's name later became famous because of the 1995 Oklahoma City bombing with tragic loss of life at the federal building bearing his name.)

The Federal Rules of Civil Procedure, now adopted by the majority of the states in substantially the same form, provide for discovery before trial.

Depositions

I STILL remember Judge Murrah's sincere praise of the virtues of discovery—I remind, code pleading had no pretrial discovery. He emphasized how depositions (deposition is a witness's sworn, out-of-court testimony) would strip a case to its essentials for trial, making litigation much less expensive for litigants. Hah! What a poor prognostication! The judge was indeed correct in theory: the purpose of and useful potential for depositions were laudable. In practice, however, the use—and misuse—of depositions have substantially increased the cost of litigation. To put it kindly, the judge did not anticipate that the number of depositions and the abuses in their taking would proliferate like rabbits.

Production of Documents

ANOTHER ASPECT of pretrial discovery is the demand for the production of documents. The number of documents demanded for production from the opposing party may be abusive by their large number and their requested span of years. In some large cases, demands are made for thousands or even millions—yes, millions—of documents going back an unreasonable length of time. Now document production includes emails, and I could write a separate long essay on the ethical problems that inhere in electronic discovery. Filing protests against such demands, or compliance with the demands, can greatly increase the cost of litigation.

Limitations Needed

SUFFICE IT to say that, although unquestionably, pretrial discovery could be a beneficial efficiency for litigation, I believe discovery badly needs changing to achieve its goal of benefiting our system of justice. As now practiced, pretrial discovery is like an infection in fair and affordable litigation. Regrettably, some lawyers have inflicted deplorable abuses on the discovery process. For example, some lawyers proliferate depositions beyond a reasonable number and drag them on beyond a needed length of time. Thriving corporations can absorb the cost; poor litigants cannot. I have known much deposition abuse: too many depositions, and undue, useless prolonging of depositions to run up the lawyer's fee. The majority of my fellow lawyers have professional integrity, and I believe that they will admit that we have serious discovery abuses.

A long-time friend, a retired judge, asked me what I thought would improve our court system. My response was quick: "Strictly limit the number of depositions and the number of pre-trial motions." You would not believe the number of motions that some lawyers file before trial: motions to dismiss, motions for summary judgment (before any discovery), motions to strike various allegations in the pleadings, motions to exclude certain evidence at trial, and so on almost ad infinitum. Opposing counsel must respond to each of the motions or risk an adverse ruling. I stress the "strictly" in "strictly limit" the number because permitting exceptions to the limitation being allowed to the "discretion" of the judge would not cure or even alleviate the problem. Experience with judicial "discretion" has proved being subject to judicial bias for the opposing lawyer, a judge's belief that granting the request to exceed the limit is more likely to prevent being reversed on appeal, or a judge just wanting to be nice.

Please, no "discretion" as to the numbers: limit those depositions, limit those motions, and firmly control demands for production of documents, including discovery both paper and electronic.

To end this description or diatribe, whichever you may consider, it is based on my experience and emphasizes my belief that every citizen and small business, too, should always be able to afford suing or defending when worthy—and never be deprived of the right to seek justice because of procedural costs.

THE PARTS OF A CIVIL JURY TRIAL

I SHALL describe the components of a civil jury trial, which differs from a trial to the judge in one important respect: in a jury trial, the jurors are the finders of facts, and the judge instructs them on the law. In a trial to the judge, the judge is the sole finder of facts as well as the decider of applicable law. Facts in a court of law are established by testimony and exhibits.

Every trial—whether to the court only or to a jury and whether a civil or criminal trial—is subject to rules of evidence. Fortunately, in 1975 the Federal Rules of Evidence were adopted, and many state courts have adopted them with substantially the same content, including their amendments. I believe that most members of the legal profession would agree that the Federal Rules of Evidence are excellent and a welcome addition to trial practice.

Voir Dire: Selection of the Jury

THE TRIAL begins with *voir dire*, which is the selection process for a jury from the jury panel. All my trials were to a jury of twelve, but now in many states civil jury trials are to a jury of six. Because selecting a jury is a key part of the trial and a fascinating inquiry into the thinking of our fellow human beings, you will find later a discussion about *voir dire*, which you may find useful if you are called for jury duty.

Opening Statements

AFTER THE jury has been selected and sworn, lawyers for the plaintiff and the defendant may each make an opening statement. In a criminal trial, the defense usually waives opening statement. I consider opening statement to be the most underused weapon in the trial lawyer's arsenal and have written for you a separate discussion of an opening statement.

Plaintiff's Case: Witness Testimony and Exhibits

WITNESS TESTIMONY is typically the major part of the evidence at trial. My view: witnesses giving testimony are always fascinating—a never-ending study in human nature. Because I wanted to share with the Reader a behind-the-scenes look at the many facets of the interaction between witnesses and lawyers, I have included a separate short essay about the topic of witnesses. I predict that you will find some surprises, not based on theory or studies but the reality of trials.

Plaintiff begins the trial by calling the first witness. Every witness on behalf of the plaintiff is subject to Direct Examination by plaintiff's lawyer. No leading questions are permitted in Direct Examination. Reminder: a "leading question" is one that is worded so as to suggest the answer.

At the conclusion of the Direct Examination, plaintiff's lawyer states to defense counsel: "You may cross examine." On Cross-Examination, the cross-examining lawyer may ask leading questions. Plaintiff then may have "re-direct-examination," and defendant may be allowed "re-cross examination." After completing the examination of the first witness, plaintiff may call other witnesses, and the same procedure is followed. Also, in a separate essay, I have written about Direct and Cross-Examination and had to restrain myself from writing more and more about it.

Testimony and exhibits . . . which include documentary evidence (such as contracts and letters), audios, videos, photographs, physical items, and demonstrative evidence (such as charts, graphs, and diagrams) may be part of plaintiff's case, commonly referred to as "case-in-chief." A well-established protocol governs the introduction of exhibits into evidence. The lawyer "lays the foundation" for an exhibit to be received into evidence by asking a few short questions of a witness, giving the opportunity for opposing counsel to object, and being prepared to argue briefly for its admission.

I share with you an odd story about the protocol. I was in a simple little trial to the court, and opposing counsel was an over-confident, rather arrogant young son of a distinguished lawyer, and he did not know how to introduce a document into evidence. The judge tried to help the young man, but to no avail. Finally, the judge turned to me and said: "Counsel, will you please get that document into evidence for him?" I responded: "Yes, Your Honor, but I ask that my putting it into evidence for him not be a considered a waiver of my protest to its admissibility." "Granted." I put the document into evidence for the inept lawyer, and the judge intoned "Thank you."

Motion for Directed Verdict

AT THE end of plaintiff's case-in-chief, prudent defense counsel will, in my opinion, always move for a directed verdict. This motion and its argument are done out of the presence of the jury—that is one of the reasons for trial recesses that may annoy the jury. Each of plaintiff's claims in a lawsuit requires at least *prima facie* evidence (evidence sufficient to establish a claim) that could support a verdict for plaintiff on the claim. Each claim has required proof of its prescribed elements by a preponderance of the evidence.

Failure to meet even *prima facie* this burden of proof by a preponderance of the evidence entitles the defendant to have the judge grant the motion for directed verdict and also to enter a verdict in favor of the defendant. Motions for directed verdict are difficult to have granted, because many trial judges justifiably believe that they are less likely to be reversed on appeal if they let the case go to the jury to decide about the sufficiency of the evidence.

Presentation of the Defendant's Case

IF THE Motion for Directed Verdict is denied, the next event in the trial is the presentation of the case for the defendant. The procedure is the same as for the plaintiff's case-in-chief: calling the witnesses for direct examination by defendant's counsel and cross-examination by plaintiff's counsel and introducing exhibits into evidence.

Rebuttal Evidence

AT THE conclusion of the defendant's case, the parties are allowed rebuttal evidence, again with direct questioning followed by the right to cross-examine.

Closing Arguments

THIS IS my favorite part of a trial. I firmly believe—and have learned from both post-trial jurors' comments and independent research—of the importance of an effective closing argument. So, of course, another short essay on this topic was irresistible, and I have included it later in this Part Three.

Judge's Instructions to the Jury

IN ALL jury trials, the trial judge instructs the jury on the applicable law by reading the instructions aloud to the jury. Written copies of those instructions are given to the jury to take with them for reference in their jury deliberation room. In federal court, closing arguments usually precede the judge's instructions.

In many state trials, including where I tried most of my cases, the judge instructs the jury on the applicable law before the lawyers' closing arguments. I like this order of events much better for two reasons: (1) it broadens the scope of closing argument to include reference to the instructions;

(2) it increases the jury's understanding of the evidence to have the closing arguments after the instructions. Also, biased judges, or those ill-versed in the law, can "kill" counsel with the judge's inflections and tone of voice used when reading aloud the instructions to the jury. A prime example of this is the report that I received from a friend who had been on a jury. She told me "I don't know why there was a jury. When the judge read the instructions to us at the end of the trial, he made plain that we were to return a verdict for the plaintiff and in a generous amount." Even though not a lawyer in the case, I was deeply saddened by this report, because the victim of such judicial conduct has no protection. This trial had been in federal court, and hence defendant's counsel was helpless because the judge had the last word.

Jury Deliberation

AFTER THE judge's jury instructions and the attorneys' closing arguments, the case goes to the jury for deliberation and deciding on a verdict. All the exhibits received in evidence and the judge's written jury instructions go with the jury to the jury deliberation room.

The first item on the jury's agenda is the election of a foreperson (formerly called the "foreman"). Then the jury deliberates. A court bailiff sits outside the room and guards against intruders. If the jury has a question, it is written and given to the bailiff for delivery to the judge. When the judge receives a question from the deliberating jury, the lawyers are called into the judge's chambers or courtroom to be apprised of the question and to agree to the judge's proposed answer. Yes, more argument ensues. The judge then sends the written answer to the jury via the bailiff.

As I write this I am reminded of an incident involving a jury question and me. As the first woman trial lawyer in Wyoming, I had become accustomed to arousing curiosity in my first-time appearance as a lawyer in a jury trial held in a small town. During jury deliberations, the jury sent out a question. After the usual consultation with counsel, the judge sent back his written answer. The bailiff returned quickly and reported, "The jury doesn't want your answer, Your Honor. They want the little woman lawyer to answer." The judge angrily replied, "The jury gets my answer or no answer." The bailiff departed, and the judge directed his anger toward me. Being candid, I had thought the judge was less than mediocre during trial, but I don't know if the jury thought the same or were just curious about me.

Well, after that long paragraph of digression, here we are back with the jury. The jury's deliberations are secret—justifiably and historically long-protected by a shield of confidentiality. Nothing is perfect, however, and many years ago a prestigious mid-Western university law school secretly recorded a jury's deliberations as part of a study that it was conducting. Of course, word leaked out about the recording and controversy erupted. I was fortunate enough to hear the recording. I was attending the annual judicial conference of the Tenth Circuit, which was being held in Estes Park, Colorado. The old cliché accurately describes that large, filled conference hall when the recording was played: "you could hear a pin drop." When it had ended, I think that all of us were surprised. Why? The amount of time and attention that the jury spent referring to the instructions and analyzing the evidence in light of those instructions was amazing.

When the jury's deliberations are ended and the verdict agreed upon, the jury notifies the bailiff who then notifies the judge and the lawyers.

Verdict

COUNSEL FOR both plaintiff and defendant are expected to be in court when the verdict is received. This humble item of procedure reminds me of another story from long ago. I was lawyer for the defendant in a jury trial held in Jackson, Wyoming, then a rustic town. Notice of the verdict came shortly after 10:00 p.m. Plaintiff's lawyer was a New York lawyer who had retired to Jackson. When he came to the courtroom for the verdict, the time was almost 11:00 p.m., and he was wearing pajamas, a brocade dressing gown, and leather slippers—a nighttime sartorial vision. The judge was horrified as was I. He barked, "You can't come to court dressed like you are." To this the lawyer replied, "This is the way we do it in New York." The judge ordered him to go home, get dressed in a suit, and then return. The verdict was finally received at midnight. Years later, when I met my second New York lawyer, a distinguished corporate lawyer, I asked about this custom of New York lawyers. He was shocked that such a false representation had been made, and worse that we all had believed it.

Now, we return to a civil jury trial. The judge receives and announces the verdict. The lawyer for the losing party then moves for "Judgment Not-withstanding Verdict." Not having ever lost a verdict in a civil jury trial, I have never made that motion, but have observed that it is rarely granted. When the motion is granted or denied, judgment is entered by the court and placed in the court's file; the trial is over. Within a prescribed window thereafter, the losing party may decide whether to file an appeal in the appellate court.

Now you've been introduced to the parts of a civil jury trial from start to finish and have a guide to the following essays about *voir dire*, opening statements, direct and cross-examination, witnesses, closing argument; and an essay about appeals.

VOIR DIRE: AN INSIDER'S LOOK AT JURY SELECTION

IF YOU have ever wondered how jurors are selected, or if you are called for jury duty, you may be particularly interested in this explanation.

What and Why Is *Voir Dire*?

VOIR DIRE in law is translated as "to speak the truth." The phrase refers to the process of questioning prospective jurors under oath to find out if they are suitable to be jurors in a particular case. The process begins with calling the required number of jurors from the jury panel into the jury box. The jury panel is comprised of the persons who received summonses from the court to report for jury duty. The number of prospective jurors called from the panel into the jury box for *voir dire* may vary from six to twelve, depending on the jurisdiction and type of case. In federal courts now and in many state courts, the trial judge or the lawyers may conduct the *voir dire*. When I was actively engaged many years ago in trial practice for over two decades, the lawyers always conducted the *voir dire* in Wyoming state courts and only the trial judge did so in federal court.

I tell you frankly that I did not like when the judge did the *voir dire*. You were allowed to submit written questions to the judge to ask the prospective jurors, but the judge had discretion as to whether to ask the requested question. And, of course, the lawyer had no control over the inflection or tone of the judge's voice when asking a question of a prospective juror. A true example of what I mean: a woman friend of mine who had just served as a juror in a federal court trial told me that she did not understand why the jury had to sit through the trial, because the judge had made clear when questioning them before the trial started what their verdict should be. The other reason I so disliked not being able to conduct the *voir dire* was my inability to have direct contact with the prospective jurors. Directly questioning them on *voir dire* gives the lawyer a much better ability to make a correct determination of a juror's suitability. Determining bias of a prospective juror is never easy. I could not ask, for example: "Do you have a bias against a large foreign corporation (my client) doing business in Wyoming as a competitor of the plaintiff (small local company)?" Of course, no bias; no one will openly admit in the jury box to a bias or a prejudice. If you suspect the prospective juror may harbor such feelings adverse to your client, you have to proceed indirectly and carefully to elicit enough information for a challenge for cause—a difficult task. Also, when the judge did the *voir dire*, I lost the fine early opportunity that direct personal contact provides to "sell" myself and my credibility to the jury.

The lawyer's determination of a person's suitability to serve as a juror—the whole purpose of *voir dire*—is generally based on two sources. First, sometimes in a major case the lawyer can obtain from the court in advance of trial a list of the persons called to report for jury duty and from which list the prospective jurors will be called into the jury box for *voir dire*. The lawyer then can hire an investigator to find out their backgrounds and any other information relevant to whether the person investigated would be appropriate to serve as a juror in the forthcoming trial. The second source, and the typical source in most civil cases, of finding out whether a person should serve as a juror is that person's responses given under oath to questions on *voir dire*. Do the responses reveal any biases detrimental to the lawyer's case?

The Reader may have noticed that I have *twice* mentioned that a prospective juror's answers to questions on *voir dire* are given under oath. I now go to a criminal case for an example of how important it is for a prospective juror to answer truthfully on *voir dire*. An able prosecutor who is a friend of mine prosecuted a case involving an especially heinous murder, and the state was seeking the death penalty. In such a case, the *voir dire* must include careful inquiry of each prospective juror seeking to ascertain if any of them is firmly opposed to the death penalty. He received assurance from each of them that the person would vote in favor of the death penalty in an appropriate case. The result was a guilty verdict on the murder charge. Then, jury deliberation about the sentence took a very long time, spanning several days. Finally, the jury returned their verdict, rejecting the death penalty in favor of life imprisonment. Afterwards, one of the jurors then came to my friend and told him that she was totally opposed to the death penalty. She had lied on *voir dire* to make sure, if she were on the jury, that the death penalty could not be imposed. She would have been a "hold out," if necessary, until a hung jury resulted. I was outraged, because being a liar under oath in a trial—whether as a prospective juror or as a witness—taints the integrity of our system of justice.

I have always thought that a couple of well-publicized prosecutions for blatant perjury should be brought at least once a year in every jurisdiction. As it is, I personally have been confronted with, and also have known about, many persons who are liars under oath in our courts—and they lie with impunity. We have a right to a fair trial—and that is impossible when liars can safely infect our judicial system.

What Are Proper Questions on *Voir Dire*?

I BEGIN my answer with a confession. My first attempt at *voir dire* is still an unresolved problem for me. At that time, books on "how to do" trial practice were not available and now mandatory Continuing Legal Education (CLE) was far in the future. I did not know any of the local Wyoming lawyers, who pointedly ignored the new woman lawyer. So, I listened to the *voir dire* at several trials. For my first jury trial, which was in a state court, I worked very hard to prepare the questions to ask. When I finished, it was about twenty minutes to noon, I was satisfied, but opposing counsel stood up and uttered the grave words, "May counsel approach the bench?" I knew just enough to know that I should join him there. The judge said sternly, "I was waiting for you to object. Clearly improper *voir dire*." Again, "Clearly improper *voir dire*." My heart sank to my toes, but then opposing counsel said, "That's not why I asked to approach the bench, Your Honor. It's now almost a quarter to noon, I'm hungry, and wondered if we could adjourn early for lunch." Whereupon the judge got so angry at him that he forgot to still be angry with me. For almost my entire legal career, I did not know what I did that was such "clearly improper *voir dire*." Then while I was writing this book, a dear friend, who is an eminent lawyer, was visiting me and I told him of this experience. After all this time, my friend gave me solace. He said: "Brooke, maybe the judge was wrong!" And that is the way that I shall now think of my first *voir dire*.

So now I return to my question: What is proper *voir dire*? The answer is simple: the questions should be relevant to finding out whether the prospective juror can be a competent, fair, and impartial juror in the case to be tried. Certain preliminary but important inquiries should always be made, and here is a list of them. Ask if anyone of the prospective jurors knows any of the following persons:

» Opposing party's(-ities') counsel or his/her relatives or persons in his/her law firm?
» Opposing party's(-ties') relative(s) or, if business entity, what contact(s)?
» Any of the opposition's witnesses (read and identify each person)? By court rule, the witness list is exchanged before trial.
» Any knowledge about this case to be tried? The source of that knowledge?

Also, the lawyer may want to explore if the person has had previous experience with a lawsuit, either as a party or as a juror.

Early in my legal trial career, I learned the importance of these preliminary questions. I was trying a commercial case involving two former partners in a bitter dispute with each other. I had told my client that my opinion was that he was "in the right" but in a trial the odds of victory were 50–50. He was a fine but high-strung, tense man, and very upset about being the defendant in a lawsuit brought against him by his ex-partner. I worried about my client's demeanor as a witness at trial. *Voir dire* was rather routine, but I noted that in asking the preliminary questions, opposing counsel did not ask the usual "Does anyone know the defendant (the opposing party)?" I was surprised and pleased by how well my client testified at trial, both on direct and cross-examinations. He seemed serene and confident. He was right. The jury returned a verdict in his favor. Then he turned to me and said, "I wasn't worried. My cousin was on the jury, and we have been close friends all our lives. I knew that he would hold out to favor me." Result: I never forgot a preliminary inquiry on *voir dire*.

The last question many lawyers ask is "Is there any reason, about which I have not asked, why you cannot serve as a fair and impartial juror in this case?" And, of course, a juror never—in my experience or to my knowledge—answers "yes." My last question, as the first woman trial lawyer in Wyoming, was "Have any of you noticed a basic difference between me and opposing counsel? If you have not, please raise your hand—I don't want you on the jury." No hand was ever raised, but I looked at each of the twelve jurors because of my quite reliable "antenna" for detecting an adverse bias attributable to my being a woman lawyer.

What Is Improper *Voir Dire*?

I THINK that overlong, irrelevant questioning is the most common form of improper *voir dire*. A vice of some trial lawyers is conducting an interminable *voir dire* about irrelevant trivia. I have never understood why some trial judges seem to have unlimited and unjustified patience with the lawyer who drags on *voir dire* at length with trivial questions. Here is a typical example. I remember suffering through a smarmy, lengthy *voir dire* with questions such as "Do you have children? How many? Boys? Girls? What grades are they in? How are they doing in school?" None of this was relevant to this which involved a commercial contract dispute. The judge, as too often occurs, failed to rein in the lawyer. I took fifteen minutes for my *voir dire* and believe that its brevity was a material aid to my trial victory.

I remember with joy, and invite you to share my pleasure, a lawyer friend who sat through one of these lengthy, irrelevant *voir dire* by opposing counsel in an alleged breach of contract case. When my friend's turn came, he asked the jury as a whole, "Is there anyone on this jury who does not like dogs? If so, please raise your hand." No hands. His next question, "Anyone on this jury not like the Broncos (the local NFL football team)? If so, please raise your hand." No hands. He turned to the judge, "Defense accepts this jury as is." Relevant questions? No. Endearing brevity of *voir dire*? Yes. He won the jury's verdict.

How Does the Lawyer Get Rid of an Unwanted Prospective Juror?

A TRIAL lawyer has two kinds of "challenges" to get rid of a prospective juror who the lawyer does not want: a Peremptory Challenge and a Challenge for Cause.

PEREMPTORY CHALLENGE

A LAWYER is not required to state a reason for a peremptory challenge. And the number of peremptory challenges allowed is fixed by statute or court rule. Thus, in the federal trial court in a civil case a party is allowed three peremptory challenges; in a criminal case seeking the death penalty, the defendant is allowed twenty peremptory challenges.

When does a lawyer use a peremptory challenge? The answer varies according to the circumstances or the lawyer. I would use a peremptory when I was concerned whether I could establish what I believed was a ground to challenge for cause, the most notable example being proof of gender bias against me—a pioneer in the state where I practiced. Some lawyers have told me that a prospective juror's demeanor or glint in the eyes made him distrustful enough to get the person dismissed from the jury.

Customarily, at the conclusion of initial *voir dire*, the trial judge would announce the dismissal of the jurors as to whom peremptory challenges had been made. In making the announcement, the trial judge should be neutral in tone and not state which lawyer had caused the dismissal. Sadly, this customary procedure was not always followed in our federal trial court (we had only one federal trial judge in Wyoming when I was trying cases there). Our federal trial judge was fine, both judicially and personally—but no one is perfect, and sadly he also announced which lawyer had used peremptory challenges to dismiss particular potential jurors.

I feel strongly that a rule should prohibit the judge from announcing which lawyers caused dismissal by way of a peremptory challenge. Let me give you an example of why the challenging lawyer's anonymity should be preserved. I had a federal court trial involving a substantial amount of money in a dispute between two large nonresident corporations, and I believed firmly that the merits and supporting evidence favored my client. When I looked out at the jury panel, I saw to my horror the wife of one of my husband's best friends. We two couples would quite regularly dine out together. Her husband was a pleasant, interesting person but she was neither and disliked me because I was a lawyer. Although I was always very careful never to mention my being a lawyer or anything remotely connected to law, the wife never failed on each dinner occasion to wait until the husbands were out of earshot to say such unpleasantries to me as: "I suppose that you think you are special because you are a lawyer" and "I think that it is disgusting for a married woman to practice law." I fervently hoped that she would not be called into the jury box for *voir dire*, but she was. I was confident that she would never vote for a verdict that would favor my client—no matter what the evidence. Loyalty to my client required my using a peremptory challenge to obtain her dismissal as a juror—which, of course, the judge announced. The trial lasted five days, and the woman sat through the whole event. Every day of the trial, at the morning and afternoon recess, she would pounce on me and say: "I demand that you tell me why you had me dismissed from the jury." I had no time for her during these "breaks" and so perforce ignored her demands, took a bathroom break, and then concentrated on my trial duties. After a short deliberation, the jury returned a verdict in my client's favor. I was, of course, very pleased and after making an appointment to see my client the next morning, I left the courtroom. Yes, the woman was still there, talking to one of the jurors. I heard her say, "Well, I would never have returned a verdict for the defense." Feeling weary and snappish, I paused and said to her: "You have just answered the question with which you hounded me throughout the trial." Mean? Probably, but accurate. Final reminder: the lawyer is never required to state the reason for a peremptory challenge.

CHALLENGE FOR CAUSE

A CHALLENGE for cause is just what its name states. For example, when on *voir dire* I asked a prospective juror the usual preliminary question, does he know opposing counsel and he replied, "Yes, he has been my lawyer for the past ten years." Then I would turn to the judge and say, "Your Honor, counsel challenges this juror for cause." The trial judge would probably accept the challenge because presumably the person would be biased in favor of opposing counsel's credibility. Sometimes, whether the cause suffices to support the challenge results in a short argument.

Invoking the right to challenge for cause is not always a good choice, even when the cause seems warranted. I cannot say whether what I am about to write applies also to a six-person jury so common today, but all my jury trials were to a twelve-person jury. For "my" size jury, I tell you that when the twelve jurors are in the jury box for *voir dire*, a symbiotic effect occurs. I think that this symbiosis is almost palpable to the questioning lawyer. The persons in the jury box seem a cohesive whole so that any offense or hurt to one of them is resented by the other eleven. Here I give you an example of firm ground to challenge for cause, but I did not because I sensed the others would be resentful.

I was defense counsel in a personal injury trial in a town of about 5,000 population. By this time, we had women on the juries in Wyoming. When I questioned the woman in the second row, she said that she was a registered nurse. Plaintiffs were a woman who had been seriously injured in an accident and her husband who was joined, as then common, claiming loss of consortium (legalese for loss of conjugal companionship and aid). The wife was also a registered nurse. When I questioned, I learned that the juror worked at the local hospital on the night shift and the plaintiff nurse was the only other nurse on the night shift; they had worked together and been friends for years.

One theory of jury selection dictates that in such a circumstance the safe thing is to say: "Challenge this juror for cause." This juror was a pleasant and sincere person, and I had a feeling that the other eleven jurors would somehow resent my having her removed. So, I asked, "Wouldn't you find it difficult to bring in a verdict against your friend? Even though you thought the defendant was not to blame?" She said, "No, I'm sure I could be fair." "Well, please think about it while I ask the other jurors some questions." I came back to her a second time, reminding her they worked together, the only two on the night shift. "Would you like to reconsider?" She said, "No, I'm certain I could be fair and impartial." I smiled and said I'd give her a little more time. After a few more questions of others, I came back for the third and last time, "Have you made your decision?" "Yes, I'm certain. I know I can be fair and impartial." I said to the judge: "Defense accepts the jury." I thought that I could feel relief from the jury that one of their own had not been rejected. Fortunately, the jury returned a defense verdict despite the risk I had taken.

My Ending Remarks about *Voir Dire*

I NEED to bring you up to date with information about a new development in jury selection since my era of trials. Now, except in smaller cases, a trial lawyer may hire jury consultants, non-lawyers who are considered experts in determining the types of jurors who should and should not be selected for jury service in a particular case. This service, of course, increases the cost of litigation. Also, there is "focusing": this is hiring up to three sets of persons as jurors to test their reaction to testimony by experts or key witnesses whom the lawyer plans to use at trial. I would not be comfortable using either method of "jury testing." I guess that I am wrong. On three separate occasions, in conversations with three different retired trial judges, each of whom is a good friend, the practice of using jury consultants arose in discussion. When I said that I would not use them, each of my friends said, "Brooke, I can't agree with you." When I asked why, each gave me the same response. They all said that many lawyers needed the help, especially women lawyers. Why? The same reply: "Women lawyers don't seem able to detect bias against them." I was and still am shocked. How can you be an effective trial lawyer if you lack sensitivity to people, either as prospective jurors or as witnesses?

Another comment on jury selection about which I have strong feeling is an old adage prevalent in my day that one should "never leave only one minority on a jury." I didn't pay any attention to that adage or to any other adage of jury selection during my trial era. My guidance came from the prospective jurors themselves. I depended solely on my person-to-person relationship when I questioned each one. I cared about only one attribute: Would the person be a fair and impartial juror. l believe that this is the best way to select a jury, and I still believe that the average American when serving as a juror wants to do the "right thing" based on the evidence and the law and helped by fair argument. I dare to close with an old adage: "The proof of the pudding is in the eating"— and I never lost even one of my many civil jury trials.

OPENING STATEMENTS: PLEASE, ANYTHING BUT A "ROADMAP"!

THE LAWYER always has the right to make an opening statement at the beginning of a trial. Some criminal defense lawyers prefer to waive their opening statement until they start the defense. About 95 percent of my trials were civil rather than criminal cases, and I always made an opening statement. I believe that the opening statement is probably the most underused persuasive weapon in the trial lawyer's arsenal, because too often it is a dreary summary of the evidence promised to be presented to the jury.

Some lawyers in their opening statement drone a dull summary of their pleadings in the case; others step over the line into argument and can be reprimanded by the judge for doing so. When you are the lawyer on the other side, your objection to the offending lawyer's improper use of argument has to be carefully worded so as not to irritate either the judge who will rule on your objection or the jury who might think that you are being "picky." Here is an example of an objection that worked well: "With all due respect to Your Honor and to opposing counsel, I object to opposing counsel's now arguing the case, and this counsel asks the court to enforce the rule of 'no argument' in opening statement."

After sixty-five years at the Bar, I can report that opening statements still sometimes suffer from a lawyer saying to the jury the tiresome cliché: "I am going to give you a roadmap of the evidence you will hear." Opening statements should fairly summarize the evidence that the lawyer will present to prove the lawyer's case. I also often preferred to include adverse evidence that I knew the opposing party would present. Why? So that I could put my "spin" on that evidence and to weaken or even cancel its impact on the jury.

To the lawyer: please just summarize, don't argue—and don't give a "roadmap."

To the jury: ignore any argument and don't blindly trust a roadmap; it may misdirect you. Most important to the jury: when you retire to deliberate, make sure that the lawyers have fulfilled their promises made in opening statements as to the evidence that the jury would receive.

TESTIMONY: DIRECT EXAMINATION AND CROSS-EXAMINATION

Direct Examination

AFTER OPENING statements comes the presentation of evidence: evidence by testimony of witnesses and evidence by exhibits. The plaintiff, as the party bringing the lawsuit, goes first; and so you'll know the term, plaintiff's case may be called "case-in-chief."

Plaintiff has the "burden of proof," which in a civil case is by a "preponderance of the evidence." The judge will instruct the jury on the meaning of preponderance of the evidence. I always think of it as any amount of favorable evidence over 50 percent. In a criminal case, American law cloaks the accused in a presumption of innocence, and the prosecution's burden of proof is evidence of guilt "beyond a reasonable doubt." Appeals abound by defendants who have been found guilty, alleging reversible error in the judge's instruction to the jury on the meaning of beyond a reasonable doubt in a criminal case.

Plaintiff's lawyer conducts Direct Examination of each of plaintiff's witnesses. Direct examination means that plaintiff's lawyer is forbidden to ask a question worded so as to suggest the answer. Plaintiff's case-in-chief is supposed to present all the evidence that plaintiff relies on for a victory—proof by a preponderance (over 50%) of the evidence in a civil case.

Plaintiff's lawyer needs to be prepared to argue credibly for the admission of testimony and exhibits to which defendant's counsel raises objection, so that the judge will rule "Objection overruled" instead of "Objection sustained." At the close of the case-in-chief, defendant's counsel always (or should always) move for a directed verdict for the defendant on the ground that plaintiff's case-in-chief has failed to establish even a *prima facie* case. In the case-in-chief, plaintiff needs to present sufficient evidence to avoid the judge granting the defendant's motion directing a verdict for the defense. So, plaintiff's counsel may seem to present too much evidence. Direct Examination can, as a result, become boring to the jury and even to opposing counsel. Suggested cure: try to make direct examinations interesting. This is often difficult for a lawyer because a key witness for a corporate client or the injured plaintiff may be inarticulate or just plain dull.

Some plaintiff's lawyers still resort to the trial tactic of calling the defendant or chief witness for a defendant entity as plaintiff's first witness; and examination of that witness is deemed a form of cross-examination so leading questions are permissible. The court rule permitting this tactic was adopted many years ago, so it has long lost any element of surprise. Prudent defense counsel nonetheless still warns a key defense witness of the risk of being the first witness plaintiff calls in the case-in-chief. Although some lawyers think this a clever "twist," I never agreed with that view but thought it a rather obvious trick—and I believe that jurors are quick to perceive trickery and distrust the trickster.

I remember many years ago one of the few cases when I was plaintiff's counsel in a personal injury case. The plaintiff had sustained a serious whiplash (yes, that is a legitimate injury), with resultant blinding, hideously painful headaches as well as a painful cut on her knee. In my office during trial preparation, I told her that on direct examination I would ask her to describe to the jury what her headaches were like. She told me, "They are bad." My heart sank. I believe, and our professional rules of ethics support the belief, that it is unethical to tell a witness what words to use in testifying. I said, "Thank you. So, they are bad." She said, "Yes, very bad." A puny jury verdict was looming. I gently prodded by saying in a flat tone: "So, you can tell the jury that your headaches are very bad." My tone of voice apparently made my client angry because she snapped: "You don't seem to understand. When I get one of these headaches, it's just like a lot of tiny men are inside my head hitting it with hammers!" "Aha!" I said, "Because of how you said that, now I can understand." And thus she described the headaches to the jury.

After the accident, the driver and his fellow teens in the car—who had been drinking—had to stop because of damage to their car. They had approached my client to make fun of her and had laughed at her. Although not a hefty sum, our plaintiff's verdict included money for what are now called "punitive damages" (formerly called "exemplary damages"). And I was later told that this was the first such award in Wyoming—but I am not sure this is so.

Postscript: When my phlegmatic client came to my office to collect her excellent judgment in that era, I thought that she would be pleased. I was wrong. She pulled her skirt up to her knee, bared it from her stocking, and showed me the tiniest scar you can imagine—and said, "Look at this. Think how I will look in a bathing suit." I looked at her and decided I would rather not imagine such a sight.

Well, back to the topic of direction examination. An important limitation on direct examination is that the plaintiff's lawyer is not allowed to ask the plaintiff or plaintiff's witnesses a "leading question," which suggests the answer to the person being questioned. For example: "Then you went to the restaurant, didn't you?"

After examination of a witness, plaintiff's counsel says to defendant's counsel, "You may cross-examine." And that is my next topic: cross-examination.

Cross-Examination

CROSS-EXAMINATION IS not subject to the prohibition of leading questions. Hence, some lawyers like to phrase their questions on "cross" (the lawyers' colloquial word for "cross-examination") with the hackneyed "Isn't it true that . . ."

I could write a separate book about cross-examination, but many other lawyers have preceded me with books, articles, and seminars about cross-examination. One of the few books giving examples of trial interrogations was Francis Wellman's now classic *The Art of Cross-Examination* which gave dazzling examples from famous cases in history. In reading the book, I thought it amazing how the witness always seemed to crumble under a withering cross-examination. I never had that experience. Indeed, I have never known a lawyer who has had a witness crumble on cross-examination when caught in a lie. Instead, the prevaricating witness just seems to be stimulated to create more lies. Ah, well. Eventually, the lawyer can elicit enough inconsistencies for the jury to decide correctly that the witness is a liar.

As I was writing this essay, a lawyer friend visited me—always a treat now that I am retired. We were swapping stories and when I told a couple about cross-examination, my friend asked, "Have you put those in the book that you are writing?" I replied "No," and he said, "I think that you should." So here they are.

The first had sad struggles for me but a good outcome for my client. I had been in practice only several months when I had a contested trial in our lower trial court. I did not know how to cross-examine and was scared about the prospect. Please remember that I was perforce practicing "solo" as a woman lawyer. No helpful "how-to" law books or lectures on trial practice were then available. So, I practiced at home saying "Counsel has no questions for this witness," with a tone of voice conveying that I thought this witness was not worth cross-examining in view of her incredible testimony. I practiced over and over, and then tried it on my husband. When I asked what it sounded like to him, he said that it meant I thought the witness was not worth the bother of cross-examination. And that's what I did at the little trial—and it worked—with a victory for my client!

Styles of cross-examination vary from lawyer to lawyer. Some believe in intimidation as an effective style. Based on my observation, I believe that this is a usually ineffective style. The average juror resents this approach to a witness, and I think the resentment spills over on the lawyer. I lacked the physical presence to intimidate and didn't want to do so anyway. Other lawyers use what I deem "trickery" and seem to underrate the intelligence of the jury. I never had a jury that failed to perceive tricks and artifice by opposing counsel. One of the most successful trial lawyers I have ever known was always courteous in cross-examination. By request, I wrote a professional "obituary" about this lawyer, and all the opposing counsel I spoke to said "He was always a gentleman."

This is an appropriate place for the second example of a memorable cross-examination that my friend thought the Reader would enjoy. I have always thought that a woman lawyer should be very careful to avoid seeming aggressive—and it is easy to cross the line if trying to be forceful. My story ends with the most heartfelt praise that I ever received for a cross-examination. I was defending a major car accident case in which the husband-and-wife plaintiffs were severely injured. The jury trial was in federal court because the accident had happened in Yellowstone National Park. On behalf of the insurance company, I was defending a young woman driver of the other car, a German national who had returned to Germany and was not coming back to Wyoming for this civil trial.

The day the trial began was a cold and snowy one. The large old federal courtroom had never looked more oppressively impressive with four-foot-high maroon-red marble wainscoting, very high ceilings and high judge's bench. The plaintiffs were a tall handsome couple and their lawyer, whom I knew, was over six feet. I never felt more small and insignificant sitting alone at counsel table with my client in Germany. I had no "live" witness because the Park officer who had investigated the accident had been transferred to Organ Pipe Cactus National Monument. When I had looked the place up on the map, I found that it was in Arizona about a mile from the Mexican border. I decided against taking his oral deposition because I did not want to go there, especially in winter cold, so took his testimony by written interrogatories. This man could use fewer words to answer questions than any witness whom I had ever encountered. So, I planned to read his skimpy answers slowly—starting as close to noon as I could, thinking that if I could read a little more after lunch, the jury might remember that we put on a defense.

As the trial progressed, I realized that any chance I had of prevailing depended on an effective cross-examination of the husband and a closing argument that, to be effective, depended on that cross-examination. When the time came for me to cross-examine the plaintiff husband, I could sense that he was contemptuous of me. I could almost feel when the witness began to put down his guard. Good! I played his cross-examination low-key until I had him in the noose—and then I pulled it tight. I pounced with the questions that "boxed in" the witness. He had really entangled himself with inconsistencies between his sworn deposition testimony and testimony at trial. Closing argument became a pleasure, and the defense verdict a happy event.

As I was packing my briefcase at counsel table after the verdict, I looked up to find the plaintiff husband standing next to me. He said abruptly, "Are you married?" I replied, "Yes." And then followed the most heartfelt compliment that I ever received on my cross-examinations. He said, "Well, when you get home, tell your husband that I'm sorry for the poor son-of-a-bitch."

My recommendation to young trial lawyers: be "natural" in your demeanor on cross-examination, free from any affectation. I always tried to be courteous and gradually to make the witness feel that cross-examination by this lawyer was "not so bad." Another recommendation: tailor your demeanor to the witness. Although always courteous, your demeanor in cross-examining a seemingly gentle little old lady will not be the same as when examining a large, bully-type man. Finally, and most difficult to heed, never ask a question on cross-examination to which you do not know the answer.

To all Readers: *I believe that cross-examination is a valuable tool for achieving justice. The reason: cross-examination tests the credibility and accuracy of the testimony by the witnesses.*

OF COURSE, I could not discuss with you the components of a trial without writing more details about witnesses. I write here only about "lay" witnesses, as distinguished from "expert" witnesses. The diversity of witnesses never ceased to amaze me: in all shapes, heights, colors, and abilities. Some spoke clearly and audibly; others mumbled. Some answered each question with a torrent of words; others were as brief as if each word would be costly and answers had to be pried out. Witnesses were a fascinating study for me, sometimes impressive and other times frustrating occasionally bordering on maddening.

The unalterable fact is that witnesses are an integral part of a trial. The trial lawyer needs always to be alert to the risk of an unpleasant surprise by the witness. I will defend my view that the lawyer, no matter how many trials, can never precisely predict the difficult witness. My law partner during my trial era in Wyoming was a very expert trial lawyer. We often defended major personal injury cases together. Our custom was to trade-off on difficult witnesses in forthcoming trials, unless some compelling tactical reason dictated otherwise. I remember one case when it was "his turn" to have the good key witness when we were defense counsel in a personal injury case. The key testimony would be the defendant's testimony about rushing out of her home to jump (bravely) into her driverless vehicle, trying to stop it from speeding downhill where it struck and severely injured a small child. The defendant was a personable and articulate woman who was a senior government scientist. What went wrong with her at trial, I don't know. My partner never could even get her to testify as to leaving her house!—much less having rushed to her vehicle.

In the next case that we had together it was obviously my turn for the difficult witness, after my partner's prior catastrophic witness. This key witness could not answer the most simple question without flooding you with a lengthy response. I privately thought that if I were to ask her what day came after Monday, she would reply, "Well, of course later comes Wednesday, Thursday, Friday, Saturday, Sunday, and then after Monday comes Tuesday." My partner said that he just couldn't stand the prospect of dealing with that woman as a witness. As proof of how experienced trial lawyers can never predict, I tell you here that I never had a better witness than the woman proved to be at trial. Her responses were brief, to-the-point, well-articulated—ah, what blissful relief! I guess the answer to how a witness will be at trial is comparable to betting on the red or black of a roulette wheel.

I cannot leave the topic of witnesses without some cautionary words about witness preparation. Although today depositions routinely precede trials, the physical premises where the depositions occur lack the formality of a courtroom. When I was trying cases, depositions were still rare, and our courtrooms were usually large and very impressive. If I had witnesses unfamiliar with the world of courts, judges, and lawyers, I would take such a witness after-hours to the courtroom where the trial would be held. I would say to that prospective witness: "That is where you will sit as a witness. Sit in the chair, which is on that platform, so it won't seem so strange at trial."

In preparing the witness to testify, I firmly believe that the lawyer should not "coach" the witness in what to say—I think that this is highly unethical. I could ethically, however, prepare the prospective witness for my areas of inquiry and the type of questions to expect on cross-examination by opposing counsel. Today's deposition practice gives the lawyer the opportunity to appraise the witnesses on whom the lawyer will have to rely at trial. I do not consider it "coaching" to talk to a witness about demeanor—although sometimes this can be a delicate task.

For example, I recall an executive of a large corporation, headquartered in the East, who at his deposition in Wyoming was well prepared with all the necessary facts and figures and testified with assurance—and arrogance. His self-esteem was as a very-important-person, a VIP. When we returned to my office after the deposition, he told me, "I believe that I gave you all the testimony that you needed and am well-prepared for trial."

When he said that, I suddenly had an irrelevant and irreverent memory of a humble little case in Justice of the Peace Court in my very early years as a lawyer. My client was a young farmer whose "pride and joy" was the family car which he used instead of his battered pickup to take his family to church and to visit relatives and was always kept "real neat and clean." He took it to the service garage for its first oil change and said his car looked "terrible" inside when he picked it up. At trial, I asked him to describe the condition of his car when he picked it up. He replied: "It looked just like a pair of bear cubs had been let loose to play inside it." We won, or more accurately, he won his case.

Well, back to my Eastern VIP executive. I looked at him as he described how well he had testified at his deposition. After my happy recollection of the young farmer's winning testimony, I decided that I wanted to keep intact my unbroken record of civil jury trial victories, so I told my corporate client's VIP the truth: "You gave all the necessary testimony, but you failed to conceal your contempt for the obviously rural people at the deposition and your country lawyer, who worse, is a woman. Your testimony was complete and competent, but the jury will not like you. I think their dislike of you may be fatal to our case. The twelve jurors are all honest, hard-working, loving family people. We folks out here deserve your respect as decent, intelligent Americans—and I don't want you to spoil my perfect record of civil jury trial victories." He was understandably shocked and further shocked as I gave him examples from his deposition testimony of "talking down" to us at the deposition as if we were all stupid.

The happy end: My Eastern VIP was fine at trial, pleased with our victory, and his parting words to me were "I shall never forget you." Hmm . . . cryptic so I don't know what he meant, and maybe it is better that way.

Another, memorable for me, example of witness preparation involving witness demeanor is The Weeping Defendant. I undertook the defense of a woman who on a clear day hit a car head-on causing major injuries and one death. The highway patrol report convinced me that the cause of the accident was plaintiff driver's high speed, not any fault of my client, the defendant. When I interviewed my client, I was astounded and perplexed. I have never met anyone before or since who started weeping so easily and copiously. All I asked that started her flood of tears was, "About how far away was plaintiff's car when you first saw it?" Answer: "I don't know." I probed gently and finally prodded urgently—and the flood of tears began. The answer became clear: the defendant had no idea whatsoever of how far plaintiff's car was from her when she first saw it. As the flood of tears continued, I said not to worry, because her truthful answer was that she did not know. She asked me: "I know that I'll start crying. What shall I do?" Me, "Don't worry. Because you don't know, that's it—you don't know." At trial all happened predictably, including the distance question on cross-examination, followed by my client's flood of tears. Plaintiff's counsel then fell into a trap. He started pressing her to answer, backing away from her, and asking "Was it about this far?" "I don't know," and more tears. The lawyer kept backing down the courtroom until I thought that he might back out of it, while asking the same question and the tears continued endlessly. Ah, the time had come to protect my witness—and win. I stood up, addressed the judge, and said: "Your Honor, I must protest opposing counsel's abuse of this witness. She has answered the same question repeatedly and made clear that she will not depart from the truth. I respectfully move the court to stop this abusive cross-examination." The court granted the motion. I gently helped my weeping witness out of the witness chair, while opposing counsel muttered "No further questions." Jury verdict: for the defendant; judgment: for the defendant.

Postscript: In preparing my witnesses for trial, I always promised them that I would protect them from abuse by opposing counsel, and I always tried to keep that promise.

My witness preparation emphasized the breadth and gravity of the oath that the witness would be required to take before testifying. I am surprised that some lawyers still dust-off these "old chestnuts" for cross-examination. For one example: "Did your lawyer discuss with you the testimony that you are to give at trial?" And you can and should answer "yes." For another example: "What did your lawyer tell you to be sure and say?" Me to my client: "You can and should answer what I have emphasized for you to say: The truth, the whole truth, and nothing but the truth."

I end this essay with some helpful advice from an old pro on being a witness at depositions and trials. Here are some good rules to remember when you are being examined.

1. Be sure that you understand the question. If you have any doubts whatsoever about what is being asked you, you can simply say: "I'm sorry, but I am not sure what you are asking me." And the lawyer will re-word the question and ask you if that clarifies the question.

2. Some lawyers still resort to the old "yes" or "no" questions, usually preceded by the equally old "Isn't it true that . . . Answer 'yes' or 'no.'" You can say (and I have used this frustrating response at my depositions as an expert witness): "I cannot give you an accurate answer with just a 'yes' or 'no,' and I presume that you want an accurate answer."

3. Be alert to detect a "sneaky" question. The clue is when opposing counsel, who is obviously competent, asks you a question that is somewhat ambiguous—you are really not sure what is being asked of you. Listen hard always for qualifying adjectives or adverbs in questions. You respond truthfully that you are not sure what you are being asked and would counsel please re-word the question. Counsel omits the adjective or adverb and may substitute a different one, and quickly re-asks the question. Aha! The qualifying "sneaky"? Yes. Your response: you point out the key difference in the re-worded question, and your cross-examination will soon end.

4. *Last and most important: Always, without exception, be truthful. A witness who will not deviate from the truth and remains vigilant against being tricked or bullied into seeming falsehoods, is always safe. Truth for the witness is both shield and armor.*

CLOSING ARGUMENT

CLOSING ARGUMENT was always my favorite part of a jury trial. Before starting what I would write about closing arguments, I went online to find out all the latest information about "closings." How do the modern closing arguments differ from my era? Determined to have an open mind as I researched, I nonetheless was not impressed by today's instructions, recommendations, and advice about closing arguments.

I have informal credentials for writing about closing arguments. In addition to never losing any of my civil jury trials, I had an independent endorsement that they had been useful. Many years ago a prestigious law school's graduate program undertook a research project about whether closing arguments served any good purpose or would be better eliminated to shorten trials. The premise apparently was that "no closing argument" would be a better procedure. Our federal judge told me about the project, that he had been visited for "interviewing" and had referred the researchers to some jurors in my recent trials. He told me that they reported to him that every juror so visited had said my closing argument was "helpful," and some of them had even said that they had thought my client had no chance of a winning verdict until my closing argument convinced them otherwise.

So with fair warning that I lack scientific basis for my views, I am committed to the opinion that in closing argument, the lawyer must be punctilious about complying with its rules, especially prohibitions—and, most importantly, be sincere.

Some of the rules for closing argument are very old and still very good. For example, the lawyer is forbidden to express a personal opinion as to the credibility—or lack of it—as to any witness. Some lawyers try to circumvent this rule by facial expression or tone of voice, which of course cannot show in the written record of the trial as errors supporting an appeal. Closely akin to that rule is the one forbidding the lawyer to express the lawyer's personal opinion of the righteousness of the client's claims or defenses in a civil suit or client's innocence in a criminal trial.

This rule forbidding the lawyer's expression of a personal opinion is some-times obeyed more faithfully in the breach than in the observance. For an example: if opposing counsel is violating the rules for closing argument, what remedy do you have to protect your client? The answer: you may stand, address the judge, and object to the offensive tactic. An able judge will sustain your objection and warn the opposing counsel to avoid such conduct during the remainder of that lawyer's closing argument.

But is it a wise tactic to object during closing argument? Maybe yes, maybe no. The trial lawyer must always be careful not to make what the jury might consider "too many" objections during the course of a trial. This can be a seri-ous problem when opposing counsel in a trial is often "treading the line" and stepping over it. If the offending opposing counsel is a seasoned, experienced lawyer, the jury's sympathy may not be roused; and hopefully the jurors may even become impatient with the offending lawyer.

A worse problem may be a young, inexperienced attorney who needs to learn the rules. How far can you let that young lawyer stray and still keep your client safe? Answer: you don't want your legitimate objections to be so many that you make the jury sorry for that young lawyer.

When I went online, the materials warned "Prepare for closing argument." Sometimes the lawyers are fortunate, the trial is ready for closing arguments, and it is 3:00 p.m.; the judge may adjourn until the next morning. Sometimes in that time frame, the judge will grant a half-hour recess to be followed by closing arguments, ending at 5:30 p.m. Also, I have had "no break" and been grateful for being defendant's counsel instead of plaintiff's counsel who has to make the first closing argument.

How does one prepare for closing argument? I did not bother to read the online recommendations. Instead, I'll write what I did. On a then 8.5-by-13-inch lined yellow legal pad, I would draw a line down the middle of the page. On the right side of the line, I would write a note on the ongoing evidence that I might want to address in closing. I tried to keep these notes to a minimum. Then during any time window, no matter how tiny such as a five-minute "stretch" for the jurors, I would check to decide which of those notes I should include in my closing argument, and then jot on the opposite left side of the line key words I would use. A humble and primitive method? Yes, but it worked just fine for me. Now I'm told some lawyers take their notes on laptop PC's or bring an employee to court to take the trial notes. To each, his or her own! I would still do it the same way today. I would make a red check on each "left" line to show me that item was to be included in the closing.

Here is something I found important about imparting information verbally. Never try to emphasize more than three points. More will just float over your listeners. I always felt a small, mean glow of satisfaction when opposing counsel would, for example, say "I am going to count out on my fingers the eight reasons that . . ." My preference was never to stress more than three key factual issues that I believed the evidence had resolved in my client's favor.

For the Reader who has never served on a jury, and maybe those who have, I thought that you might be interested to read some examples from my closings. First, though, I tell you that I think most lawyers talk too much. The court limits the time of closing argument, and I always took care not to use my full time—even stopping five minutes short could be effective.

I always started my closings the same way. "Gentlemen of the jury"— and a few years later when women became allowed on juries—"Ladies and Gentlemen of the jury." Then, "I am no orator and am not going to argue to you. Instead, I remind you that I have lived with this case a lot longer than you and believe that I can be most helpful by summarizing the key evidence for you." Thus, I would customarily begin my closing argument quietly and modestly. Then, I would move to an increasingly lively presentation of the key evidence favoring my client. I would stress any evidence in favor of my client that had remained undisputed by the other party. What about evidence unfavorable to my client? Lawyers do not agree on the best way to deal with this problem. My preference was always to bring it up, put my "spin" on it, using my descriptive words, and hope for a neutralizing effect.

I always concluded my closing argument with my heartfelt summary of the two or three main reasons the evidence supported victory for my client. Emotional? Yes. Sincere? Always. I repeat: closing argument was my favorite part of a trial. I always believed that I could win the case with my closing argument. At the end of a trial, I always felt passionately that my client deserved to win, but I learned to curb that passion following an incident that shocked me and in which I had unprofessionally become emotionally involved in my argument. After a trial in a small community, one of the jurors came up to me and said: "Ma'am, we didn't think that you had a chance to win until that closing talk and when you rolled up your sleeves and really gave it to us, we realized that you were right." I had no remembrance of rolling up my sleeves and resolved always to be "more cool" in the future—but I don't know if I did behave better.

But this I know: the key to persuasion is sincerity.

ABOUT APPEALS

APPEALS ARE an integral and vital part of our American legal system. I consider appeals to be part of the litigation process. The losing party in the trial court has the right to appeal to a higher or appeals court. For example, the loser at a state court trial has the right to appeal to the state's appellate court, usually called the state's supreme court, or an intermediate court of appeals—with several exceptions to these titles, for example, New York where the highest appellate court is called the Court of Appeals. The loser in a federal district court trial has the right to appeal to the court of appeals for the circuit where the district is located, for example, New York is in the United States Court of Appeals for the Second Circuit, and California is in the United States Court of Appeals for the Ninth Circuit. Many people, including lawyers, usually refer to the federal circuit courts of appeals simply by number, for example, Sixth Circuit or Eighth Circuit. In my preceding discussion of *The Judiciary: What It Means for You*, there is an organizational chart of the federal courts and more explanation.

One notable exception to this right to appeal may surprise you. You have no right of appeal to the United States Supreme Court. Instead, if you want to have an adverse decision reviewed by the Supreme Court, since Congress enacted the Judiciary Act of 1925, you file a Petition for *Writ of Certiorari*. *Certiorari* has a slushy pronunciation on which not even all the justices agree, and lawyers usually call it "cert" for an obvious reason. The United States Supreme Court receives annually about 10,000 Petitions for *Writ of Certiorari*, of which the court grants about one hundred. The Court has adequate assistants to help winnow through the thousands of petitions for "cert" and make a preliminary selection. The justices decide which petitions will be granted, and four of the nine justices are required to accept the case for review before the *writ* will issue.

A federal court of appeals is the court to which you have the right to appeal resulting from an adverse judgment, civil or criminal, in a federal district court. During my many years as a lawyer, the Second Circuit, which includes the State of New York, has always been a "strong" circuit, so that a precedent from that court has more persuasive weight than does one from one of the weaker circuits. This fact has always intrigued me, because New York has never been a role model for its political purity; but the judicial appointments to the United States Court of Appeals for the Second Circuit, located in Manhattan, have always been notable for their excellence. And the United States District Court for the Southern District of New York, also located in Manhattan, has always made much of American business law. Again, my curiosity is aroused by the consistency of these courts' judicial excellence compared to New York City's political history. Other circuit courts that are "strong" in areas of law pertinent to their member states are the Seventh Circuit on business law, based in Chicago and serving states such as Illinois, and the Fifth Circuit on oil and gas law, serving Louisiana and Texas and Mississippi.

I include several not-commendatory comments, but always being noncontroversial does not paint a true picture. I remember some years ago when we had a "strong" United States Supreme Court that stated it had to reverse more decisions of the Ninth Circuit (of which California is a member state) than of all the other circuits together. The Tenth Circuit, in which my practice states of Colorado and Wyoming are located, has always been considered one of the "weaker" circuits. Hence, in writing appellate briefs for the state Supreme Court I would scurry to find precedent from "strong" courts.

"Appellate Briefs"—what a misnomer! "Briefs" ho, ho, trying to make some lawyers be brief, either on paper or orally, requires specific court rules.

I remember when courts first began limiting the number of pages for an appellate brief, and presto! Before you would believe it, some lawyers were submitting briefs typed in small print and using flyspeck-type footnotes! So now the careful lawyer checks the applicable rule in the federal circuit court or state appellate court where the brief will be filed to ensure its compliance in form. The typical appellate court rule mandates as to form of briefs: the maximum number of pages, the size of the paper, the minimum or preferred size of type, and a ban on attempted evasion of size by flyspeck-type footnotes.

Opinions differ among lawyers as to whether the appellate lawyer and trial lawyer have different skills; I think that they do. Hence, I believe that a lawyer who is both a trial and an appellate lawyer has an advantage over one who does not handle trials. I believe that the reason for this advantage is that the appellate-only lawyer cannot flesh out the skeleton that is the record of the trial. For example, the trial lawyer reading the trial record can add recollection of a witness's voice inflection and body language and bias. Because of my experience with both trials and appeals, I can verify that the skills are very different. I could tell the distinction when a case was referred to me to handle the appeal, after the referring lawyer had lost at trial.

Whether the appellate lawyer should or should not also handle trials is rapidly becoming a question of historical interest. Why? Because appellate advocacy is rapidly becoming an academic exercise of a departed era.

In my personal opinion, appellate advocacy has become very often limited to the parties' written briefs that are strictly limited as to form. The advocacy to the court for the client often does not include the lawyers' oral appellate argument. Appellate courts today, generally speaking, seem not to want to hear from attorneys in courtroom appearances. For example, in some states, the oral argument is not automatically scheduled, as formerly. Instead, a lawyer in the appeal must file a written request for oral argument. I never filed such a request, but "outwaited" the other side because I thought that the court did not want to hear us and would resent the request.

The other, and to me more serious, limitation on oral appellate argument is the reduction in allowable time by the courts. For years, the typical time was a half-hour for the plaintiff and for the defendant. I thought this a fair and reasonable time to make a useful presentation. In one appeal, testing the constitutionality of an advance-escrow type refunding statute, we were assigned two hours per side! The result was a splendid opinion selected for publication in a national series of precedent-setting opinions. I made a special effort never to use all my allowable time. I sometimes wonder if my appellate successes were due only to my introductory statement that, "This counsel will not need all of her allowable time"—and I always kept that promise.

Some appellate courts are limiting oral arguments to fifteen minutes per side. I conclude by stating undiplomatically that I think fifteen-minute arguments serve no good purpose and are insufficient to help that court to justify the cost to litigants.

I hope you will enjoy reading about several unusual and important appeals that I handled and have described earlier in this book in *The Appellate Lawyer* in Part Two.

What's Important in the Law for Us

The use of words is to express ideas. Perspicuity, therefore, requires not only that the ideas should be distinctly formed, but that they should be expressed by words distinctly and distinctly appropriate to them.
James Madison, The Federalist, *No. 37 (1788)*

WE THE PEOPLE—PREAMBLE TO OUR CONSTITUTION

T O THE Reader: I could not write this book without including the Preamble to our 1787 Constitution of the United States:

We the People of the United States, in Order to form a more perfect Union, establish Justice, insure domestic Tranquility, provide for the common defence, promote the general Welfare, and secure the Blessings of Liberty to ourselves and our Posterity, do ordain and establish this Constitution for the United States of America.

Without an extra word or phrase, the Preamble's goals are magnificent and timeless.

Over 200 years later, the goals remain goals not yet converted into achievements. But one thing is sure: we shall never attain nor even progress toward those goals if we do not improve our legal system. And I fearlessly include lawyers and judges and legal education in the meaning of "legal system."

Constitution: The Interstate Commerce Clause

IS THE Interstate Commerce Clause interesting? Well, I think so and hope that you will agree with me. I was shocked when I recently re-read, after many years, the entire, very short Commerce Clause. Article I, Section 8, Clause 3 of our Constitution grants Congress the "Power To . . . regulate Commerce with foreign Nations, and among the several States, and with the Indian Tribes"— all in only seventeen (17) words! The twelve (12) words pertaining to interstate commerce read:

> The Congress shall have Power To . . . regulate Commerce . . . among the several States.

That's it—only twelve (12) words—the entire power of Congress over interstate commerce!

I cannot help but think of the millions of words that the courts in this country have written about this clause. I leave to the Reader's imagination how many words it would take today for the members of Congress to write an interstate commerce clause.

The Interstate Commerce Clause has engendered thousands of judicial opinions. I have always thought that tension between federal power and states' rights is inherent in all these opinions. I begin our look at the fate of the Interstate Commerce Clause in the courts with the landmark 1824 United States Supreme Court opinion in *Gibbons v. Ogden*, 22 U.S. 1. The first chief justice of the Supreme Court, the great and still unsurpassed American jurist John Marshall, wrote this first opinion by the Supreme Court about the Interstate Commerce Clause. He apologized for the opinion's length. Reading it, I think not only of its excellence but also having no law clerks (unlike today's Supreme Court justices) to do his research or to write a draft of the opinion. I also think about the physical labor required. Imagine writing all that by hand—before computers or typewriters, even before fountain pens. Instead, he wrote by dipping a quill pen into ink and with no electricity to provide light for his task.

The opinion in *Gibbons v. Ogden*, written in pleasingly precise language, served for 113 years as a reliable guide—not always followed—to a useful and sensible application of the Interstate Commerce Clause. The facts of the case are briefly stated. In 1808, Robert Fulton and Robert Livingston held a monopoly granted by the New York state legislature to operate steamboats on the state's waters and extending to waters that stretch between states. Aaron Ogden operated steamboats under a Fulton-Livingston license. Thomas Gibbons operated steamboats between New Jersey and New York, in competition with Ogden under a federal coastal license granted by a congressional act. Ogden sued to have the court restrain Gibbons from operating his steamboats and won in the lower courts, but Gibbons prevailed in the Supreme Court.

Gibbons v. Ogden held that the federal power to regulate interstate commerce included the power to regulate interstate navigation. Marshall's opinion confirmed that our Constitution is one of "enumeration, not of definition" and then defined "commerce" to include navigation. The opinion states:

> Commerce, undoubtedly, is traffic, but it is something more: it is intercourse. . . . [A] power to regulate navigation is as expressly granted as if that term had been added to the word "commerce." . . . [T]he power of Congress does not stop at the jurisdictional lines of the several States. It would be a very useless power, if it could not pass those lines.

The impact of *Gibbons v. Ogden* was to establish the Commerce Clause as a plenary and exclusive federal power. Before 1900, more than 400 cases reached the Supreme Court that involved the Interstate Commerce Clause. The expansive breadth of the federal power over commerce became more evident through the years. For example, the 1890 Sherman Anti-Trust Act was upheld, based on the Interstate Commerce Clause.

A new era of Commerce Clause judicial interpretation began in 1937 with the New Deal legislation of the Franklin Delano Roosevelt (FDR) presidency. A series of Supreme Court decisions struck down as unconstitutional certain New Deal legislation based on the court's narrow view of the extent of federal power over commerce. FDR's reaction to these decisions was his famous effort to "pack" the Supreme Court with more justices who could outnumber the justices with that narrow view. Instead, the result was an amelioration of the judicial view, and the federal power over interstate commerce served as the basis for upholding much of the New Deal social legislation.

What Is the "Dormant Commerce Clause" for Federal Powers?

THE DORMANT Commerce Clause is a judicially created doctrine that the Supreme Court decided based on the Constitution's grant of federal power to regulate interstate commerce. The court decided this power to be exclusive and implies federal power to restrict the states' legislative acts that burden or discriminate against or have negative effect on interstate commerce. This is the Dormant Commerce Clause, or some call it the "negative commerce clause."

The Dormant Commerce Clause was fully awakened during FDR's administration, beginning in 1937. For example, in 1937, the court upheld the National Labor Relations Act. From 1937 until 1995, much of the New Deal legislation and subsequent federal social legislation was upheld as constitutional, based on the Dormant Commerce Clause. From 1937 to 1995, the Supreme Court broadened the applicability of Congress's power over interstate commerce to apply the Dormant Commerce Clause to restrict state legislation resulting in discrimination and to uphold the Civil Rights Act of 1964.

The Supreme Court's decisions reflected the court's view that the federal power over commerce was as broad as the economic and social needs of our country.

For example: important to people of diverse races when traveling on interstate highways: in *Heart of Atlanta Motel v. United States*, 379 U.S. 241 (1964), the court held that Congress could regulate under the Commerce Clause a business that served mostly interstate travelers on an interstate highway—even if all of the motel's business activities were in Atlanta. The court held that the provisions of the Civil Rights Act of 1964 banning racial discrimination in places of public accommodation applied here. The court declared that, even conceding the motel's acts were entirely local, interstate commerce felt the "pinch" of illegal racial discrimination.

In 1995, the Supreme Court reversed course and reverted to its narrower view of federal power granted by the Commerce Clause. The William Rehnquist Court in *United States v. Lopez*, 514 U.S. 549 (1995), in a 5–4 decision held—for the first time in sixty years—that Congress had exceeded its power under the Commerce Clause. *Lopez* held that Congress did not have power under the Commerce Clause to enact The Gun-Free School Zones Act of 1990.

I thought that I had written probably more about the Commerce Clause than the Reader wanted to know. Then, on June 28, 2012, the Supreme Court issued a blockbuster of an opinion that included an important discussion of the Commerce Clause. The case is *National Federation of Independent Business v. Sebelius*, 567 U.S. 519 (2012). The author of the opinion is Chief Justice John Roberts, and I recommend that the Reader at least skim this opinion for its excellent organization and detailed analyses. The opinion considers constitutional issues raised by the 900-page Patient Protection and Affordable Care Act of 2010 (known as the Affordable Care Act or ACA, and commonly called Obamacare). Justice Roberts's opinion provides reassuring reliance on sensible precedent about the scope of the Commerce Clause and persuasive analysis of its role in evaluating the Affordable Care Act.

Well, dear Readers, the Supreme Court has decided hundreds and hundreds of cases involving the Court's interpretations of and views about the Commerce Clause in our Constitution. For what legal scholars would consider an adequate evaluation of this huge mass of judicial opinions, several tomes would be needed. I trust that these few pages will create or renew your interest in the Commerce Clause and how it affects each of us.

I intend no disrespect for our judiciary, but in concluding this essay I share with you my lawyer's opinion of the Supreme Court's decisions about the Commerce Clause: they are like Lewis Carroll's Humpty Dumpty, who said, "When I use a word, it means just what I choose it to mean—neither more nor less."

Constitution: The Great Writ to Protect You—*Habeas Corpus*

Reader, you ask: "Why do we need to care about the writ of habeas corpus?"
My answer: "Because it is the best protection of our individual liberty."

WHAT IS a *writ*? A written command from a court requiring the person to whom it is addressed to do some specific thing as stated in the command. Writs are of ancient origin in England and were of many different kinds. Our focus here is the *writ of habeas corpus ad subjiciendum*, usually (and for obvious reason) referred to simply as *habeas corpus*, which dates to the Magna Carta in 1215.

What does the Latin phrase *habeas corpus* mean? Its literal meaning, ignoring the tenses, is "you have the body." What does a writ of habeas corpus do? It commands whoever is detaining a person in prison or other place of restraint to bring that person before the court for a hearing as to the lawfulness of the detention. *Habeas corpus* is a guarantee against a person languishing in a prison for an indefinite length of time with no charges pending and no right to a hearing on whether the detention is lawful.

Why is *habeas corpus* called the "Great Writ"? The answer has been the same for centuries. In 1755, William Blackstone, famed author of the classic *Commentaries on the Laws of England*, described the 1679 Habeas Corpus Act as the "stable bulwark of our liberties." Our founding fathers were familiar with the history of habeas corpus and considered it a vital protection for individual freedom. I urge every American to know about, cherish, and vigilantly preserve the right to petition for a writ of habeas corpus.

Does the United States Constitution guarantee our right to habeas corpus? Not directly, but the right to petition for habeas corpus is part of the common law which all the states in the United States have adopted, except Louisiana, where law is based on the Napoleonic Code, but does include a habeas corpus protection. (Please refer to my *Bedrock of Justice: The Common Law*.) The Constitution's single reference to habeas corpus is in what is called the "Suspension Clause," Article I, Section 9, Clause 2. The Suspension Clause establishes that habeas corpus is an implicit constitutional right and reads:

> The Privilege of the Writ of Habeas Corpus shall not be suspended, unless when in Cases of Rebellion or Invasion the public Safety may require it.

The right to habeas corpus has been suspended very rarely in our history. President Abraham Lincoln ordered suspension in the early years of the Civil War, but the public outcry against this exercise of authority caused the president to seek congressional approval, which he received. In 1866, a year after the end of the Civil War ended, the United States Supreme Court declared habeas corpus restored and military courts illegal where civil courts had resumed their operations. The Supreme Court declared that only Congress, not the president, had the power to suspend the right to habeas corpus. Congress has suspended the Great Writ only three more times and then but briefly: (1) in 1871, in eight South Carolina counties to combat the Ku Klux Klan; (2) in 1905, in the Philippines; and (3) in World War II, in Hawaii.

I skip the governmental attacks on habeas corpus as part of its war on terrorism until 2008, when the Supreme Court considered for the first time whether the aliens detained at Guantanamo have the constitutional privilege of habeas corpus. In *Boumediene v. Bush*, 553 U.S. 723 (2008), by a 5–4 decision, the court held that the detainees do have the privilege of habeas corpus. The *Boumediene* opinion, with its majority of only one justice, declared that the Framers of our Constitution viewed freedom from restraint as a "fundamental precept of liberty," and they understood the writ of habeas corpus as a vital instrument to secure that freedom. Also, the court confirmed its precedent that the Constitution protects persons as well as citizens, including foreign nationals. The majority opinion concludes with these words:

[T]oday's decision is no judicial victory, but an act of perseverance in trying to make habeas corpus review, and the obligation of the courts to provide it, mean something of value to both prisoners and to the Nation.

Thus, by a narrow majority of one justice, the Supreme Court reaffirmed our country's basic commitment to human liberty.

Now I shall disclose my lawyer's involvement with habeas corpus. In the 1960s the Earl Warren Court in a series of United States Supreme Court decisions expanded the right of state prisoners convicted in state courts of state crimes to file petitions for a writ of habeas corpus in the federal district (trial) courts, which became flooded with these petitions. Prisoners often have the time to prepare these petitions, many without legitimate grounds. The federal district courts, therefore, usually justifiably denied the petitions. I have not checked the current status of appeals from these denials, but in the 1960s appeals from the denials inundated the circuit courts, which are the federal courts of appeal.

I don't know what other circuit courts did with the surge of appeals from denials of habeas corpus petitions, but I know what the United States Circuit Court of Appeals for the Tenth Circuit did because Wyoming and Colorado are both in the Tenth Circuit. That circuit appointed lawyers in all states in its region to serve as lawyers in these appeals by state prisoners, who always claimed to be without money to hire a lawyer. The Tenth Circuit appointed senior, respected lawyers to represent the prisoners to avoid later prisoners' claims of "incompetent counsel." The lawyers whom the court selected to represent the prisoners in these appeals received no compensation whatsoever from anyone—client, court, or other government agency. The Tenth Circuit also distributed the cases so that the lawyers in each of its states had cases from a state other than the lawyer's own state. As a then Wyoming lawyer, I received a case from New Mexico and shall share with you my saga with it.

I have always found the right to petition for a writ of habeas corpus to be inspiring—a shining example of what law can and should do to protect our individual liberties. Yet the only time that I ever represented a client to obtain a writ of habeas corpus was in a worthless appeal without any merit. Yes, the Tenth Circuit appointed me for the case. I was delighted that the record was only a single rather slim volume, because I was very busy with paying legal business. When I read the record of the proceeding in the federal district (trial) court, however, I was shocked and dismayed. The petitioning prisoner had no lawyer, so the judge had to appoint one for him. Let me tell you what the record stated, almost exact in my memory:

> *The Judge.* Ah, good. I see that (name), one of our most distinguished lawyers, has just entered the courtroom. I am going to appoint you to represent (naming my now client).
>
> *The Distinguished Lawyer.* Your Honor, with the utmost respect, I must decline the appointment. I know about this case and I would not touch it with a twenty-foot, no, a forty-foot barge pole.

This was the case to which the Tenth Circuit had appointed me!

The facts underlying my client's conviction were so disgusting and horrid that I omit them here because, if included, my book would not be acceptable for public reading. The client had absolutely no basis for an appeal of anything, according to my analysis of the record.

The Tenth Circuit met in different states within its region, except then never in Wyoming. Previously, I had always driven the one hundred miles from Cheyenne to Denver for my appellate arguments before that court. For these assigned habeas corpus cases, the court was making an exception and coming to Cheyenne to hear the lawyers' arguments. This would be quite an occasion for our local Bar, and we planned a banquet to be held after the court had heard all the arguments by the Wyoming lawyers. The judges were very gracious to the lawyers for their free work and thanked each lawyer with a really nice little speech at the conclusion of each lawyer's argument. When my turn came, the judges looked shocked and embarrassed as I made my argument, and I didn't feel comfortable either, but I did the best I could. When I finished, the presiding judge made no nice little speech, just a mumbled "Thank you, counsel." At the banquet, however, the judge came to me and said that he and the other judges apologized for appointing me to serve as the lawyer in the case and appreciated, "indeed, respected, my able representation." Thus ended my only direct involvement as a lawyer with the Great Writ of habeas corpus that has always meant so much to me.

> Here, I conclude this small discussion with a big plea: the next time any Congress or any President acts to suspend the right to petition for a writ of habeas corpus, and there is no rebellion and no invasion,

raise your voice loud and clear in protest. The Great Writ is the Great Protection of our Liberty.

Constitution: No "Bill of Attainder" Allowed—Your Protections

WHEN I confided to a friend that my book was going to include a short discussion on a bill of attainder, the reply was, "Why? And what is it?" In the next several pages, I shall answer those two questions and also why you should care.

WHY THIS DISCUSSION?

FREEDOM FROM a bill of attainder is one of the basic principles undergirding our republic. *The framers of our Constitution deemed banning attainders so important that the ban is one of only two individual liberties that the Constitution protects from both federal and state violation*, the other being *ex post facto* laws, about which you may read in *The Judiciary: What It Means for You.*

Here is our right to freedom from attainder given to us in very plain language in our Constitution:

No Bill of Attainder . . . shall be passed [by the Congress].
ARTICLE I, SECTION 9, CLAUSE 3

No State . . . shall pass any Bill of Attainder . . .
ARTICLE I, SECTION 10

Prohibiting them a third time in our Constitution, our founding fathers wanted to make sure that no attainders would be tolerated:

The Congress shall have Power to declare the Punishment of Treason, but no Attainder of Treason shall work Corruption of Blood, or Forfeiture [of property] except during the Life of the Person attainted.
ARTICLE III, SECTION 3, CLAUSE 2

Alexander Hamilton warned with respect to the need for banning bills of attainder:

Nothing is more common than for a free people, in times of heat and violence, to gratify momentary passions, by letting into the govern-

ment, principles and precedents which afterwards prove fatal to
themselves.

FROM *THE PAPERS OF ALEXANDER HAMILTON*, VOL. 3, 1782–1786

Surely we should welcome an introduction to or reminder of a valuable
right that is a constitutional guarantee: bills of attainder are prohibited by
our federal Constitution.

WHAT IS A BILL OF ATTAINDER?

IT IS a legislative enactment that, without trial or conviction, condemns a
specific person, persons or group to death or lesser punishment including
confiscation of property. An additional penalty, "Corruption of Blood," could
be imposed in medieval England, which meant that the "attainted" person's
property could not pass to his heirs. Attainders were first used in England in
1321, and were often invoked there in the sixteenth, seventeenth, and eighteenth centuries. In addition, "bills of pains and penalties" were also used,
and they differed from bills of attainder only in the penalty not being death
but lesser, such as forfeiture of all property and banishment.

"WHY SHOULD I CARE ABOUT THIS FUSTY OLD BILL OF ATTAINDER, TODAY?" YOU MAY NOW BE ASKING.

ANTICIPATING THIS question by you, Readers, I checked online to find out
if a bill of attainder were still an issue in recent years. I was surprised to learn
that in just the two years from mid-2007 to mid-2009, 272 cases involving a
bill of attainder as the determinative issue were important enough for written
opinions by courts.

Our constitutional protection against bills of attainder will always be
important to Americans so long as we are a free people. An example is *United
States v. Brown*, 381 U.S. 437 (1965), which the United States Supreme Court
decided at the height of the American people's fright about Communism,
fueled constantly by then prevalent McCarthyism. The Supreme Court held,
in a 5–4 decision, that a section of the Labor-Management Reporting and
Disclosure Act of 1959 was an unconstitutional bill of attainder. The unconstitutional section provided that no member of the Communist Party could
serve as an executive officer of a union. The *Brown* court noted:

> Bills of attainder, *ex post facto* laws, and laws impairing the obligations
> of contracts, are contrary to the first principles of the social compact,

and to every principle of sound legislation. . . . The sober people of America are weary of the fluctuating policy which has directed the public councils. They have seen with regret and indignation, that sudden changes, and legislative interferences, in cases affecting personal rights, become jobs in the hands of enterprising and influential speculators; and snares to the more industrious and less-informed part of the community.

How is our right to freedom from attainder doing more recently? In 2008–2009, when the federal government paid $182 billion "bail-out" funds to American International Group Inc. (AIG), AIG then paid substantial bonuses to some executives, causing public indignation. The media reported that Congress had considered imposing a surtax on the bonuses but would not because of its expressed concern that it would be an unconstitutional attainder.

In 2010, the United States Court of Appeals for the Second Circuit held in *ACORN v. United States*, 618 F.3d 125 (2d Cir. 2010), that ACORN, a nonprofit corporation, being barred from receiving any further federal funding was not an unconstitutional bill of attainder. In June 2011, the United States Supreme Court denied ACORN's petition for *writ of certiorari* (Docket No. 10–1068), thereby refusing review of the lower court's decision of "no bill of attainder."

As the bill of attainder ban has been applied, so it is with all our constitutional freedoms. They are granted to the people, they are our freedoms, and they are not to be arbitrarily doled out by any one branch of our government. In *United States v. Brown*, 381 U.S. 437 (1965), the Supreme Court declared:

> **[T]he Bill of Attainder Clause was intended** not as a narrow, technical (and therefore soon to be outmoded) prohibition, but rather as an implementation of the separation of powers, **a general safeguard against** legislative exercise of the judicial function, or more simply—**trial by legislature**. (My emphasis added.)

Thus, our United States Constitution grants us the right to due process, including judicial determination, before any of our rights can constitutionally be abridged or denied to us.

THE BILL of Rights in our Constitution is one of the main reasons that I wrote this book. My earnest desire and fervent hope are to arouse in every Reader a renewed appreciation of our guaranteed rights as Americans to live as a free people. When I see inroads being made on that freedom in different ways, and under different guises, something within me cries out "No! No!" and wants the American people to become quickly aware of any impairment of our constitutionally guaranteed rights—and wage a victorious battle to retain our rights.

I remember many years ago, when I had been invited to speak at a university about some law-related topic, that I observed with dismay a then prevalent attitude at that university. The main speaker was a guest from Washington, DC, prominent in the then administration, and his thesis was the desirability of entrusting major decisions for our country to an elite group that would be free from any input or disagreement by the people. I was deeply offended and tried politely to stifle my anger. Those feelings turned to sorrow as I observed the students nodding their heads and apparently fully satisfied to abdicate their rights to the "elite." Ever since that evening, in all my lectures I have wriggled in the need for people to be vigilant and vocal to preserve our rights.

Now let us look at our basic rights as Americans. They are embodied in the Bill of Rights in our Constitution of the United States. Our Constitution was adopted in 1787 but had few individual rights. Instead, the original 1787 Constitution was primarily devoted to establishing the structure of our government. By 1791, what is commonly known as the Bill of Rights had been ratified by three-fourths of the states and adopted.

The Bill of Rights refers to the first ten Amendments to the Constitution. And this part of my book for you includes a discussion about a few of them, after the following convenient brief explanation of each of them.

FIRST AMENDMENT

HERE IS the First Amendment in full, and I invite you to admire its elegant brevity and plain meaning.

> Congress shall make no law respecting an establishment of religion, or prohibiting the free exercise thereof; or abridging the freedom of speech, or of the press; or the right of the people peaceably to assemble, and to petition the Government for a redress of grievances.

What a cornucopia of rights! All those basic rights for a free people guaranteed in only forty-five—yes, 45 words! In contrast, the Congress of the United States has rarely proved itself capable of writing an important legislative bill in fewer than hundreds of pages.

SECOND AMENDMENT

A well regulated Militia, being necessary to the security of a free State, the right of the people to keep and bear Arms, shall not be infringed.

Yes, this is the full text of the Second Amendment—all its twenty-seven words—that underlies the ongoing legal controversies about gun regulations and laws relating to an American's right to have guns.

A discussion that fairly described gun control legislation and fate in the courts would be too long to be appropriate in this book.

THIRD AMENDMENT

No Soldier shall, in time of peace be quartered in any house, without the consent of the Owner, nor in time of war, but in a manner prescribed by law.

This is the least cited of any of the Amendments in the Bill of Rights because it has not been an issue since our Revolutionary War for independence against England.

FOURTH AMENDMENT

ALERT! PLEASE read this one carefully because it is another cornucopia filled with important rights for all Americans.

The right of the people to be secure in their persons, houses, papers, and effects, against unreasonable searches and seizures, shall not be violated, and no Warrants shall issue, but upon probable cause, supported by Oath or affirmation, and particularly describing the place to be searched, and the persons or things to be seized.

I handled many an appeal involving the Fourth Amendment during my years as Chief Appellate Deputy District Attorney. The Public Defender was quick to invoke a defense of "lack of probable cause," and when the claim seemed specious, I would fight for the State of Colorado. When a lack of probable cause seemed obvious, I always recommended so to admit and to be more careful to have legitimate "probable cause." I submit that the Fourth Amendment is important for each citizen to be safe from over-aggressive police tactics or politically motivated persecution.

FIFTH AMENDMENT

THE FIFTH Amendment in a single paragraph grants us these rights: (1) we cannot be tried for a capital offense (death penalty case) or infamous crime except after a grand jury indictment (except in time of war or public danger); (2) no person can be tried twice for the same offense (the double jeopardy ban); (3) we shall not be compelled to be a witness against ourselves (the right against self-incrimination); (4) *a vital right, we are not to be deprived of life, liberty, or property without due process of law*; and (5) private property shall not be taken for public use without just compensation.

If you are thinking that this is all rather boring, and I overdo the importance of our constitutionally guaranteed rights, be fair. Shut your eyes and imagine being wrongfully involved in a criminal proceeding, or your property being "condemned" by the government, and not having the rights that the Fifth Amendment gives us.

SIXTH AMENDMENT

THIS IS another gift of rights the Constitution bestows on us and makes me renew my gratitude for being an American. The Sixth Amendment guarantees the accused in a criminal case (1) the right to a speedy and public trial; (2) the right to trial by an impartial jury; (3) the right to be represented by legal counsel (the source for public defenders representing defendants in criminal cases); and (4) the right to be informed of the charges against the accused. It also grants us the right of confrontation of the witnesses against us if we are the accused. This is indeed a protective right—so much so in my opinion that I have written more about in this part's, *Bill of Rights: Sixth Amendment —The Confrontation Clause.*

SEVENTH AMENDMENT

THE SEVENTH Amendment guarantees our right to a jury trial in cases at common law—meaning that a jury will be available to the litigants in a civil case.

EIGHTH AMENDMENT

THE EIGHTH Amendment grants three important rights in a single short sentence:

> Excessive bail shall not be required, nor excessive fines imposed, nor cruel and unusual punishments inflicted.

I have had no personal experience with this Amendment. I do recall one of our federal judge's ruling that the cells for prisoners were so small as to be "cruel and unusual punishments." The ruling was not well-received because the cells' dimensions were larger than the small offices the State of Colorado was able to provide for its deputy prosecutors.

NINTH AMENDMENT

THIS IS what I call "The Forgotten Ninth Amendment" and reads in full:

> The enumeration in the Constitution, of certain rights, shall not be construed to deny or disparage others retained by the people.

"The people" is us—and no politicians can strip that from us. We have inalienable rights. The Ninth Amendment's forgotten status led me to grant it a short discussion, *Bill of Rights: "The Forgotten Ninth Amendment."*

TENTH AMENDMENT

THIS AMENDMENT has also suffered a poor fate, and I could call it "The Neglected Tenth Amendment." It reads in full:

> The powers not delegated to the United States by the Constitution, nor prohibited by it to the States, are reserved to the States respectively, or to the people.

Also, pitying its neglect, I have included in this book's part a short essay, *Bill of Rights: 'The Neglected Tenth Amendment."*

To the Reader: I hope you join me in being grateful for our Bill of Rights and now invite you to read more about some of them, as follows.

Bill of Rights: Let's Guard the First Amendment!

THE UNITED States "Patriot Act" is a short name for the act's very lengthy title, "Uniting and Strengthening America by Providing Appropriate Tools Required to Intercept and Obstruct Terrorism Act." The Patriot Act, enacted by Congress shortly after the September 11, 2001, attack on New York City's World Trade Center, has over 300 pages. The Dodd-Frank Wall Street Reform and Consumer Protection Act was enacted by Congress in 2010 and quickly became known as the "Lawyers' and Consultants' Full Employment Act of 2010." The act has 2,319 pages!

Now I go back to 1791, when the First Amendment to our United States Constitution was adopted as the beginning of our Bill of Rights. In few words, here is the full text of the very important First Amendment:

> Congress shall make no law respecting an establishment of religion, or prohibiting the free exercise thereof; or abridging the freedom of speech, or of the press; or the right of the people peaceably to assemble, and to petition the Government for a redress of grievances.

That's all of the First Amendment: forty-five, yes, *in 45 words not pages.*

The six freedoms granted to us and essential for a free people:

1. Freedom from a government-supported church;
2. Freedom to worship according to our beliefs;
3. Freedom of speech;
4. Freedom of the press;
5. Freedom of the people to assemble peacefully (yes, we can protest lawfully!); and,
6. Freedom to petition our government to redress grievances (yes, we can and do sue our government).

What a generous bundle of freedoms for us! We shall not be able to keep them, I fear, unless we are mindful of what freedoms we were given and of the need for our vigilance to keep them.

OUR RIGHT to freedom of speech is guaranteed in the First Amendment to the Constitution of the United States: "Congress shall make no law . . . abridging freedom of speech." There it is—our priceless right to freedom of speech is guaranteed in less than ten words.

The late great jurist, United States Supreme Court Justice Oliver Wendell Holmes Jr., wrote the memorable statement that freedom of speech includes "freedom for the thought we hate." He also pointed out that our constitutional right to free speech has some boundaries. Justice Holmes stated the sensible limit succinctly in *Schenck v. United States*, 249 U.S. 47 (1919):

> The most stringent protection of free speech would not protect a man in falsely shouting fire in a theatre and causing a panic.

I believe that this simple recognition is an excellent example illustrating that the right to freedom of speech is not intended to include a right to flout the standards of the community: the generally accepted sensibilities of the people should serve as boundaries. Put another way, *I believe that our constitutional right to freedom of speech does not mean "anything goes."*

Or, does it? What happened judicially in 2011 with respect to freedom of speech? That year, the United States Supreme Court rendered its 8–1 decision in a case named *Snyder v. Phelps*, 562 U.S. 443 (2011), that seems to endorse "anything goes" to suffice as the sole standard for protected free speech.

The facts of the *Snyder* case are simple. Members of Westboro Baptist Church (Westboro) believe that God punishes the United States for its tolerance of homosexuality, particularly in the military. They have protested at hundreds of military funerals. In this case, Westboro members picketed a procession of mourners on their way to a Catholic church memorial service for Matthew Snyder, a United States soldier killed in Iraq in the line of duty. The picketers were on public land adjacent to a public street approximately 1,000 feet from the church. Only the tops of the picketers' signs were visible to the mourners. The signs were shown, however, on the television news that evening, and included: "God Hates You!" and "God Hates Fags" and "Don't Pray for the USA" and "Thank God for 9/11" and "Thank God for Dead Soldiers" and others of similar offensive ilk. The soldier's grieving father, Albert Snyder, sued the picketing sign-bearers and Westboro church.

The federal district court trial resulted in a jury verdict in favor of Mr. Snyder on state tort claims, including intentional infliction of emotional distress. The United States Circuit Court of Appeals for the Sixth Circuit reversed the judgment entered on the trial court's verdict. Later, the Supreme Court held that the signs were protected free speech.

The Supreme Court stated that "[w]hether the First Amendment prohibits holding Westboro liable for its speech . . . turns largely on whether that speech is of public or private concern." The court explained that "[s]peech deals with matters of public concern when it can 'be fairly considered as relating to any matter of political, social, or other concern to the community,' . . . or when it 'is a subject of general interest and of value and concern to the public.'" The court reiterated that "debate on public issues should be uninhibited, robust, and wide-open;" and "speech on public issues occupies the highest rung of the hierarchy of First Amendment values and is entitled to special protection." After examining the "content, form, and context of the speech," the Court held that Westboro's speech was of public concern and protected by the First Amendment.

The majority opinion of the Supreme Court in its concluding section states, "Our holding today is narrow." The balance of that section is inscrutable to me. Stating the opinion to be "narrow" does not make it so when applied as precedent in the real world.

I respectfully submit that picketing in public carrying signs reading "God Hates the USA" and "Don't Pray for the USA" and "America is Doomed" are messages to arouse public concern. As I read the signs that the protesters were carrying, I thought it obvious that some of the signs involved public concern and others private concern—surely two kinds of speech can co-exist. I am left with the feeling that I am incapable of discerning the basis for the court's delicate distinctions. I am convinced that the protesters' signs impermissibly abused the right to freedom of speech by their signs' vicious attacks on the United States and also on a dead United States soldier.

You may want to read the Supreme Court opinion in *Snyder* as well as Justice Samuel Alito's thoughtful, lone dissenting opinion. Justice Alito began his dissenting opinion by stating that *"[o]ur profound national commitment to free and open debate is not a license for the vicious verbal assault that occurred in this case."* (My emphasis added.) Regarding Westboro's speech, Justice Alito noted:

Signs stating "God Hates You" and "Thank God for Dead Soldiers" reiterated the message that God had caused Matthew's death in retribution for his sins. . . . Others, stating "You're Going to Hell" and "Not Blessed Just Cursed," conveyed the message that Matthew was "in Hell—sine die."

He also noted that some of the "signs would most naturally have been understood as suggesting—falsely—that Matthew was gay. Homosexuality was the theme of many of the signs."

As Justice Alito stated, "While commentary on the Catholic Church or the United States military constitutes speech on matters of public concern, speech regarding Matthew Snyder's purely private conduct does not." After strongly criticizing Westboro's conduct and addressing the reasoning in the Supreme Court's majority opinion, Justice Alito concluded that Westboro's speech was not protected by the First Amendment. He stated that "[i]n order to have a society in which public issues can be openly and vigorously debated, it is not necessary to allow the brutalization of innocent victims like [Matthew Snyder's father]."

I have decided that better judgment is for me to stop writing about this *Snyder* case, reminding myself that this is an essay in a book—not a court brief with hopefully persuasive arguments.

I believe that the right to freedom of speech imposes a responsibility not to violate community standards. I digress, to use legalese, "to lay a foundation" for discussion of *Snyder v. Phelps*. Community standards have been invoked by the Supreme Court as a test for determining alleged obscenity in *Miller v. California*, 413 U.S. 15 (1973). I submit to you, the Reader: wouldn't community standards be an appropriate test for determining whether a restraint on freedom of speech is justified under the circumstances?

I conclude this essay by assuring the Reader of my fervent dedication to the right of freedom of speech—including speech "for the thought we hate." I also fervently believe that to uphold the right to freedom of speech when the speech is cruelly abusive is a perversion of a splendid and precious right.

Bill of Rights: Fifth Amendment—Due Process of Law

What Is It? What Are Its Uses?

DUE PROCESS is a right that the United States Constitution doubly guarantees to all persons. Both the Fifth Amendment, which is in the Bill of Rights, and the Fourteenth Amendment to the Constitution adopted post-Civil War expressly bestow the right to due process.

The Fifth Amendment in the Bill of Rights gives us a bundle of rights including in just fifteen (15!) words this precious right to due process:

> No person shall be . . . deprived of life, liberty, or property, *without due process of law*; nor shall private property be taken for public use, without just compensation. (My emphasis added.)

Important to note is that the right to due process is not limited to a citizen of the United States but is all-inclusive: "no person." In addition, Section 1 of the Fourteenth Amendment provides that no state shall "deprive any person of life, liberty, or property, without due process of law; nor deny to any person within its jurisdiction the equal protection of the laws."

WHAT IS DUE PROCESS?

I WOULD not be so reckless as to attempt an adequate definition of "due process." It is a concept based on noble human morality. The fundamental principle of due process is fairness. Fairness is not, however, an absolute standard. The great jurist, the late Oliver Wendell Homes Jr. of the United States Supreme Court gave this definition, with which I agree, in *Moyer v. Peabody*, 212 U.S. 78 (1909):

> What is due process of law depends on circumstances. It varies with the subject-matter and the necessities of the situation.

This view of due process accords with fairness as both a noble and flexible concept. The Constitution, in assuring due process, granted the right to jury trial in all criminal cases. I submit that as Americans we can be proud that our constitutional guarantee of due process is not limited to ourselves but includes all persons who are within our jurisdiction.

ORIGIN OF DUE PROCESS

LET ME share with you the matrix in which the American right of due process is embedded. Yes—the great Magna Carta—in 1215, England. Chapter 39 of the Magna Carta is a declaration of a person's right to fairness when involved in the criminal process of the law and (in one version, as English language has changed over 800 years) provides:

No free man will be taken or imprisoned or disseised [property taken] or exiled in any way ruined, nor shall we go or send against him, save by the lawful judgment of his peers or by the law of the land.

Over three centuries later, in 1608, the great English jurist Sir Edward Coke wrote that according to the Magna Carta and the common law (the law of the land) no man could be deprived of his liberty except by the due process of law.

DUE PROCESS OF LAW IN THE UNITED STATES

NOW I turn to the great right of due process of law in the United States of America, and its current use and abuse. I begin with three reminders.

First, the Magna Carta almost eight hundred years ago recognized the right to due process of law is essential for personal liberty.

Second, the United States Constitution, Bill of Rights, Fifth Amendment, provides that "[n]o person shall be . . . deprived of life, liberty, or property without *due process of law*." And the post-Civil War Fourteenth Amendment provides that no state shall "deprive any person of life, liberty, or property without *due process of law*." (My emphasis added.)

Third, our constitutional guarantees of due process are all-inclusive in their application: both federal and state governments are bound by its strictures and the due process guarantee applies to all persons—*all persons, without regard to citizenship, who are within the jurisdiction of the United States.*

TERRITORIAL JURISDICTION

WITHOUT TURNING this into a law textbook, I point out that the United States has jurisdiction over persons in its territories such as Puerto Rico, its foreign embassies, and yes—its foreign bases such as its Cuban-based Guantanamo Bay Prison. Prisoners have been detained for years at that prison without charges being brought against them. *Hamdi v. Rumsfeld*, 542 U.S. 507 (2004) held that a Guantanamo prisoner detained there for two years without charges was entitled to petition a United States District Court for a writ of habeas corpus. This close 5–4 decision of the Supreme Court is unfortunately a narrow precedent because the prisoner had been born in Louisiana but moved to Saudi Arabia with his family when still a very small child. The *Hamdi* court, therefore, did not have to address the question of a person who is not a US citizen.

USES OF THE RIGHT TO DUE PROCESS OF LAW

THE DUE process right is intertwined with all our other personal rights, and I submit is necessarily invoked in enforcing other vital rights. The determination of the right to habeas corpus, the criminal trial of one's guilt or innocence with its integral right to confront adverse witnesses, the legality of a sentence imposed, and whether one has received equal protection of the law, all require the person affected to receive the due process of law in making the determination needed. I submit that our Constitution gives all persons within its jurisdiction the rights necessary to be protected by due process of law.

ABUSES OF DUE PROCESS OF LAW

I HAVE always feared that some of our most precious personal rights may be subject to erosion and ultimate loss because of being abused.

For example, a person convicted in a state court of a serious felony has the right to appeal the conviction. If the conviction is affirmed at the state appellate court level, the convicted person may apply to begin the appellate process in the federal court system. Some states have the death penalty for first degree murder convictions, provided a number of statutory-specified conditions are met. Yet the number of defense motions filed in a death penalty appeal may vary from 300 to 700! Public Defenders are the defense counsel in many of these cases and, upon affirmance of the conviction they, as well as private defense counsel, begin the process that will lead to filing a petition for *writ of certiorari* in the United States Supreme Court. Sometimes these criminal appeals involve repeated filings—and, yes, more motions. I respectfully submit that such practices are a dangerous abuse of the right to due process of law. When a jury returns a verdict of guilty, *and* the judge enters judgment on the verdict after ruling on the defense motion for judgment notwithstanding verdict, *and* that conviction has been affirmed on appeal because no error is found in the trial proceedings, *then* that convicted person has received due process of law. Further appellate proceedings without favorable result for the person appealing should end the matter. But it does not—the appellate maneuvers may continue for years. I hope that you join me in considering this abuse of the right to due process of law.

MANY YEARS ago on a holiday visit in Lima, Peru, we toured ongoing excavations under the city's library. The objective of the excavations was to reveal the rooms and their artifacts of the Peruvian Inquisition (based on the Spanish Inquisition) that was established in 1570. I remember well the excavated courtroom where the Inquisition trials had been held because it looked much like courtrooms in which I had tried cases: an elevated judge's bench and two counsel tables. There the resemblance ended. To my right was a solid wooden door with a peephole. In answer to my question, our guide said, "The witnesses against the accused would look with one eye through that peephole and identify the accused as the guilty person. Of course, the accused could not see whose eye was peeking through that peephole." As I looked at that tiny aperture in the door, a chill ran down my spine, and then I gave thanks for the Confrontation Clause in our United States Constitution.

What is the Confrontation Clause? Part of the Bill of Rights of the United States Constitution is the Sixth Amendment, which in part provides: "In all criminal prosecutions, the accused shall enjoy the right . . . to be confronted with the witnesses against him." That's it, a big right, with common law roots, granted in those few words. The words are so plain and few that I thought no judicial interpretation would be needed or imposed. I was wrong.

Now I must digress to mention a component of that judicial interpretation: hearsay evidence. The general rule is that hearsay evidence is not admissible into evidence at trial for lack of trustworthiness. The general rule that hearsay evidence is inadmissible, however, was subject to thirty-five (35!) exceptions the last time that I checked.

Hearsay evidence is easily explained by an example. At trial, Witness A seeks to testify about a statement that Witness A will say that he heard Person B make, and the statement is being offered as evidence to prove a fact. Person B is not at the trial and is unavailable. Not being there, Person B cannot be cross-examined to test Person B's credibility and to test the truth of Person B's statement, or whether Person B would deny making the statement.

Hearsay evidence is sometimes termed "second-hand evidence" because it is not what the witness knows personally but instead is what the witness claims to have heard from another person, and that person is not available for cross-examination. The exceptions to the hearsay rule are all based on the assumption that the circumstances of the out-of-court declarant's statement establish credibility and truthfulness. The exceptions to the hearsay rule can become intertwined with the Confrontation Clause, as we shall soon see.

I debated with myself about how far back in date I should go to review with you the United States Supreme Court's interpretations of the Confrontation Clause. I decided to limit myself to the twenty-first century and, yes, our highest court has been active in deciding what the Confrontation Clause means.

I begin with the 2004 decision in *Crawford v. Washington*, 541 U.S. 36 (2004), which ushered in a new era of judicial interpretation following decades of what some lawyers and legal scholars considered a judicial erosion of the constitutional right of an accused person to confront the witnesses against that defendant. The *Crawford* court overruled one of the Supreme Court's own decisions made almost twenty-five years previously in *Ohio v. Roberts*, 448 U.S. 56 (1980). In *Roberts*, the defendant had been charged with forgery of a check, and the witness who had testified at the preliminary hearing during which defendant's attorney had the opportunity to examine her under oath, became unavailable at trial. The *Roberts* court held that the statements of the witness at the preliminary hearing were admissible in evidence against defendant at his trial. *Roberts* announced a new test: an out-of-court statement by an unavailable witness is not admissible in evidence against the accused at trial *unless* it (1) "bears adequate indicia of reliability"; or (2) is "within a firmly rooted hearsay exception." And under *Roberts*, the trial court judge determines whether the statement is sufficiently reliable to be admitted into evidence at trial. In 2004, however, the Supreme Court in *Crawford* ruled that "a judicial determination of reliability" does not meet the constitutional right of confrontation.

Crawford reversed the conviction of the defendant for attempted murder that occurred when he stabbed the victim whom the defendant claimed was trying to rape his wife. At trial, the wife's statement to the police during investigation was admitted into evidence despite the wife's unavailability to testify at trial, because of the husband-wife evidentiary privilege which protects the privacy of marital communications between spouses. *Crawford* held that statements of a witness absent from trial are admissible "only where the declarant is unavailable, and only where the defendant has had a prior opportunity to cross-examine" the witness.

The *Crawford* opinion is an interesting read, because it includes the history of an accused's right to confront witnesses, dating back to ancient Roman law and early English common law, and broadly defines "witness" to include a testimonial statement. *Crawford* underscores the importance of the accused having the right to test the testimonial evidence in the "crucible of cross-examination."

In 2009, the Supreme Court issued another major decision interpreting the Confrontation Clause, *Melendez-Diaz v. Massachusetts*, 557 U.S. 305 (2009). *Melendez-Diaz* again gave rise to some professional outcries of "the new Confrontation Clause." The confrontation issue in *Melendez-Diaz* was the admissibility at trial of "certificates of analysis" in the nature of affidavits, made after tests in a government laboratory, that stated the substance found in the accused's car tested as cocaine. The analyst who conducted the tests was "unavailable" to testify at trial, because he was suspended from his job for reasons his employer stated were "irrelevant" to the test.

In a 5–4 decision, the Supreme Court in *Melendez-Diaz* reversed the defendant's conviction, because his right under the Confrontation Clause had been violated by admission of the affidavit stating the test result of a substance found in defendant's car was cocaine—with the defendant having had no opportunity either before or during trial to cross-examine the analyst who conducted the incriminating test. Thus, the court held that the Confrontation Clause, giving defendants in criminal cases the right to confront the witnesses against them, applies to analysts who conduct and report on forensic laboratory tests. This decision and its opinion caused another stir, especially among prosecutors, about the Supreme Court's interpretation of the Confrontation Clause.

I had thought that the *Melendez-Diaz* case would end this essay on the Confrontation Clause. In 2011, however, the Supreme Court again interpreted the Confrontation Clause in a major 5–4 decision, *Bullcoming v. New Mexico*, 564 U.S. 647 (2011). Bullcoming was charged with aggravated driving while intoxicated (DWI), and the analyst who had performed the blood sample test was not called as a witness. Instead, the prosecution called as a witness an analyst who was familiar with the laboratory's testing procedures but had not participated in or observed the test of Bullcoming's blood sample.

At the outset of the majority opinion, the court identified the issue:

> The question presented is whether the Confrontation Clause permits the prosecution to introduce a forensic laboratory report containing a testimonial certification—made for the purpose of proving a particular fact—through the in-court testimony of a scientist who did not

sign the certification or perform or observe the test reported in the certification.

Whew! That is indeed a very long question, but it lays out the issue with laudable clarity. The next sentence in the court's holding, again stated with unmistakable meaning:

> The accused's right is to be confronted with the analyst who made the certification, unless that analyst is unavailable at trial, *and the accused had an opportunity, pretrial, to cross-examine that particular scientist*. [My emphasis added.]

With the *Bullcoming* case, I end this essay's brief review of the Confrontation Clause and its journey through the Supreme Court by saying these heartfelt words to the Reader:

> *Trust me, the Confrontation Clause, given its sensible meaning, is an essential component of our liberty.*

Bill of Rights: "The Forgotten Ninth Amendment"

"We the People" have rights that are not stated in our Constitution.

SNOW HAS been falling all day. Staying home from the office and keeping warm is an agreeable way to spend the day. Dismal news in this morning's newspaper started my thinking about the Ninth Amendment to the Constitution of the United States and the provocative small book given to me years ago titled *The Forgotten Ninth Amendment* by Bennett Peterson. When I first received the book, I was ashamed that I certainly had forgotten the Ninth Amendment—no scrap of memory hinted at what it was about. And I have since found out that none of my friends, both lawyers and judges, remembered anything about it either. So presumably you will not be offended by my saying, "You probably also don't remember the Ninth Amendment." So here it is—all twenty-one (21) words which acknowledge that "We the People" have natural or inherent rights that belong to no government.

> The enumeration in the Constitution, of certain rights, shall not be construed to deny or disparage others retained by the people.

Almost daily we can read in the reported events of our United States and the world about encroachment, abridgment, violation, or abrogation of our basic rights as people. Sometimes we are told that we must give up rights (for how long?) for "security"; sometimes rights are trampled on with no reason required or given, and always the world is afflicted with despots who decree that people have no rights.

I became curious about the Ninth Amendment and its place in American law. I learned that the Ninth Amendment came into being because of the proposed Bill of Rights. The Bill of Rights is comprised of the first ten amendments to the Constitution of the United States. They enumerate certain rights that are not included in the grant of power to the federal government. The Federalists were opposed to including a bill of rights in the Constitution for fear that the enumeration of certain rights could be deemed to grant unenumerated rights to the federal government. This objection is a restatement of an old legal maxim, taught in its original Latin to me in law school: *inclusio unius est exclusio alterius*, meaning the inclusion of one is the exclusion of another.

The Anti-Federalists countered the views of the Federalists with three arguments. First, the Constitution expressly guarantees certain liberties, even without a bill of rights, for example: freedom of religion, freedom of the press, ban on *ex post facto* laws, and right to writ of habeas corpus. Second, even though a complete list of liberties is impossible, the essential liberties could be specifically stated. Third—and I believe underlies the Ninth Amendment—that an amendment should explicitly protect for the people any and all other liberties that the Bill of Rights has not specifically stated. Put another way, each individual and "we the people" retain rights, even if "unlisted" or not enumerated.

James Madison drafted the Ninth Amendment, which served to meet the objections to the proposed Bill of Rights and thereby expedited the states' ratification of our Constitution.

Why is the Ninth Amendment "forgotten"? I don't know but guess that one reason is that it has been infrequently mentioned by the United States Supreme Court. Indeed, almost 170 years elapsed between the adoption of the Ninth Amendment and its first discussion by the Supreme Court. The most attention that the court has paid to the Ninth Amendment was in the 1965 opinion in *Griswold v. Connecticut*, 381 U.S. 479 (1965). *Griswold* declared unconstitutional a statute that prohibited the dispensing or use of birth control devices. The Court voided the statute as an invasion of the right of marital privacy. In its written opinion, the Court stated that its prior decisions "suggest that specific guarantees in the Bill of Rights have penumbras, formed by emanations from those guarantees that help give them life and substance." The Court ends the paragraph containing this quotation by quoting the Ninth Amendment.

With all due respect to the Supreme Court, I do not find an emanation from a penumbra a helpful explanation of what the Ninth Amendment means.

Controversy exists among legal scholars as to whether the Ninth Amendment states a rule of construction or of substance. I do not give myself the status of a legal scholar and so frankly tell you I do not have a definitive answer. Instead, I shall share the two views with you, each with its own group of judicial adherents. One group of courts and scholars interprets the Ninth Amendment as merely providing that the Bill of Rights does not extend the power of the federal government over unenumerated rights; hence, the Ninth Amendment does not within itself grant or protect any other rights. Another group of courts and scholars considers the Ninth Amendment to be an independent source of guaranteeing the people's rights. The *Griswold* case expressed this view by stating:

> The language and history of the Ninth Amendment reveal that the Framers of the Constitution believed that there are *additional fundamental rights, protected from governmental infringement, which exist alongside those fundamental rights specifically mentioned in the first eight constitutional amendments.* (My emphasis added.)

In 2008, the Supreme Court issued its decision in *District of Columbia v. Heller*, 554 U.S. 570 (2008), which held unconstitutional the district's ban on possessing an operable handgun in the home. The court placed its primary reliance on the Second Amendment to the United States Constitution, which includes the statement that "the right of the people to keep and bear Arms, shall not be infringed." The court pointed out that the First, Fourth, and Ninth Amendments all refer to "the people" and declared:

> All three of these instances unambiguously refer to individual rights, not 'collective' rights, or rights that may be exercised only through participation in some corporate body.

The court bluntly stated, however, that the Ninth Amendment was not an independent source of any right, but instead shows that the Framers of the Constitution believed in the existence of fundamental rights not expressly mentioned.

A criticism of the view that the Ninth Amendment is a source of guaranteeing us "unlisted" fundamental rights is that it leaves to a judge unrestricted power to decide what is a fundamental right. But this is not a valid criticism because the Supreme Court has imposed restraints on judges' determination of what is a "fundamental right." For example, the court prescribed and reiterated an important standard for determination of whether the right involved "is of such a character that it cannot be denied without violating those 'fundamental principles of liberty and justice which lie at the base of all our civil and political institutions'" in *Snyder v. Massachusetts*, 291 U.S. 97 (1934), quoting *Herbert v. Louisiana*, 272 U.S. 312 (1926).

Based on its history, I believe that the Ninth Amendment simply means what its plain words say. They assure us that just because a basic right is not expressly included in the Constitution's enumeration of rights does not mean the government has the right—instead of us. Basic unenumerated rights belong to each of us, the people. That's good enough for me—and hopefully satisfies you, too.

I submit that the best quotation for conclusion is to repeat the Ninth Amendment itself, no interpretation needed:

THE ENUMERATION IN THE CONSTITUTION, OF CERTAIN RIGHTS, SHALL NOT BE CONSTRUED TO DENY OR DISPARAGE OTHERS RETAINED BY THE PEOPLE.

Bill of Rights: "The Neglected Tenth Amendment"

Again—"We the People" and Our Rights

I HOPE that you agree with me that George Washington was correct when he wrote in 1787 that the: "power under the Constitution of the United States of America will always be with the people." Also, I hope that you will agree with me that the Tenth Amendment to the Constitution of the United States of America is important for each individual American. The Ninth Amendment expressly makes the ultimate power of government reside in "we the people." If you still have doubts, the Tenth Amendment assures you that every American is a residuary of that power. The Tenth Amendment reads:

> The powers not delegated to the United States by the Constitution, nor prohibited by it to the States, are reserved to the States respectively, or to the people.

Yes, there we are again in the terse Tenth Amendment: "the people." I remind you that the first three words of our Constitution's Preamble single us out, "We the People."

I have never thought that a person needed a law degree to know that "We the People" meant individuals such as you and me. Sadly, I was wrong.

In June 2011, however, the United States Supreme Court breathed some needed new life into the Tenth Amendment with a unanimous opinion in *Bond v. United States*, 564 U.S. 211 (2011). Carole Anne Bond had been prosecuted, tried, convicted, and sentenced for violating a federal statute. At her trial in the federal district court, she moved to dismiss the case against her, asserting that Congress had exceeded its power in enacting that statute; her motion was denied, and she was sentenced to six years' imprisonment. On appeal, Bond again asserted her right to challenge the validity of the statute that had resulted in her conviction, relying on the Tenth Amendment. But the United States Court of Appeals for the Third Circuit agreed with government counsel's argument that Bond did not have standing to rely on the Tenth Amendment to attack the validity of the statute. In 2011, the Supreme Court reversed the lower courts and remanded the case back to decide on its merits her claim of the statute's invalidity.

What is this legal doctrine of *standing* that determines whether an individual American may challenge the validity of a federal statute? It has been judicially decided that standing has a three-fold requirement: (i) the person challenging the statute must have suffered harm or harm is imminent; (ii) the harm is fairly traceable to the conduct complained of; and (iii) the harm is redressable or can be remedied. In addition, standing has what the courts have named "prudential limitations."

I agree that standing, when applied sensibly, is necessary to curb abuses by individuals who, without ongoing particular harmful connection to a statute, decide to challenge it. I believe that the Supreme Court's unanimous 2011 opinion in *Bond* is worthy of our attention: it modified the doctrine of standing when it vindicated the right of an individual to challenge the validity of a federal statute, in reliance on the Tenth Amendment.

Much language in the opinion goes beyond that ultimate holding by its reaffirmance of the rights of individuals under our Constitution. I quote you a few heartwarming examples.

After reviewing our country's system of federalism, the opinion states:

> Federalism also protects the liberty of all persons within a State by ensuring that laws enacted in excess of delegated governmental power cannot direct or control their actions.

After a declaration that the states are not the sole beneficiaries of a system of federalism is this recognition by the Supreme Court:

> An individual has a direct interest in objecting to laws that upset the constitutional balance between the National Government and the States when the enforcement of those laws causes injury that is concrete, particular, and redressable.

For a final quotation, I have selected one that underscores our rights as individuals:

> Whether the Tenth Amendment is regarded as simply a 'truism,' . . . or whether it has independent force of its own, the result here is the same.

The Court then held that there is no basis in precedent or principle to deny Bond standing to challenge the validity of the statute under which she had been prosecuted, tried, convicted, and sentenced.

I hope that you agree with me that the Supreme Court's 2011 opinion, confirming the rights of individuals to rely on the Tenth Amendment, is both reassuring and heartwarming.

Yes, my Readers, you and I are indeed part of "We the People" whose Constitution protects our rights to "life, liberty, and the pursuit of happiness."

Your Inalienable Rights

Although "memoirs" is too pretentious for me, I claim the right to use "epilogue." The dictionary defines "epilogue" as "a concluding section that rounds out the design of a literary work." But, like Humpty Dumpty, when I use "epilogue" it means what I choose it to mean, neither more nor less. And I conclude with the radiant first sentence of the second paragraph of the Declaration of Independence by the original thirteen United States of America, July 4, 1776:

> We hold these Truths to be self-evident, that all men are created equal, that they are endowed by their Creator with certain inalienable Rights, that among these are Life, Liberty, and the Pursuit of Happiness

I believe that enjoyment of our inalienable rights depends on a good legal system. I hope that this book helps you to decide whether our legal system needs improvement for our protection—and, if so, how.

Brooke Wunnicke
Curriculum Vitae
1918–2014

> There are lawyers among us who have led such extraordinary lives
> and careers that—in time—stories will grow around their memories
> like vines covering the walls of Old Main. They are the stuff of legend.
> Brooke Wunnicke is one of these. The Truth? She Loves The Law.
> *From* The Docket, *Denver Bar Association, March 1995*

> I truly believe that law is civilization's hope for the world . . . We have three
> branches of government, but it is the judiciary that speaks for the law.
> Congress, presidents, can't protect freedom. But lawyers and judges can.
> *Brooke Wunnicke*

BROOKE VON FALKENSTEIN Wunnicke exemplified the pioneering spirit of the West. After her undergraduate education at Stanford University, she moved to Wyoming with her husband whom she met at college. When he left for WWII, she attended the University of Colorado Law School, where she graduated Order of the Coif in 1945. She opened her Cheyenne practice in 1946, representing clients in front of juries when women in Wyoming (the first state to allow women to vote) were not allowed to be jurors. She had years of substantial experience in a broad range of legal areas: trials and appeals in state and federal courts (over 250 appeals, many being referrals from other lawyers); business law; general law, including probate, wills, and taxes; real estate; and securities law.

Moving to Colorado in 1969 with her husband, she gave twelve years of public service as Chief Appellate Deputy District Attorney in the Denver District Attorney's Office where she mentored many "children" who excelled in service as lawyers, judges, and a Governor. From 1978 to 1997, she was Adjunct Professor of Law, University of Denver College of Law, teaching oil and gas law and the law of future interests and received DU Law's first honorary adjunct professorship. In 1986, Brooke affiliated Of Counsel to Hall

& Evans and also was a consultant, expert witness, and a frequent lecturer nationally about legal ethics and professionalism. She was an active member of the Business Law Section, American Bar Association.

Brooke was the recipient of many honors, including: William Lee Knous Award, 1997, Colorado University School of Law (school's highest alumnus annual award, for outstanding achievements) and the first woman to give a CULaw commencement address (1981); Life Fellow, American Bar Foundation; 2004 Denver Bar Association Award of Merit; 2003 a DU Law Star, 1997 Excellence in Teaching Award, University of Denver College of Law; 1999 Defense Research Institute's national Louis B. Potter Lifetime Professional Service Award; 1999 Colorado Bar Association's highest honor Award of Merit and in 2010 its first Colorado Legal Legends speaker; Honorary Life Fellow, Colorado Bar Foundation; honorable life member, Denver and Colorado Bar Associations; Wyoming State Bar certificates of recognition for distinguished service; the Hall & Evans Colorado Law scholarship in her name and memorial addition to that endowed scholarship. Brooke Wunnicke was in six *Marquis Who's Who*. In January 2021, CU Law established the Dean's Choice, Brooke Wunnicke Outstanding Mentor Award to recognize honored attorneys who also are outstanding mentors.

Brooke coauthored annually supplemented *Legal Opinion Letters Formbook* (3rd ed. 2010) and *Standby and Commercial Letters of Credit* (3rd ed. 2002) (both Wolters Kluwer); *Corporate Financial Risk Management* (John Wiley & Sons, 1992); and was author of *Ethics Compliance for Business Lawyers* (Wiley Law, 1987). She was the author of many articles for business and professional periodicals and received the Defense Research Institute's G. Duffield Smith Outstanding Publication Award.

Brooke was a graduate of Stanford University, BA (1939), Phi Beta Kappa, and University of Colorado School of Law, JD (1945), Order of the Coif.

Denver Public Library Western History and Genealogy Archive Index of the Brooke Wunnicke Papers

[COMPILER'S NOTE: The Brooke Wunnicke Papers are part of the Denver Public Library Western History / Genealogy Department collection and include papers and photographs. The Compiler in 2015 was introduced by Thomas J. ("Dr. Colorado") Noel to James Kroll, then Manager, and the department agreed to consider materials for its archive. For patient guidance as I scanned and catalogued file folders, and then for transporting many boxes, the Compiler is grateful to Jamie Seemiller, Acquisitions Specialist. Abbe Hoverstock, Senior Archivist, decided selections that were accepted for archive and, graciously, was efficient for all our arrangements.]

The Brooke Wunnicke Papers can be found at https://archives.denverlibrary .org/repositories/3/resources/8958 or by an internet search of "Brooke Wunnicke Papers."

Index

Locators followed by *f* indicate figures.

bankruptcy cases, 112, 131
bankruptcy courts, 214
Bar associations, 205, 220; membership in,
   199; service to, 197
Bar examination, 35, 36, 126, 138, 167
Bar of the United States Supreme Court,
   90
Bar meetings, a first in Cheyenne, 58
Barrett, Frank (Wyoming senator,
   1953–59), 11
Beethoven, Ludwig van, 8
bias, 231; freedom from, 76–78; gender,
   235
Bill of Attainder Clause in Constitution, 264
Bill of Rights, xvii, xx, 65, 66, 209, 265–84;
   liberties and, 280; U.S. Constitution
   and, 264, 276, 280
bills of attainder: unconstitutional, 262,
   263–64
Blackstone, William, 178, 196, 201, 206, 258
Blackstone's Commentaries, 196
Blake, William, 194, 201
Blume, Fred H. (Wyoming Supreme Court
   Justice, 1922–63; Latin translation
   scholar), 36, 59, 86
Board of Governors (Colorado Bar Association), serving on, 133
Board of Trustees (Denver Bar Associa-
   tion), serving on, 133
Bond Dealers Association, IDRBs and, 97.
   See also Industrial Development Reve-
   nue Bonds
Bond v. United States, 564 U.S. 211 (2011)
   (regarding the Tenth Amendment),
   283–84
bonds: issuing, 95, 156; refunding, 94,
   95*f*; repaying, 97. *See also* Industrial
   Development Revenue Bonds; public
   bond statutes
Boumediene v. Bush, 553 U.S. 723 (2008)
   (regarding topic of habeas corpus), 259
Bowen v. Smith, 838 P.2d 186 (1992), 176.
   See also *Ethics Compliance for Business
   Lawyers* (Wunnicke)
Brandeis, Louis D., 216
briefs, 86, 87; appellate, 91, 252; trial court,
   139, 163
Brooke, Lula LeNora: family history of
   mother, 10–12; siblings (Arthur Lee,
   Jasper, O. A., Roxanne), 10–11; Pinckney,
   Zachariah, maternal grandfather's home,
   11
"Brooke's Children," 137–38; message to,
   144–45

Bullcoming v. New Mexico, 564 U.S. 647
   (2011) (regarding the Bill of Rights confrontation clause), 278, 279
Bulova Watch Co. v. Zale Jewelry Co., 371
   P.2d. 409 (Wyo. 1962), 92. *See also* Wyoming Fair Trade Act
burden of proof, 222, 226–27, 239
Bureau of Land Management (BLM) and
   Wyoming Ranchers, 109
Burke, Edmund, 91, 195, 201
business law, 252, 286; various types of
   cases in, 102–5
Business Law Section (ABA), 287
Byrne v. Boadle (1863) (regarding an
   important old English case in Bedrock of
   Justice—The Common Law; negligence
   and the rule of *res ipsa loquitor*), 211, 212

California Court of Appeals, 211
California Gold Rush, 110
California Supreme Court, 212
Canons of Professional Ethics, 181
Capone, Al, 85
Cardozo, Nathan (former SCOTUS Jus-
   tice), 178, 196, 216
Carroll, Lewis, 258
casebook system for teaching law, 164, 171
Casper, Wyoming, 86, 88, 113, 115; jail, 69;
   Wild West and, 114
Castro, Fidel (regarding the importance
   of protecting the Judiciary's independence), 213
cemeteries, "burying" a law for level grave
   markers, 154–55
challenge for cause, described, 236–37
Chamber of Commerce, 97; article about,
   50*f*. *See also* Cheyenne Chamber of
   Commerce
chemistry, 20; "lemon meringue pie" and,
   82–83
Cheyenne, Wyoming, 33, 35, 55, 61, 62, 63,
   68, 71, 72, 73; jail, 69; moving from, 89,
   130; moving to, 41, 286
Cheyenne Action, 53*f*
Cheyenne Chamber of Commerce, 49–50,
   53; Board of Trustees, first woman
   elected to, 97; commendation letter
   from, 51*f*; report by, 49*f*
Cheyenne Post Office, 107
Chief Appellate Deputy District Attorney,
   xviii, xix, 145, 156, 266; serving as, 80,
   136, 137, 149, 286
Chief of Police, story about, 188, 189
child abuse, an attorney confronts, 187–91

Choate, Joseph Hodges, 194, 201

circuit courts, 65, 101

civil cases, 65, 68, 209, 267; burden of proof and, 239

Civil Rights Act (1964), 257

civil suits, 64–65, 248

Civil War, habeas corpus and, 259

civilization, law and, 286

CLE. *See* Continuing Legal Education

Clerk of the Supreme Court of Wyoming. *See* Fobes, Fred S.

closing arguments, 43, 71, 227, 228, 230, 248–51; preparing for, 249; time limit for, 250

Code of Professional Responsibility, 181, 198

Coke, Sir Edward, 196, 274

collateral estoppel case, 101

college: attending, 25–31; snap course: "Life and Times of Jesus" and meeting "A Kraft Cheese," 25–26; working in Great Depression at stock exchange, 27–28. *See also* debates

Colorado Bar Association, xviii, 69, 116, 132, 135, 137, 151; admission to, 125–26, 130; award from, 133, 134*f*; invitation from, 192

Colorado Bar Association Convention, luncheon program of, 134*f*

Colorado Court of Appeals, 140

Colorado Criminal Code, 146

Colorado General Assembly, 211

Colorado Lawyer, 69

"Colorado Legal Legends: A Fireside Chat with Brooke Wunnicke," 192, 202*f*

Colorado Revised Statutes, 211

Colorado Supreme Court, 140, 146

Colorado v. Connelly, 479 U.S. 157 (1986) (Brooke's successful petition to the U.S. Supreme Court regarding a murder confession), 142

Colorado v. Quintero, 464 U.S. 1014 (1983) (example of a petition for *writ of certiorari*), 142

Commentaries on the Laws of England (Blackstone), 206, 258

commerce, 206; interstate, 255, 257; regulation of, 255

Commerce Clause (in Constitution), 256, 257, 258

Committee of 100 (in Cheyenne 1966), 50*f*

common law, 209–13; English, 110, 211, 277; indigenous, 109; justice and, 213

Common Law (Holmes), 211

communication, 182, 277; effective, 139; oral/written, 139

community standards, freedom of speech and, 272

confidentiality, 182, 229

conflict of interests, 182–83

Conflict of Laws (course), 169

Confrontation Clause (in Bill of Rights), 66, 276–79

Confucius, 178

constitutional issues, 91–93, 167

Constitutional Law (law school class), teaching, 167–68

Continuing Legal Education (CLE): lectures, 180–86; requirements, 137

Cooper, James Fenimore, 176

corporate clients, wins for, 103–4

Corporate Financial Risk Management (Wunnicke), 287

Corpus Juris Civilis, 206

counsel: bond, 94, 156, 157; defense, 77, 80, 82, 226, 236, 240, 244, 275; securities, 131; wise and resourceful, 195

Court of Appeals for Armed Forces, 214

Court of Appeals for Veteran Claims, 214

court packing, 215–16, 256

Crawford v. Washington, 541 U.S. 36 (2004) (regarding the Bill of Rights about confronting witnesses), 277, 278

criminal cases, 79, 209, 267; court appointed to defend, 68; defending, 80; early, 66–69; violent, 85

criminal trials, 136, 222, 248; *Miranda* and, 80; opening statements for, 225

cross-examination, 78, 153–54, 226, 230, 239–43, 276, 278; abusive, 246–47; described, 241–43; memorable, 242; preparing for, 245, 246; pretrial, 279

dancing shoes, bank teller thinks a luxury, 28–29

Dante, 195

Davenport, Robert (former SEC regional director), 129

death penalty, 231, 267, 275

debate college coach, 26, 27

Debate and Oratory high school class, 21

debates, 18–24, 27, 39

decision to become a lawyer, age twelve, 17–18*f*

Declaration of Independence, 10, 285

Defense Research Institute (DRI): award letter from, 123*f*; dinner invitation, 122*f*; luncheon invitation from, 120*f*

Hollywood High School: attending, 18–24; class of, 22*f*; physical education ("Fizz-Ed") at, 39

Holmes, Oliver Wendell, Jr. (former SCOTUS Justice), 178, 195, 196, 201, 205, 211, 216, 270; due process and, 273

Homer, 195

honor guard, serving on, 58–60

Hoover Dam, 74

Horace (Quintus Horatius Flaccus), 178

Horn, Tom, famous homicide and trial in Wyoming, 55

Hotel Henning in Casper, unusual events while staying at, 113–14

human rights, 207, 208

Humpty Dumpty (Carroll), 258

Huntington Library and Art Museum, 4

IDRBs/IRBs. *See* Industrial Development Revenue Bonds

illegal advice/conduct, 187, 189–90

Immigration and Naturalization Agency, 84

immigration case, 83–85

incest, 188, 189

inclusio unius est exclusio alterius (legal maxim about inclusion and exclusion), 280

Industrial Development Revenue Bonds (IDRBs/IRBs), 94–97; prospectus for, 96*f*

infanticide, appeal on for Wyoming Supreme Court, 86

Inquisition trials, 66, 276

integrity, xix, 112, 133, 183, 197, 200, 214, 221, 232; professional, 93, 224; serving with, 186

interlocutory appeal, 136

Internal Revenue Code, IRBs and, 95

International Practicum Institute (IPI), national lecturer legal ethics, 180

Interns at Denver District Attorney appellate division, 140, 142; law school, 68, 138; work of, 139

InterOcean Hotel (in old Cheyenne), 55

Interstate Commerce Clause, 254–56, 257

IPI. *See* International Practicum Institute

Jackson, Wyoming, 229; described, 104

James, Brooke, and Diane Wunnicke Library Room (Auraria Library), 125

James, W. A. "Billy" (former State District Clerk of Court in Cheyenne), 73

JD. *See* Juris Doctor

Jerusalem (Blake), text from, 194

John, King: Magna Carta and, 207

John Wiley & Sons, 175, 176, 177

judges: appellate, 91; appointment of, 218; bankruptcy, 131; biased, 228; district court, 140; federal, 158, 214; merit selection of, 220; qualified, 221; state supreme court, xix; trial, 227–28, 237; *voir dire* and, 235

Judgment Notwithstanding Verdict, 229

judicial activism, 141, 216–17

judicial appointments, 252; grave warning about, 221; merit system of, 220–21

Judicial Commission (Colorado), 221

judicial discretion, 224, 230

judiciary, 208; fearless, 213; federal, 213, 214; meaning of, 213–14; public confidence in, 197; state, 213, 219–21

Judiciary Act (1925), 251

Julius Caesar, 199

juries: fair/impartial, 77–78, 267; faith in, 78; hung, 232; trusting, 69; weeping, 69–70

Juris Doctor (JD), described, 201

Jurisprudence and philosophers, Brooke lists (Plato, Aristotle, Homer, Shakespeare, Bacon, Milton, Dante, Montaigne, and Montesquieu and the great writers on jurisprudence Lord Coke, Blackstone, Pollock, Maitland, Cardozo, and Holmes), 195–96

jurors: fair/impartial, 237, 238; intelligence of, 242; prospective, 232, 238; unwanted, 234–37

jury deliberation, described, 228–29

jury duty, 250; women in Wyoming and, 56–57

jury instructions, 229, 239, 248; described, 227–28

jury selection, 70, 225; look at, 230–39

jury trials, 79, 85, 116, 210; civil, 69, 88, 101, 222, 224–25, 230, 233, 238, 242, 246, 248; right to, 267–68

justice, 72, 205; common law and, 213; enforcing, 206; "inspiring phrase" about, 99; integrity of, 232; miscarriage of, 99; serving, 89, 209

Justice of the Peace Court, 64–65, 90, 245

Justinian Code, 36, 206, 210

Kapelke, Bob ("A Song about Brooke"), xxiv

Kennedy, T. Blake, 58; Horn and, 55, 56

Kerr, Ewing T. (former District Court Judge for District of Wyoming), 55, 70,

Peremptory Challenge, using, 234–36
personal computers (PCs), 176, 211, 249
Peruvian and Spanish Inquisitions (in
    contrast to the Confrontation Clause in
    the Bill of Rights), 276
petition, right to, 259, 260, 261, 265, 269
Phi Beta Kappa, 35, 139, 287; election to,
    28, 31; necklace with key, 20*f*
Phoenix, Arizona: conference in, 185
physical education, 20; "Fizz-Ed" problems
    with, 38–43
plaintiff's case, described, 225–26
Plato, 195
Police Court, 64–65, 66, 90, 188
Pollock, Sir Frederick, 196
poverty, 19, 71
prejudice, 64, 231; freedom from, 76–78
press, freedom of, 269, 280
pretrial process, uses/abuses of, 222–24
prima facie evidence, 226–27, 239
private property, taking, 273, 274
probate. *See* wills and probate
probation, 70, 71–72
Problems in Legal Practice (law school
    course), teaching, xviii, 162, 163
Prohibition, 21–22
public bond statutes, 93–94, 94–97
public defenders (PDs), 66, 140, 266, 275
public safety, 140, 141
punishment, 209, 262, 263; cruel and
    unusual, 268

questions of witnesses: leading, 241;
    re-worded, 247; sneaky, 247; yes/no, 247

Rawlins, Wyoming, 115, 184; courthouse,
    76
Real Property Law (law school course),
    teaching, 171
reasonable doubt, 80, 239
recommendation letters, 127*f*, 128*f*, 129*f*
Rehnquist, William (former Chief Justice
    of the United States Supreme Court),
    257
relationships: attorney-client, 107, 183;
    person-to-person, 116, 238
reliability, judicial determination of, 277
religion, freedom of, 265, 269, 280
representation, 64, 67, 69, 81, 83, 92, 261;
    competent, 182; loyal/zealous, 70
res ipsa loquitur ("the thing speaks for
    itself"; regarding common law and neg-
    ligence), 195, 201, 211–12
res judicata, doctrine of, 100–101

Rhetoric, Book III (Aristotle), 222
rights: constitutional, 265, 282, 284; main-
    taining/regulating, 207, 282; security
    and, 280; violation of, 280
Riner, William A. (Wyoming Supreme
    Court Justice), 59, 60
RMMLF. *See* Rocky Mountain Mineral
    Law Foundation
roadmaps, 238–39
Roberts, John (Chief Justice of the United
    States Supreme Court), 257, 258
Rock Springs, Wyoming, 60, 61, 62
Rocky Mountain Mineral Law Foundation
    (RMMLF), 110; special award, 164
Rocky Mountain News Spotlight, 205;
    front page from, 44*f*
Rodin v. State, 417 P.2d 180 (Wyo. 1966)
    (regarding Wyoming constitutionality of
    advance escrow refunding bonds and a
    financing for the University of Wyo-
    ming), 94, 95
Roosevelt, Franklin Delano: court packing
    and, 215; Dormant Commerce Clause
    and, 256–58
Rosewood Grammar School, attending,
    13–14
ROTC, 32
Rule 1.1, competent representation and,
    181–82
Rule 1.6, confidentiality and, 182
Rule 1.7, conflicting interests and, 182
Rule against Perpetuities, 170
rule of law and ethics, 179. *See also* Part
    Three: The Law, 203–84
rules of evidence, 225
Rules of Professional Conduct, 198

San Francisco Chronicle, 9
Schenck v. United States, 249 U.S. 47
    (1919), 270. *See also* Bill of Rights about
    freedom of speech
Schiller, Friedrich, 8
SCOTUS (Supreme Court of the United
    States). *See* U.S. Supreme Court
SEC. *See* Securities and Exchange
    Commission
Second Amendment, Bill of Rights:
    described, 266; reliance on, 281
Securities Bar, 131, 133
Securities and Exchange Commission
    (SEC), 131
security: national, 9; rights and, 280
self-incrimination, 267
Sensitive Plant, The (Shelley), 12

TIMBERLINE BOOKS

STEPHEN J. LEONARD AND THOMAS J. NOEL, EDITORS